DATE DUE

SEP 19'9	OCT 13 94	OCT 29 '90
NOV 29 '91		MAR 18 9
APR 20 '92	JUL 10 '94	SEP 15 '99
NOV 16 '92	FEB 23 '95	FEB 19'00
	APR 03 '95	JUN 12 '01
MAY 20 '93		
JUN 05 '93	JUN 26 '96	JUL 31 98
		MAY 0 5 200
OCT 28 '93	JUN 08 96	NOV 15 01
DEC 27 '93	SEP 14 '96	JUL 19 02
	DEC 02 '96	MAR 11 2004
APR 05 '94	MAY 13 '97	NOV 1 2014
JUL 02 '94	AUG 16 '97	
SEP 30 '9	SEP 05 98	

GAYLORD   PRINTED IN U.S.A.

The Cajuns

From Acadia to Louisiana

The Cajuns

From Acadia to Louisiana

William Faulkner Rushton

FARRAR STRAUS GIROUX
New York

The line drawing on page 177 is reproduced
with permission from Natural History Magazine,
February 1977; copyright, American Museum
of Natural History, 1977

Library of Congress Cataloging in Publication Data
Rushton, William Faulkner.
The Cajuns: from Acadia to Louisiana.
Bibliography: p.
1. Cajuns—History.   2. Cajuns—Social life and
customs.   3. Acadians—History.   I. Title.
F380.A2R87   976.3'004'046   78–21580

For my parents,
George and Evelyn Rushton,
who first brought
me into Louisiana

Contents

All maps prepared by Bernard Leblanc

The Cajuns

From Acadia to Louisiana

James Daisy lives on Bayou du Large, near where the road ends in coastal marshes stretching on for several more miles to the Gulf of Mexico. For most of the year, James Daisy harvests oysters from the shallow brackish lakes scattered through the marshes; for most of the rest of the year, he traps muskrats. James Daisy is a Cajun.

Gladys LeBlanc Clark lives on a rice farm a few miles outside Louisiana's Cajun capital, Lafayette. The modern laundry room just off her spacious country kitchen is neatly lined with appliances: washer-dryer, sewing machine, loom. Loom? In the evenings, using a mysterious brown cotton she grows in her garden, Gladys Clark watches television and weaves Cajun cloth in the manner of her mother and her grandmother before her. Gladys LeBlanc Clark is a Cajun, too.

Ambrose Thibodeaux is perhaps Louisiana's most recorded living French accordion player. At age seventy-four, he still finds the time and energy to get up early and drive an hour through the Cajun prairie to the village of Mamou for a live music program broadcast out of Fred's Lounge every Saturday—from 8 A.M. onwards. He never learned to read music as a young man, but a few years ago he taught himself to use a tape recorder to "compose" folk music from fragments remembered from his youth—an ideal technique to make finished songs for commercial records, and also a clever way to create "documents" he can "read" by listening. The resourceful Ambrose Thibodeaux is most definitely a Cajun.

These three characters and an estimated 900,000 more residents of primarily rural areas of south Louisiana constitute the largest French-speaking minority in the United States. Through a series of astonishing historical flukes, they are also descendants of some of the very first European North Americans, who established their first permanent colony in 1604—three years before Jamestown, four before Quebec, and fifteen before Plymouth Rock. But that first Cajun colony was to be founded in Canada, not in southern Louisiana. The

Cajuns were called Acadians then—"Cajun" being a frontier American corruption of the word "Acadian," as "Injun" is to "Indian."[1] Though there are still Acadian cousins in French areas of Canada and a few other parts of the world, they number less than half the total of those whose ancestors ended up in Louisiana after their farms were seized and burned by the English governor of Nova Scotia in 1755. The Acadians were forcibly dispersed to ports all over the Old and New Worlds, in an act of genocide memorialized by Henry Wadsworth Longfellow's narrative poem *Evangeline* almost a century later. A grade-school reading of *Evangeline* is often the first (and sometimes the only) encounter Anglo-Americans of either the United States or Canada have with the history and culture of these scattered and still largely unheralded American pioneers.

Evangeline—and it may also be general knowledge that contemporary Cajuns play an exotic-sounding folk music and eat even more exotic foods that they lure out of the swamps and bayous. Indeed, since Cajun music was first popularized outside Louisiana by the likes of Jimmy Newman and Doug Kershaw, it has been carried along on the rest of the country's country/folk/Austin music branch of the national nostalgia craze and gone on to attract a cult following all its own. And as for Louisiana's fabled food: whenever you eat domestic seafood in America these days—whether or not it's mixed into a jambalaya—chances are one in four that a Cajun caught it.

Confused perceptions of this unparalleled American subculture result partially from the fact that there are *three* separate but interestingly interrelated French cultures in Louisiana that together have formed a surprisingly effective resistance to the values of English-speaking North America. The Creoles of New Orleans and its immediate plantation precincts are perhaps the best-known of the three groups, for they were the wealthiest and the most flamboyant. The Creoles enjoyed America's first opera, and styled the culture and politics of Louisiana—the only state to have its own French-language daily newspapers and a French-language constitution—until well after the Civil War.

A second Louisiana Francophone culture was established by the

Creoles' former black slaves, who were allowed personal and cultural latitudes unknown in the antebellum slave societies of the Anglo-Saxon South. Their mixed-blood offspring (the quadroons, octaroons, etc.) were prosperous, cultured, and sometimes emancipated in the phenomenally diverse and wide-open New Orleans golden age that preceded the Civil War. And the black Creoles' ranks have included voodoo Queen Marie Laveau, the originators of jazz, and, most recently, the first black mayor of New Orleans.

The Cajuns, who have extensive blood and cultural ties to both the Creoles and their former slaves, are perhaps the least well understood, though they are the largest and most historically significant of the three groups. By virtue of their early isolation in Canada and their subsequent isolation in the swampy, so-called French Triangle of Louisiana, the Cajuns are the living repository of a unique set of pre-industrial agrarian values that have otherwise disappeared in the modern West. Their journey from Acadia to Louisiana is full of secrets that could not be eradicated by the Expulsion of 1755, Le Grand Dérangement, the act that in large measure laid the foundation for the Anglo-dominant structure of modern North America. The Cajuns are still very close to the earth and to the material reality of life, and their culture is full of provocative alternatives to the modern life style.

Attempts have been made over the years to characterize the difference between Cajuns and the rest of America, with varying degrees of perspective and with varying degrees of success. Because of the same biases in the dominant Anglo-American culture that afflict the subcultures of the Quebecois, the Hispanic Americans, the Indians, and the blacks, those comparative assessments of the Cajuns have not always been flattering. One especially caustic and deprecatory evaluation was made by a Marguerite A. Pecot for the Federal Writers' Project in 1939, at a time when the Cajuns were still being described as North America's last unassimilated minority. The Cajuns, she begins innocuously enough, are a "simple, uneducated, uncultured, yet intrinsically genuine and lovable people . . . The Cajun temperament is impulsive, impetuous, highly inflammable, ultra-sensitive, unrelenting in hatreds, ardent in affections." But she goes on: "The men are, as a rule, of medium height, robust, sinewy, with heavily tanned skin, coarse irregular features, dark bushy hair, and dull, rather unimaginative eyes; the women during adolescence and girlhood possess a certain youthful charm, but four or five years of connubial felicity unfailingly take the glow from their eyes and the delicate flush from their cheeks." The Cajuns who live on the bayou enjoy "a life without stability, responsibility or conventionality . . . one in which the sole purpose and solitary desire is the satisfaction of fundamental necessities and emotions." Education, charges Pecot, is considered "quite superfluous," because the "sole purpose" of children is "to assist in the duties of the farm, marry early, rear a large family, and thus perpetuate the same unchanging cycle of rustic beatitude."

Other observers, such as Glenn Conrad, are beginning to speak out against this still common caricature of the Cajuns as "ignorant, therefore superstitious swamp dwellers living in squalor in a moss-draped, reptile-infested wilderness." Conrad, director of the Center for Louisiana Studies at the Cajuns' own University of Southwestern Louisiana (USL) in Lafayette, has edited a major new collection of academic essays on Cajun history and culture. He takes note of the common perception of the Cajuns as a "minority incapable of coexisting with the American majority—a socially rebellious breed," but suggests a new way to understand the vital truth that is masked by such a caricature. The Cajuns' culture, he declares, is "founded on French tradition, but [is] almost entirely superstructured by themselves"— emphasizing an adaptability and resourcefulness that the dominant culture would do well to respect and learn about and cultivate. Behind the myths and superstitions that abound about the Cajuns, there are not a few such hidden truths—for the Cajuns and their reality are often as exotic as they appear to be. They are the standard-bearers of a lost chapter in European-American history, a chapter full of rich departure points from which to better understand the true course of the history of us all.

Some authorities believe that as many as two-thirds of the original Acadian immigrants came from the coastal regions of France, lured to the New World by the tales of fishermen who had been in the area pursuing the interests of that country from no later than 1504. French fishermen and their relatives from the surrounding towns and country-side constituted an unusual breed of social and political refugees in this period of Western history, because they possessed both the means of escape from the old country and a means of maintaining an independent livelihood afterwards. And it was the northern fishing coast of France from which a particularly large number of Acadian immigrants came.

Brittany is the most heavily Celtic cultural region of France. It was an independent duchy until a strategic royal marriage of 1515—when the fishermen were still scouting the New World coast—so the Brittany of that day would have been the Acadian emigration pool with the least social and political ties to the emerging "metropolitan" regime centered on royalist Paris and its nationalist Catholic Church. The Cajun patois of today is full of nautical terms and antique usages from that place and period, as well as a number of grammatical and other linguistic evidences of Celtic influence.

The Cajuns come from a specific pre-industrial European agrarian tradition that differs markedly from the tradition of most Anglo-Americans. The Cajun tradition is nominally Christian and predominantly Catholic, yet still retains a surprising range of pre-Christian values and perceptions. Even when forced by later circumstances to make their historic adaptations, the Cajuns have courageously preserved from a now-distant era of the Western past a wide range of human attitudes and experiences that would otherwise have been altogether lost. The Cajuns are the founders of a form of North American neo-paganism which, for want of a better term, we might as well call Cajunism.

Cajunism derives its pagan roots from a variety of geographical and ethnic sources, including France and Scotland, as well as the American Indians and Louisiana's blacks. There is even a large batch of Huguenots, French Protestants, in the early Acadian social mix, though all end up adopting in the New World an eccentric form of nominal Catholicism that was a major factor in the Puritan-led expulsion campaign of the mid-eighteenth century.

The Huguenots tended to rise to economic and political power in the very coastal areas that had longest been political holdouts to the centralized modern French state established by the Catholic monarchy of Paris. John Calvin was convicted of heresy in 1533, and throughout the remainder of the sixteenth century, opponents of the Paris regime often styled themselves Protestants—regardless of their true religious convictions. Some theologians speculate that Protestantism in its early formative stages may have been greatly influenced by holdover pagan values. The Protestant is asserting his right to make his own pact with his own god(s), without any uninvited human intervention.

The pagan connection is amply, if somewhat indirectly, reinforced by the work of Geneviève Massignon, a French scholar of Acadian origins. She speculates that a smaller but earlier migration from the inland regions of the old province of Poitou, along the southwestern coast of France, exerted a proportionately greater influence on the life style of later immigrants. The Poitou area she targets is bounded on the north by Loudon, the scene of bedevilment memorialized by Aldous Huxley and Ken Russell; and toward the coast, by the seaport of La Rochelle, a Protestant citadel that was the last military stronghold to fall to Paris. The largest Poitou immigrant group arrived in Acadia just four years after the fall of La Rochelle. Massignon's thesis gains added credence from a detail turned up recently on a 1720 map in the archives of a New Orleans museum. That map shows the New World drawn from a French perspective and identifies the heavily populated Chignecto isthmus of Nova Scotia—the Canadian province that was in large part the original Acadia—as Poitou.

In addition to Brittany and Poitou, other major areas of early French-Acadian immigration include Normandy (the next province east of Brittany along the northern coast, heavily settled by Vikings in the ninth and tenth centuries) and Picardy (with its influential inland village of Noyon, where Charlemagne was crowned to end one era of conflict and John Calvin was born to begin another).

Brittany, Normandy, Picardy, Poitou: regardless of how the various authorities rank them, these are the provinces that, together, are thought to account for about half the population of pre-Expulsion Acadia, although refugees from forty-three other provincial areas across France are also said to be represented in the mix. Given such

Graveyard at night, All Saints' Eve, 1945 ELEMORE MORGAN, SR.

a diversity of backgrounds, the Acadian immigrants may well have discovered that certain pagan cultural elements formed a more convenient and accessible base for interaction—an interaction that was to be, in USL authority Conrad's words, "entirely superstructured by themselves." Such an open, democratic sensibility would have been reinforced by frequent and intimate contact with the indigenous "pagan" Indians—who got along with the Acadians better than they did with any of the other early-American immigrants. The Acadians' Puritan New Englander neighbors, for example, feared the Indians, regarding them as "tawny serpents." One historian writes that "contact with the Indians had a traumatic effect on the Puritan, revealing to him what he was in spite of himself." But Cajunism didn't find the Indian culture threatening at all, and the tolerance and pagan base of early Acadian society may, in fact, explain the extraordinary elasticity and absorptive quality which continue to characterize this culture today.

One example of that flexibility comes immediately to mind. A group of Scottish immigrants from one of England's earliest colonizing efforts stayed on in Acadia when political control reverted to France. They gallicized their name to Melanson—a detail that confirms suspected links between Cajunism and the culture of the Scotch-Irish Anglo-American rebels of Appalachia who are the Cajuns' Celtic cousins. After the Expulsion, that elasticity continued in Louisiana: the bayou state's Guillory Cajuns are said to have Irish roots. Then there are the people from the so-called German Coast area of colonial Louisiana, established by John Law in 1717; though these settlers preceded the Cajuns in coming to the state, they eventually became French-speaking and thoroughly Cajun. All over the French Triangle of Louisiana now, you can find Cajuns who started out as Indians, Africans, Anglos, Spaniards, and even Lebanese. *Mamou Prairie* editor Revon Reed claims to count fifteen different kinds of Louisana Cajuns, including Yugoslavs and Filipinos. Professor Patricia Rickels, a French Triangle folklorist from USL, quotes an old folk saying that you can become a Cajun three ways: "by the blood, by the ring, and by the back door."

Out in the country a two hours' drive from New Orleans, a seeker of Cajunism will find the unexpected shrine of Our Lady of the Butane Tank, one of many folk shrines in the Cajun countryside. She guards the fuel supply of a small pink house next door—appropriately enough, at the boundary line between Ascension Parish (county) and Assumption Parish. Our Lady of the Butane Tank reminds us that there is about the Cajuns of Louisiana a thin but well-defined Catholic swamp mist that contributes much to the culture's separation from the American mainstream. And a closer examination will reveal that Cajun Catholicism differs quite remarkably from the standard brand. The leading Nova Scotia authority on the history of Acadian culture, Professor Alphonse Deveau of Collège Sainte-Anne, observes that "religion, to the Acadian, was based on inner convictions and [was] not imposed from the outside." These inner convictions have been generously interlaced with ritualistic holdovers from the pagan rural areas of seventeenth-century France, and reinforced by the episodic lack of orthodox clergymen to dispute the inevitable result. Those Cajuns who were allowed to return to Nova Scotia's so-called French Shore after the Expulsion, for example, had to wait another thirty-three years for their first Catholic priest, and in the meantime had to make do spiritually on their own. Professor Rickels notes that in post-Expulsion Louisiana, by as late as 1835, there were only six functioning churches, and two resident priests—and, she concludes without hesitation in a recent paper on early religion in Louisiana, "pagan elements continue to survive." In an 1857 book, landscape architect Frederick Law Olmstead wrote that, during his travels in antebellum Louisiana, he found "frontier Catholicism not so pervasive as he had expected it to be." By 1918, when the separate Cajun diocese of Lafayette was carved out of the New Orleans Archdiocese to serve all of southwest Louisiana west of the Atchafalaya Basin swamp, there were only forty organized parishes, with fifty priests, to cover a geographical area whose widely dispersed population exceeded 300,000. Even today in some areas, observes USL French professor Mathé Allain, in an essay in Glenn Conrad's book on the Cajuns, Cajun men customarily get up during the sermon and go outside for a smoke. This practice seems to survive intact from the original Acadia, where, according to a letter that one bitterly complaining priest sent back to his bishop at Quebec, the Acadian men would sometimes run horse races around the church during the sermon.

These are merely bits and snatches from the historial record, but they are sufficient to suggest that traditional assumptions about the role of Catholicism in Cajun culture will have to be reevaluated in light of surviving widespread religious practices that verge on heresy and voodoo. The witch-doctor role in Cajunism has historical roots other than purely religious ones, of course, for in early Canadian Acadia there were only four doctors that we know about. This medical setting required the services of midwives, many of whom also performed medicinal duties, with whatever was at hand, including spells and incantations. No successful orthodox resistance to this straying of the Cajun flock was offered, and unlike Europe or nearby Puritan New England, there were no witch burnings in Acadia. "There is one witch trial on record," notes Nova Scotia's Deveau, and it was declared a mistrial. In Acadian Canada, these special practitioners, all women, are known as *sage femmes,* and in other French-speaking areas of Canada as "angel-makers," for they are also abortionists. In Louisiana, the Cajun folk-medicine practitioners are known as *traiteurs,* or "treaters." Herbs from the surrounding countryside, many gathered from the Indians, plus holy water and prayers, are their stock-in-trade —but all "practice" is personal and personally tailored and unique, without the benefit of an organized body of literature. In the Acadian areas of New Brunswick, black-magic Bibles known as the Petit Albert and the Grand Albert were once in wide use, despite ruthless attempts at suppression by the Church. Early in the twentieth century there was a part-Acadian, part-Indian (métis) sorceress in Maritime Canada by the name of Marie Comeau who has received revived interest at the hands of New Brunswick novelist Regis Brun—but, in general, the woman-magician phenomenon is one of the Acadian culture's most closely guarded secrets.

In Louisiana, this tradition was enriched by the presence of African voodoo. The black slaves of colonial Louisiana were allowed a surprising amount of ethnic autonomy and integrity, as witnessed by the weekly bamboula dances in New Orleans' Congo Square (now Louis Armstrong Park), where a black Creole composer by the name of Louis Moreau Gottschalk would one day adapt tribal rhythms to symphonic instrumentation, and from where jazz can also trace its roots. The black Creoles—slave or free—were also adept at paying homage to selected Catholic saints who reminded them of the African gods they had left behind. St. John the Baptist, with his crooked shepherd's stick, became a visually suitable substitute for the Yoruba god of thunder, Shango, a ram. St. Peter, with his keys to heaven, was and is idolatrized in sections of Louisiana as the Dahomean voodoo god Legba (also sometimes known as Limba, Lebat, and Papa La Bas). The *Code Noir* of 1724, a book of rules and regulations for the administration of slavery during the French regime, required all owners of slaves to baptize them and their offspring as Catholics—which merely served to bring the blacks' voodoo gods into a legitimate church setting. By 1830, free mulattoes, known as the *gens de couleur,* could be found

"The Solidity of Shadows," No. 2, 1953. CLARENCE J. LAUGHLIN, © 1972

listed in the baptismal registry of every church in Louisiana, as were all slaves. Blacks and whites, and the growing numbers of those in between, attended the same church services in the same rooms together in Louisiana before there ever was a United States of America, and in spite of the turbulence of the Civil War and the Reconstruction, black and white Catholics in Louisiana continued to worship together until Jim Crow finally came to church in the years just before the First World War. Moreover, the predominantly Cajun diocese of Lafayette also administers the geographical area with the largest per capita population of black Catholics in the country. Among the states of the Union, Louisiana has the third-highest per capita black population (after Mississippi and South Carolina). The full national impact of this French-cultured, black Louisiana population has yet to be reckoned with and can only be suggested here.[2]

Suffice it to say that the exchange of black secrets and white secrets was inevitable in colonial Louisiana, and continues today in Louisiana's French Triangle in the way clients cross over for the services of treaters. Treaters are often specialists, necessitating a referral network entirely handled by French word-of-mouth. The ability to treat is usually inherited from an ancestor who will pass on his/her secrets. Most treaters are left-handed—another link between modern Cajun culture and pre-Christian European paganism, where left-handedness was considered a sign of magic powers. Another direct link, speculates Rickels, is the survival of pre-Christian attitudes toward dead babies. Babies that die before they are baptized become *couchemals,* or evil spirits, which lurk around like lesser ghosts. According to elderly Cajuns of today, a house with a dead unbaptized baby requires the following ritual: you must drain the contents of the roof's rain-gathering cistern and other such containers of any liquid in which the *couchemal* might settle to cause trouble. To guard against creation of *couchemals,* Cajun mothers and midwives customarily keep vials of holy water handy. Inevitably, some of that holy water gets splashed around, gets used in what Rickels delicately calls "para-ecclesiastical" or "extra-official" ceremonies: placing vials of holy water in fig trees, to assure productivity; administering holy water to cure sick people, especially for sore throats; taking extra palm fronds to be blessed at Palm Sunday services so as to procure a year's supply of ashes for various weather-control rites—rituals, she notes, "to buttress an un-seen God [by] carrying around physical objects."

Foremost among these objects, scattered among the rosaries and burning candles and novenas, is the totem of the Virgin Mary: Our Lady of the Butane Tank, our lady of so many projects and purposes that she seems to play an overly exaggerated role in Cajun Catholi-cism. She is, perhaps, evidence of a continuing neo-pagan matriarchal social structure sublimated into fetishism. The Virgin Mary hovers in churches and Catholic schools and in front yards and grave groupings all over the French Triangle, often hand-painted in dazzling poly-chrome. Near the Southern Pacific's railroad track as it winds along the Bayou Teche, a factory turns out raw statues of the Virgin Mary by the gross, and lines them up unpainted in a huge, shoulder-to-shoulder arc surrounding an enormous pool of rainwater. Wherever they stand around the ring of water, whatever direction they face, all the virgins have their arms open wide—welcoming all comers into the fold, in an appropriate sculptural embodiment of the culture they nourish and safeguard.[3]

The importance of the Acadian family unit as a determinant of culture is stressed by all observers, and USL sociologist Sarah Brabant de-clares that the family is "the ultimate bulwark in this remarkably resilient culture." But she's not talking about the patriarchal, nuclear family unit common to the Anglo-American-dominated, post-indus-trial West.

The distinctive character of the Cajun family is its extended net-work, through intermarriage, into all the other families of the immedi-ate community. "Our manner of living in Acadia was peculiar," recalls the grandmother of a St. Martinville judge, in his 1907 classic oral-history account, *Acadian Reminiscences,* "the people forming, as it were, one single family." Such a family—extended by the blood, by the ring, and by the back door—forms a community where no one is left out and where institutions like mental hospitals and old-folk homes were never developed to allow one class of people to throw another class out.[4] Indeed, one team of researchers has concluded that seventy-six surnames—which, because of variant spellings, become one hundred separate families—account for 86 percent of all Acadians today.[5] In the days before the Expulsion, when the Acadian extended family still lived together in one unit, they devised a form of communal entertainment with music and dancing that has survived and has accompanied their descendants through their various separations and transformations over the years. Perhaps the most important positive result of this consanguinity is to be seen in the development of the Acadian political economy and the Acadian perception of property. Communal task-solving projects included the *piocherie* (a hoeing bee) and the *couvrage* (a shingling party)—forerunners of the more contemporary community-wide Louisiana festivals at Chauvin with its "Lagniappe on the Bayou" or at Mamou with its "Courir de Mardi Gras." An admiring Longfellow wrote: "Alike were they free from Fear, that reigns with the tyrant, and envy, the vice of republics./Neither locks had they to their doors, nor bars to their windows;/But their dwellings were open as day and the hearts of the owners;/There the richest was poor, and the poorest lived in abundance."

This sense of psychological security is perhaps nowhere revealed more clearly than in the plans of houses built by the Expulsion refugees in New Brunswick. Homes of that era usually featured two ground-floor rooms—a communal sleeping area on one side of the central, stone fireplace, and a combined kitchen–dining–living room on the other side. The fireplace did not extend from wall to wall but, instead, left two end gaps—one for an enclosed ladder or a very steep stair reaching into the attic *grenier,* where the food was stored, and the other for a small passageway forming an air-lock to the world outside. The air-lock opening was usually wide enough to accommodate a long bench or storage trunk along the warm wall of the fireplace. In the winters of the Acadian north, any overnight traveler caught in a storm might spend the night in the air-lock space, sheltered from the weather. The kitchen and food-supply areas were locked—mainly to keep out animal intruders—as was the sleeping room, where the family retired at night. But the following morning the family would rouse their guest and invite him to join them for breakfast.

A similar custom in Louisiana is recorded in the so-called Anonymous Breaux Manuscript, one of the earliest extant folklore commentaries about the Louisiana Cajuns written by one of their own. "If overtaken by nightfall or a storm while travelling," the manuscript tells, "one need not fear to knock at the door or call to the farmhouse from the road." In return for news or a story, there would be lodging, and breakfast the next morning.

Such social customs imply the lack of a constabulary, and also the lack of a need for one. Social orderliness in the early Cajun extended family did not require outside force or authority. And one's immediate surroundings, one's "property" of various sorts, were not viewed as something to be hoarded from others and protected by a "state." In early Louisiana, when community conflicts over property or other grievances arose, the Cajuns would convene an informal court, called a *plaid*. Presiding would be a temporary judge or *doyen* ("eldest"), chosen by acclamation. The practice is similar to that reported by the Reverend Hugh Graham, a Protestant minister and pre-Expulsion visitor to Acadia, who late in his life wrote: "They had no courts of law because they had no need of them. If any difference arose, it was soon allayed and settled by the interference and counsel of two or three of the most judicious and best respected [residents] of the neighborhood."

I had an unexpected close encounter with the communal personal politics of Cajunism in the summer of 1977 at an Acadian festival in the New Brunswick farming community of Packetville—perhaps best known as the hometown of Acadian folksinger Edith Butler. Packetville and its festival occupy the hilly highlands between two small, fjordlike river valleys in the remote northeastern section of New Brunswick known as the Acadian Peninsula. This rural area is almost as far and as isolated from the Acadian metropolis of Moncton as it is from Quebec. The encounter occurred while we were seated, talking, at a long table in an area where rows of them had been set up for a massive outdoor Acadian barbecue. A heated discussion erupted between two young men at the next table. They had both been drinking, and when the loudness began, relatives from both sides rushed to each participant's aid. But the chair-throwing melee we had wincingly anticipated did not materialize. The lone uniformed officer in the clearing walked over calmly, without an expression of temper or force. It was apparent that he knew both parties, and it may even be that he was related to one or both of them. The two adversaries and their backups formed a small circle and the cop walked into the middle of the group, asking questions of both sides and generating a spirited collective discussion. As soon as the consensus, whatever it was, was reached, they all headed their separate ways, melting back into the festivities again, leaving no marks, not even a broken beer bottle.

When we arrived at the festival, a wet, cold wind was sweeping up over the Packetville highlands from the sea. It fanned away at a bonfire visible for miles against the sky—a bonfire built in the manner of the peaceful Micmac Indians who have co-inhabited the same areas in an earlier Nova Scotia and a later New Brunswick where the Canadian Acadians have always lived. The scene was reminiscent of the Christmas season's bonfires still built on the levees of the Mississippi River parishes where the Acadian refugees first settled in Louisiana—and yet this bonfire seemed even more primordial. The light from the Packetville bonfire, some two or three stories high, filled every corner of the hillside, for the billowing clouded canopy reflected the bonfire's glow across the massive highland ridge where the festival spread out in all directions. The wind had the sound of a giant shell from a very old beach, but it was a sound interrupted with occasional shouted greeting in French and the general roar of a parking lot as celebrants from all over the Acadian peninsula drove in for the evening.

It was July of 1977, the very week of the U.S. Bicentennial plus one year, in fact, and the night was full of fireworks—though of a most different kind. Still startled and stumbling from the feel of a Canadian midsummer chill that visits the subtropical jungles of Louisiana only on the rarest of fierce winter days, I lit out immediately for the bonfire. But our guide for the occasion kept tugging in another direction—insisting that there was still more to come from another, darker side of the festival's highlighted meadow.

More to come from and through a low forest of trees that seemed to stand up only as we approached them. The trees and the rest of the festival were sunk into a glen protected by the hillside from the wrath of the sea's northerly winds, and an absolute silence enveloped us as we entered that forest. The light of the bonfire was obscured, too, but a few rows of light bulbs were carefully strung through the trees so as to illuminate the footpaths through the well-trod, almost polished ground underfoot. This lobby of trees rolled around a few turns and down the glen before sloping out into an opening ringed with high trees and echoing with the faint sounds of music. Have you ever heard a violin played in the woods?

To the right, through the clearing, people and food and tables disappeared back into the dark. To the left end, on higher ground, the clearing sprouted a wood-and-concrete pier, also filled with people. A small building partially hid the proceedings beyond, but walking over, we soon saw that it also provided one wall to this open-air meeting place—surrounded on three sides by wooden fences. In the middle, a still smaller enclosure built entirely of wood held a company of whirling dancers. Spectators watched approvingly from the four sides of the dancing terrace. Within, there were built-in benches for rests between numbers and built-in movements for each and every tune the band could play. The songs were like the Cajun songs of Louisiana, but somehow more antique, and played to a slower if still-spirited and evocative beat. Any member of the community could enter the magic ring to dance, and if you stayed there long enough, you might, conceivably, dance with everyone else in the community by evening's end.

The Packetville dancing recalled the Cajun country dancehalls back home with their Saturday-night *fais-dodo,* but in a different way, more intimate perhaps, seeming to belong to an older, more distant time closer to the earth and to the fire within us all. To encounter that dance is to discover the Cajuns' most important secret, and to join in it is to accept their greatest gift.

Canadian Roots

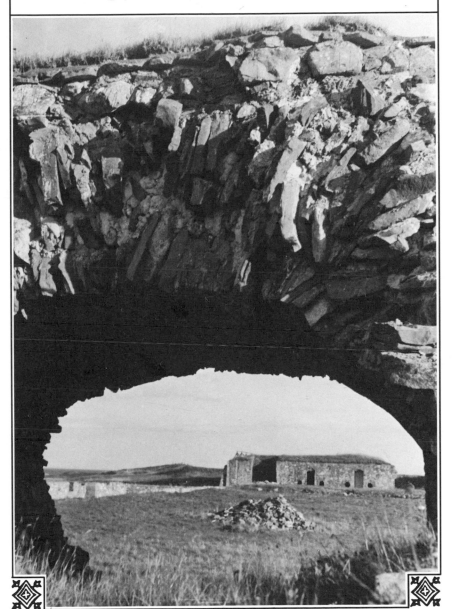

The ruins of Fortress Louisbourg   CANADIAN CONSULATE-GENERAL, NEW YORK

October 1755: Under the slate-cloud canopy of autumn in Maritime Canada, isolated and broken clumps of farmers, their wives, and their children stand shivering on a wave-lapped beach. Each cluster is surrounded by scarlet-coated musketeers, their bayonets glinting in the glow of a distant fire. Stretched out before this gathering is a haphazard fleet of secondhand sailing ships, cargo vessels brought in unexpectedly from Boston and linked to the shore by a relentless flotilla of longboats. Behind them, on a slight hill in the far distance, burns what is left of the village of Grand Pré—seven hundred houses, eleven mills, and two churches, plus various barns and outbuildings that will require six days and nights of torching to be fully consumed. Winter approaches. The water is cold, and gray like the faces and the clouds and the despairing smoke that curls its way into the very edges of the canvas.

We are looking at a huge canvas painted a century later, a mural almost the size of Picasso's *Guernica,* in the basement museum of a college library not too far from where the scene actually took place.

Both the ancient Acadian village of Grand Pré, Nova Scotia, and the Musée Acadien at Moncton, New Brunswick, are to be found in the upper tidal reaches of the Bay of Fundy—where the narrow Chignecto isthmus begins to unfold its rocky claws from New Brunswick out into the North Atlantic and around the bay to form the peninsula called Acadia. (For an explanation of the origins of the word Acadia, see the Chronology, under 1524.)

The museum and a nearby Acadian archives center, both at the Université de Moncton, contain almost all the material artifacts that survive of the early Acadian settlements of this region. The paintings —there are several of them in the museum showing several different versions of the same seaside scene—are almost all of what we have left of Grand Pré.

Grand Pré was at one time the largest village in a network of settlements housing 18,000 French-speaking inhabitants around

Fundy's marsh-filled, bayside edges. Grand Pré survives today only as a tiny, government-administered park in the middle of the Acadians' usurped but still-fertile fields, and as a historical marker along Nova Scotia's provincial Route 1—the main route from Yarmouth to Halifax. Behind that marker, down an insignificant side road from the highway, lies the "great meadow" that gave the vanished village its legendary name.

The meadow slides, as if it had been lubricated for that very purpose, down to a level area of the prairie, where stands the commemorative park—and then the land rises, ever so slightly, to fan out absolutely level and smooth into a rich, checkerboard field of man-made dikes extended gradually, over the years, out into the edges of the bay.

Where the side road in from Route 1 slopes to a sudden stop, the park explores its way along the dividing line between the natural meadow and its handmade extension. A row of gnarled and waning willow trees stands out among the midsummer growths of the tightly compacted farmsteads, which are spread back up the hill to the highway and out through the diked fields to the bay. The willows mark the edges of the park, which is divided into a visitors' center and parking lot to the right of the entrance road and, on the left, public gardens centering on a replica of the forsaken church of St. Charles de Grand Pré.

The willows were planted by the original Acadian settlers of Grand Pré. When they had finished building their dikes and houses and barns and mills and churches and roads alongside their fields, they turned to the willow tree to provide the markers and the shade for the edges of their roads. The park at Grand Pré has been squeezed in-between two surviving rows of thirteen trees, a skinny pause at the bottom of the hill, a fragment of an old road that survives now only as a rose-bushed pilgrimage path for tourists. It may be only a minor irony, but this passageway, lined with the still-living products of the Acadians' labors, slices straight through the later, English-built modern road.

.　　.　　.

Grand Pré was the largest and most central of the ancient Acadian settlements, but it was neither the first to rise in the colonial countryside nor the last to rise in English smoke.

English smoke had been billowing from Acadian settlements for a hundred and fifty years prior to the Expulsion of 1755 (as the English called it) or, as the French preferred, Le Grand Dérangement. And English smoke would continue to billow another generation beyond the incident at Grand Pré, until 1771, when Acadian possession of lands in the province of Nova Scotia was once more "legalized." By that time, imported Anglo-American settlers had already occupied all the best lands of the province, and the Acadian pioneers who had built up those lands for a century and a half were given what was left over of the worst.

From Grand Pré, the origins of the Acadian colony go back to the other side and the other end of the tumultuous Bay of Fundy, to a place where the St. Croix River now divides the Yankees' united state of Maine from the not-so-united bilingual Canadian province of New Brunswick. The St. Croix settlement traces its genesis to the early 1500's, when merchants from the independent-minded seacoast towns of France, anxious to secure both the fishing grounds that lay offshore Maritime Canada and the Indian fur trade that lay open and waiting within its shores, sought to establish a permanent administrative base somewhere along the water's edge. And in 1604, on one of the islands in the St. Croix, these merchants planted the first seeds of a colony that would spread its roots around the Bay of Fundy for the next century and a half. The hapless St. Croix settlers of this first voyage, whittled away by scurvy, and stranded far from supplies of fresh water, barely withstood the severity of the weather they encountered. Their rocky island would not yield a well, and they had no firewood with which to melt fresh water from the ice floes separating them from the lumber and running streams of the river's shore. Conditions were so desperate that the half of the colony which survived the first year packed up the following year and took refuge in a more hospitable cove across Fundy's often brutal bay. In what is now the Annapolis Valley of Nova Scotia, they began again.

Through a narrow slit in an otherwise impregnable bayside moun-sable island ⚓ (1598-160

fortress louisbourg

ile royale
(cape breton island)

atlantic

nova

halifax

pisiquid (windsor)

cobequid ○
(truro)

grand pré

ile
st.-jean

(prince edward
island)

baie
verte

missaguash r.

chignecto isthmus

beaubassin
(1672)

(16

nor

fort
beauséjour

● moncton

caraquet

new

1 = fortress louisbourg
2 = annapolis royal

québec ●

montréal ●

1

area of
map

2

boston ●

new york ●

chicago ●

english colonies

st.
louis ●

french america

bruns-

florida (spain)

new orleans ●

acadia

bird's-eye view

ocean

scotia

n.s hwy. 1

annapolis r.

annapolis royal (1635)

ountain

port royal habitation (1605)

yarmouth

"french shore"

bay of fundy

s.
e. — w.
n.

st. john (1612)

mt. desert island (1613) (maine)

wick

st. croix settlement (1604)

u.s.a.

tain range their ships went, behind the mountain to a quiet basin fed by nine rivers. Their smaller but wiser settlement was founded on a strategic promontory they resolutely named Port Royal. The Port Royal basin, the Rivière Dauphin (now Annapolis River) that collected the streams to feed it, and the verdant valley cupped around it all, run from the site of this settlement some seventy-five narrow and gently rising miles east and slightly north to another geologic formation known as the Minas Basin, the eventual site of Grand Pré.

Port Royal's hidden valley is protected by North Mountain—actually, a formation no more than 400 to 700 feet high. Behind the protection of North Mountain, the valley ranges some two to seven miles wide, squeezed in by a companion rock formation, the edge of the remaining Nova Scotia upland, known in the valley as South Mountain. Geologists theorize that glaciers carved out the valley, leaving a demi-fjord of a scale and beauty unknown anywhere else in North America. The guardian hills to either side seem high and safe, well capable, you would judge from down on the valley's floor, of shielding all within from the rafts of gray clouds that ride the winter's southward spread across New Brunswick from the far Canadian north.

Perhaps even more important than North Mountain's physical protection, however, is the intimate scale of its protected valley, with its implicit offer of improved psychological security. North Mountain's valley permitted the colony to be more confident in its ties to its new land than the St. Croix island had—more confident to experiment. To plant the first successful wheat crop in North America, for example, in an environment where even today only the hardiest varieties, under the closest supervision, can expect to make it. And to erect North America's first gristmill, with which to process that crop. North America's first drama was written and produced here—a tribute of thanks to Neptune for the bounty of his sea, and for bringing back the explorers for whose pleasure the play was written (see Appendix). Early Acadia was also the site of colonial America's first organized attempt at secular entertainment, L'Ordre du Bon Temps—basically an evening banquet circle, a personal project of Sieur Samuel de Champlain, navigator to the King of France and the founding engineer of French America.

The outshoots of this Port Royal colony would sometimes succeed and sometimes fail—like the attempted French settlement on Mount Desert Island, Maine, founded in 1613 and later that same year extinguished by raiding Virginia pirates. Sometimes, new colonies would take root but remain small and fragile—like the outpost fishing village of Cape Sable, where the rocky tip of the Nova Scotia peninsula reluctantly releases the Bay of Fundy back into the North Atlantic. And sometimes these offshoots would take hold and flourish beyond all expectation, like the ones in Fundy's forbidding upper reaches, centering on the village of Grand Pré. Almost always, the largest and the most successful settlements were the ones where the Acadians could both fish from the sea and reclaim enough marshland to become *petits habitants* (subsistence farmers). And in keeping with the lessons afforded by the earthen and timbered fortress range of North Mountain, the Acadians' initial colonial development centered on reclaiming and protecting their fertile marshland fields with miles of hand-formed artificial hillocks, or dikes.

Dike building does not seem to have begun in earnest until a mid-century expedition brought to Port Royal colonists who were familiar with Dutch-aided land-reclamation projects along the western coast of France. On the other hand, the Acadians may have picked up their dike-building ideas from the peaceful Micmac Indians who occupied the rest of the Nova Scotia peninsula inland, away from the French settlers' valley and their Fundy shore. The Indians would come to the shore only to rush out at low tide into the mud flats at the mouth of a small river or a large stream, to pound timbers (brought from the interior) into the ooze of the shore. These structures would be in the shape of an arc, sometimes almost a circle, and the incoming Fundy tide would wash over them, carrying salmon or other fish into the higher ground to spawn or feed. When the tide came out again, only the largest fish would be left caught against the Indian-designed trap, while the younger ones escaped to come back, larger, another day. These traps are called weirs, and all along Nova Scotia's Clare County, the so-called French Shore, small streams and rivers still sprout them. In the fall, when the tide carries dead and dying underbrush with it back into the sea, a cluttered Indian weir might have suggested the possibility of constructing a permanent barrier reinforced with mud.

During the day, groups of the men—in a communal-family or village-wide dike-building effort—would head out into the highest and nearest coastal marshes left dry by the receding Fundy tide. Those marshes would sometimes stretch out for several hundred feet, shallow enough at high tide to catch the sunlight, before dropping off to mud flats, where the sprouting roots of marsh grass would be buried too deep at high tide to grow. Through the rich thickets of long wavy grass, at half-day intervals, the Acadians would drive upended logs into the ground side by side in straight rows, and then retreat from the coming tide, to venture out a day later to drive in some more.

Eventually, this stick fort would be packed with cross timbers and mud, and after it had several times kept most of the tidewater out, the mud would stay. Packed with more mud, the dike could withstand all but the weather's worst abuse—and, especially near the mouths of rivers, would generate land deposits on its seaward side that might grow new patches of marsh grass with which to enclose yet another field.

Now the principal problem with these ingeniously reclaimed fields was the sea salt left behind in the soil. And the Acadians solved that problem with a series of hand-carved, wooden clapper valves (gates on horizontal hinges) called *aboiteaux*. The aboiteaux were installed in the dike superstructure with the logs and the mud, and posed no problem in construction because of their one-way doors. When the tide came in, it slammed shut the aboiteau door. But when the dike was finished, and a rainstorm filled its field like a pool, the aboiteau door would be forced open during a low tide, when the sea was no longer beating on it. Most every rainstorm, then, helped flush the field of salt. It was easier to dike the marshes for fields than to clear the upland forests, and besides, the Acadian cattle loved to eat the field's saltiest growths of marsh grass. The constructions could be used for raising (and penning) livestock until successive varieties of grass told the settlers their new field was ready for planting wheat, peas, and cabbage. These crops supplemented the colony's abundant diet of weir-caught fish, marsh-raised livestock, and mountainside wild game. All that grass detritus in the soil, plus livestock manure: we are talking about some of the most fertile fields on this continent, wrested back by Acadian farmers from the sea. Fields magically poised almost exactly midway between the North Pole and the equator. Fields distant from most—but, alas, not all—the havoc of Christian Europe.

The resourceful Acadians had no difficulty diking out the sea. But they could never successfully keep away the English raiding parties that periodically crossed it, intent on burning their farmsteads and starving them out. So they dug in and learned to build their early houses in much the same way they had built their dikes: low to the ground; made of big timbers; and packed with mud to keep them insulated from wind and water—as well as to make them more fireproof.

But neither North Mountain nor low-slung houses were enough. Their first attempt at a military post—a wooden palisade that has been rebuilt on its original site by the Canadian government—was burned by English raiders. (A Depression-era, museum-quality reproduction made from Samuel de Champlain's still-extant drawings, the palisade is known as the Port Royal Habitation).

In order to gain the security that the Habitation had failed to provide, the settlers decamped farther back into the valley, to a place where the main stem of the Rivière Dauphin finally emptied into the main tidal basin. There, on a bluff protected to the north by the Dauphin and to the south by a smaller but still formidable stream, they erected a new Port Royal, a *Fort* Royal. On the bluff, they piled up timber and brick-reinforced earthworks to form a star-shaped fortress that could not be burned or blasted off the land. And they filled it with muskets and cannon of sufficient range to reach and destroy ships or land-based parties of soldiers attempting to enter the valley beyond it. Fort Royal resembles a miniature version of the fortress at Quebec, but without all the rocks, and covered with a grass coat closely cropped by the prim, latter-day, English-speaking employees of Parks Canada, who are its current caretakers.

This first Acadian fort in Canada was to become, successively, the first outpost of English military intrusion into French Canada and the historic site chosen by Anglo-Canadians for their country's first national park. And it is, therefore, much better promoted and seen from nearby Route 1 than its perhaps more disturbing counterpart farther up the road at Grand Pré.

The new Fort Royal was an important spur to early colonial development, for it provided the military protection needed to make worthwhile the diking in of riverside tidal marshlands for another thirty miles inland. There the Acadian settlers could seek refuge from the turmoil visited upon the fort and its town—which were to remain a magnet for recurring American episodes of European intrigue.

Some of the early settlers went even farther than thirty miles, seeking out other, more defiantly inaccessible coves and marshlands on the upper and deepest reaches of the Bay of Fundy, where mariners unfamiliar with local tidal conditions might themselves be beached, capsized, or otherwise damaged on the vast Fundy mud flats at low tide. The colonists' migrations behind Fort Royal took them back as far as the Chignecto isthmus, that rocky, cove-encrusted land bridge between New France and the bulk of the Nova Scotia–Cape Breton land mass.

The Chignecto region is washed by Fundy's most astonishing tides, and admits the upper reaches of that body of water into two main branches, where only the most skilled pilots could successfully navigate a seaborn raiding party. The two main branches, Chignecto Bay to the northeast and the Minas Basin to the southeast, are dotted with low-lying areas where rivers empty into marshes which in turn empty into what becomes a salty expanse of mud for half the day and a glistening finger of the Atlantic Ocean—sometimes forty or fifty feet deep—for the other half.

The isthmus is narrow, so narrow in fact that, during pre-Expulsion times, these visionary French pioneers contemplated elaborate plans for a canal similar to the Panama Canal—plans never implemented—to shorten the sailing distance from Boston and Fort Royal to the St. Lawrence River and Quebec. Even without a canal, the isthmus was narrow enough to spawn a flourishing smuggling trade across it—especially after 1672, when the first of the major settlements outside Fort Royal was established at Beaubassin, a picturesque basin of Chignecto Bay located at the narrowest part of the isthmus. The trading monopoly of the home country had been a major issue in the incessant feuding between London and Paris in the American colonial era, and smuggling was an essential element of the near-autonomous economy of Acadia. Until 1710, most of the Acadian smuggling was done with the Yankee merchants of Anglo-American Boston, while the French governors looked on helplessly. After the English occupation of 1710, the English governors looked on help-lessly: the Acadian smuggling trade switched its focus to Louisbourg, the French fortress that had been erected on Île Royale (now Cape Breton Island) to secure the remainder of New France from further English advances.

The Beaubassin outpost was to prove a crucial battleground in a century of intrigue and hardships still to come. It lay by the Missaguash River, which can be navigated to the crown of the isthmus near a point where you take another river down the other side to a coastal village opening to the Gulf of St. Lawrence, a village the Acadians named Baie Verte (for its green sea grass and marshes). After the English capture of Fort Royal (for the third and final time) was permanently recognized by the Treaty of Utrecht, the French, claiming everything north of the Missaguash in their definition of the New France, built themselves another star-shaped earthwork fort across the river from the town of Beaubassin, and called it Fort Beauséjour. It looked out protectively over Beaubassin, but more importantly, like the Fort Royal and Quebec outposts it imitated, Fort Beauséjour protected a cluster of strategic villages and diked fields farther up the Petitcodiac and Memramcook River Valleys. These settlements, now part of New Brunswick, have become the suburbs of metropolitan Moncton—with its still-predominant Acadian popula-tion, its French-speaking university, and its telltale museum.

The settlements in and around the Chignecto isthmus were to grow more populous than Fort Royal for a variety of reasons, princi-pally because the on-again, off-again governments of both the French and the English ruled the isolated colony with more or less benign neglect. The garrison at Fort Royal was incapable of stopping Acadian settlers from leaving the immediate area of settlement and squatting on the open land beyond. Nor could the authorities at the fort prevent the Acadians from serving as middlemen between the Indians and unauthorized outside merchants. During the farming season, Acadian farm children not needed in the fields would build boats of their own or work the Atlantic fisheries from scattered posts along the shore north of Cape Sable—just as their ancestors from the coastal fringes of France had been doing for two hundred years. Over the years, the increasingly hungry Yankees carried away dried fish, furs, sometimes even surplus grain, in an economy that functioned entirely by barter. In Moncton's archives is a hand-penned copy of a diary kept by Robert Hale, a Harvard-trained physician and part owner of the schooner *Cupid,* detailing the mechanics of this trade. While on an expedition of his own in June of 1731, Hale reported: "When I came to inquire into the price of things, I found their manner is to give no more (or scarcely so much) for *our* goods as they cost in Boston, so that all the advances our traders can make is on *their* goods." Hale fumes on about the fact that the Acadians will take only goods in exchange for other goods, and not money, because the Indians don't want to be bothered with it, either. The Acadians "have no taxes to pay, and they trade but little among themselves, everyone raising himself what he wants, except what they have in exchange from the traders. And as a proof that they are governed by this maxim, I need only say that when I came to pay my reckoning at the tavern, the landlord had but five pence in money, though he is one of the wealthiest in the place."

And the wealth of the isthmus area was, colonially speaking, immense. The political economy of this advanced early settlement was characterized by collective resistance to outside exploitation—English or French—thus conserving and accumulating capital resources. Yet there was unlimited room for personal enterprise—and in such a system, personal enterprise ultimately serves to strengthen, rather than weaken, the community. Plagued neither by the shortages of land nor of food that held back feudal Europe and some of their less-enterprising Anglo-American neighbors, the Acadians thrived—doubling their population on an average every fifteen years after 1680. The center of population in the colony eventually shifted to Grand Pré—midway between Fort Royal and Beaubassin. But the colony continued to spread out until it had formed three spokes from its Minas Basin hub. In one direction, through the glacial rift of North and South Mountain, lay a continuous settlement of farms all the way to the military and administrative center of Fort Royal. Farther up the Minas Basin—presumably named for its "mines," actually just surface deposits of minerals that had suggested to early explorers vague and never-to-be-realized dreams of a French Peru—more settlements were scattered all the way to Cobequid (now Truro). In a third direction, the population spread out along Chignecto Bay to Beaubassin and beyond, up several river valleys into what is now New Brunswick. The two largest settlements at the Minas Basin hub were Pisiquid (now Windsor) and Grand Pré—whose broad prairie was laced with five rivers offering fresh water, dikable marshlands, and a communication-transportation system far more extensive and commodious than at any other place on the Acadian peninsula. Grand Pré prospered not only because it was the Acadian hub but also because its astounding 28,000 feet of handmade dikes reclaimed 3,000 acres of land—the largest single reclamation project in the colony, almost four times the size of New York City's Central Park. By 1755 and the Expulsion, the three-pronged Acadian colony was so self-sufficient that the agricultural production of Grand Pré's fields alone would have fed the entire colony of 18,000 people for one year. But the Acadians, not wanting to work harder than necessary, and not feeling a need for imported possessions more elaborate than a few iron pots, bottles of liquor, and bolts of red English cloth with which to supplement the wool and flax garments they wove for themselves, never went on to develop a proto-capitalist economy with its surpluses, money, government, banks, and soldiers. By 1755, the Acadians had carved out more than 14,000 acres of diked lands—an area exactly the size of Manhattan—and on that land they lived with more than 100,000 head of livestock, in quietly rude and independent and proliferating defiance of every European attempt to make them go away—or to exploit them while they remained.

In fact, it seems that the only residents of Acadia who never settled down to this life of satisfied self-sufficiency were its carousel cast of governors. The early ones—such as Charles La Tour, who arrived in the colony as a teenager in 1614, later serving two terms as an English "Protestant" governor and two more as a French "Catholic" one— tended to share in the hardships and outlook of those they governed, and usually joined in when the smugglers came around. But the later ones found themselves on the periphery of Acadia's colonial life, reduced to the status of snubbed outsiders and unable to stop the smuggling, unable to levy taxes or guarantee a steady supply of food-stuffs from those they were presumably there to govern and protect, and unable to keep up their forts, their guns, or their troop morale. The Acadians learned not to take their governors too seriously as superiors, and that tradition persists in Louisiana today: a Cajun almost never says "monsieur." It's your first name, or your nickname, or nothing.

Nothing, in the monarchial eighteenth century, was sometimes too much to bear. Groused one late-period governor, an indignant English one, after some Acadian settlements beyond Fort Royal de-clined even to answer a remonstrative letter: "The greatest part of the people desired *no* communication with us." Bellowed another, in a proclamation nailed to a church door: "It appears to me that you think yourselves independent of any government, and you wish to treat with the king as if you were so." Added a third, with candid, if brittle, resignation: "This has been hitherto no more than a mock govern-ment, its authority having never yet extended beyond cannon reach of this fort."

These and similar observations of the day snarl out from the pages of old documents, particularly the governors' handwritten letter books. These pre-Xerox copies of letters sent back to the home gov-ernment—the most revealing of them written by English governors in English—are all we have left of those who participated in the pre-Expulsion conflict and determined the course it took. A heavily edited edition of these and related documents from various govern-ment archives was issued as a small brown book by the Nova Scotia government in 1869, because "the necessity for their removal [the Acadians] has not been clearly perceived," and English motives, the book's preface defensively asserts, have been "misunderstood." Not coincidentally, this first edition appeared twenty-two years after

Henry Wadsworth Longfellow created an international literary and political sensation with his romantic Expulsion narrative, *Evangeline*, which contained quotes from some of those documents.

The central political issue in these papers is the attempt by English governors to extract an oath of allegiance to the English crown—an issue rooted in cultural conflict and branching into political tragi-comedy. After England took possession of Acadia for the third and final time in 1710, and for a determined forty-five years thereafter, English governors kept trying to persuade the horrified Acadians to take an oath of allegiance to Queen Anne and, later, three Georges, all of them Francophobes.

The oath controversy stretched over four decades, because no one could decide exactly what the official version was supposed to say. The confusion began in 1710, when the French commander gave up the Acadians' grassed-over fort to an Anglo-American invasion force after being outnumbered eleven to one for three weeks. The Acadian garrison surrendered to an improbable raiding party headed by a Virginia governor and a New York businessman. The governor was the ambitious Francis Nicholson, who had previously served as lieutenant governor in New York and as governor of the colonies of Virginia and Maryland, before brashly sailing into Port Royal's harbor to install himself as the new governor of a conquered Nova Scotia. One year before the capture of Fort Royal, and again one year afterwards, the determined Nicholson would attempt expeditions to capture the rest of Canada—but, in those more evenly matched contests, he lost. Nonetheless, Nicholson went from his modest, almost embarrassing Fort Royal success to become a lieutenant general in His Majesty's Army and ultimately commander-in-chief of all English forces in North America. While Nicholson's capture of Fort Royal tipped the balance of power by which New England would destroy New France half a century later, luck would have it that he pulled it off entirely with volunteer forces from England's North American colonies—in what proved to be a fateful rehearsal for the events of 1776.

Nicholson's articles of capitulation, still extant among Acadian colonial documents, permitted "the inhabitants within cannon shot of

Martin House, Caraquet, New Brunswick. A one-room cabin built in 1783 with pièce-sur-pièce construction VILLAGE HISTORIQUE ACADIEN

Fort Royal" to remain on their farms if they agreed to take oaths of "allegiance and fidelity to her sacred Majesty of Great Britain." All others would be permitted to leave, and Nicholson not so secretly hoped that most of them would. For he dreamed that hordes of new, English-speaking, Puritan colonists could be induced to secure the rich territory he had conquered. In a fit of cunning patriotism, he had renamed the fort for Queen Anne, and also the town (thereafter known as Annapolis Royal), the river, and the valley it drained—but the anticipated hordes of English settlers never arrived. To his considerable chagrin, one day a personal letter from Queen Anne *did* arrive,

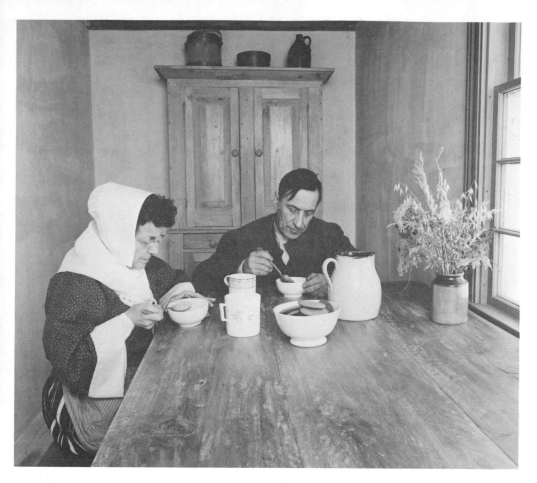

Dining-room scene, Babineau House, Caraquet, New Brunswick, reenacted by Village em-ployees VILLAGE HISTORIQUE ACADIEN

announcing the Treaty of Utrecht, which superseded his provisional articles of capitulation. That treaty confirmed English rights to Nova Scotia after 1714. Moreover, above and beyond the formal terms of the treaty, Anne's court announced that "our good brother, the most Christian king [Louis XIV], hath, at our desire, released from imprisonment on board his galleys, such of his subjects as were detained there on account of their professing the Protestant religion." In order to "show by some mark of our favour towards his subjects how kind we take his compliance," Anne agreed to permit the Acadians to have priests of their own choosing and "retain and enjoy their said lands and tenements without any molestation, as fully and freely as our other subjects do."

This agreement, particularly the clause guaranteeing the Acadians French-speaking priests sent in by the Bishop of Quebec, angered the Anglo-American Puritan extremists who had supported and financed Nicholson's expedition. Worse, they were outraged that Anne had committed her successors to pay for the farms of any departing Acadians who refused to give further allegiance to English rule. "It would entirely disappoint the settlement of that valuable country," reads one letter of protest, "because it is never to be supposed that any person will go to buy land in a new country, when in all His Majesty's plantations abroad there is such encouragement, of land gratis, to such as will come and settle in them." Besides, more to the point, such needless fiduciary complications form a "breach of public trust," charged Nicholson's gain-seeking invaders, because, by rights, these "lands are promised away to the captors" and should be given to them directly, rather than sold back to the crown.

The English crown never seriously sought to buy the Acadians out, and the Acadians never seriously considered leaving. And those outside cannon shot of the fort of Annapolis Royal never seriously considered taking the English oath without a variety of reservations that subsequent, monarch-appointed governors would find to be most *demi-républicain* and insolent. After Queen Anne died, the situation worsened—for George I, the German-born English king who himself could speak no English, was embroiled in all the continent's dynastic power struggles. His successor, George II, saw any form of Catholicism, and those who would practice it, as a dark and near-Satanic force to be destroyed. Those Acadians who would not take an unqualified oath, and who also would not leave, would shrewdly maneuver to remind their absolutely astonished governors of the promises of the "late Queen Anne of happy memory."

There were further complications: the failure of the Treaty of Utrecht to establish exact and realistic boundaries for the French and English territories after Queen Anne's War. The French were permitted to keep two islands within easy smuggling distance of the two settlement prongs along the Chignecto isthmus, where well over half the colony was living after 1710. The larger smuggling destination was Île Royale, with Fortress Louisbourg, the would-be Gibraltar of the North Atlantic, and the guardian of the gateway to their remaining North American possessions along the St. Lawrence Valley. The smaller one, Île St. Jean (now the province of Prince Edward Island), lay only ten miles off the north coast of the Chignecto isthmus. After the French built Fort Beauséjour at the Missaguash River, securing what had become the de facto boundary line, the residents within its range considered themselves still basically French, or at least at liberty to engage in passive resistance to self-inflated English governors who couldn't speak their language. And certainly at liberty to continue duty-free trading unmolested by them. At any English attempt to take them prisoner, or make them do anything by force, the Acadians would slip away, just as they had done in the earlier days when the English came among them to burn their houses. Antagonized too directly, they would be a formidable enemy, and could wage extended guerrilla warfare against imported English replacement settlers or even against regular troops. Mused the virtually helpless Governor Nicholson: "So it is to be considered that one hundred of the French, who were born upon that continent and are perfectly known in the woods; can march upon snowshoes; and understand the use of birch canoes, are of more value and service than five times their number of raw men, newly come from Europe."

Yet another complicating factor in this delicate political situation was the presence of a third force, the Indians—a force larger than either of the other two. The Indians had taught the Acadians how to use snowshoes and birch canoes, thus enabling them to survive and resist both the winter and the English assaults. The Acadian settlers achieved a relatively healthy accommodation with their Indian neighbors, in part because they stayed close to the shore and left the Indians' interior hunting grounds alone—something the land-hungry English invaders would never agree to do. Moreover, frequent miscegenation since the early 1600's had made many of the Indians half-blood relatives, or métis. One early Acadian settler by the name of Jean Vincent de Castain had even married the daughter of an

Abenaki chief, and eventually assumed leadership of the whole tribe.

Though the Indians could have continued on without any of the white settlers—French or English—the Acadians could never have survived without the Indians, who from 1605 onwards provided the fur for the small but essential French–Boston trade (legal and contraband) that brought the colony the few outside goods it absolutely needed. From the Indians, the Acadians also acquired dogs for hunting, and a knowledge of wild carrots, potatoes, blueberries, cranberries, huckleberries, and shadberries (wild pear). They also learned to gather clams, oysters, scallops, and lobsters from the Fundy mud flats during low tide, as well as how to trap salmon and other finfish in weirs. They learned to use birch bark to make canoes, and to make insulating covers for their mud-and-timber houses. Some linguists even suggest that "Acadie" comes from the Indian word for the codfish found in the offshore Atlantic fisheries, and not from the European notion of a classic, trouble-free Arcadia.

The cultural exchange of Acadia went two ways, however. Most of the Indians eventually adapted their religious beliefs to a loose Catholicism, which proved an additional inducement for them to be openly hostile to the Puritan English. Governor Nicholson's successor, Richard Philipps, constantly complained to London of insufficient presents with which to woo the Indians, especially since priests and other French agents were keeping their Indian allies well supplied from Fortress Louisbourg. Understanding that the Puritans would drive them from their land—unlike the French and the Acadians—the Indians threatened to slit the throats of any Acadians who agreed to become Puritans or fight with the English. The Acadians living outside Annapolis Royal's cannon range adamantly refused to take an oath of English allegiance without a clause exempting them from bearing arms, especially against the Indians. One of Governor Philipps's lieutenants was forced to grant the Acadians one version of this clause because he was afraid the settlers would withhold their fish catch or smuggle it off to France via Louisbourg if he refused. Philipps himself, who governed mainly from abroad and was in the colony for only two brief visits, narrowly avoided the wrath of a mass meeting of Annapolis Royal's townspeople, who almost stormed his fort when he set out to administer an unqualified oath personally. He soon found he could obtain the oaths necessary to his continued appointments to His Majesty's service only by penning in the arms-bearing provision on the margin of the French copies. Curiously, the English copies—without the arms clause appended—are the only ones to survive, but other remaining letters and records confirm the existence of the variations in the French versions.

The English remained convinced throughout this oath-seeking ordeal that the Indian problem was merely an ill-concealed ruse: oath-taking Acadians could remain "neutral" and at the same time cause the government trouble by dressing up as Indians—perhaps another tantalizing Acadian anticipation of the Anglo-American events of 1776. But even without the French, the Indians were to prove quite troublesome to the English on their own. During the four-year Indian wars (1722–26) that split Philipps's administration more than just chronologically, one insurgent group of Indians seized two armed sloops and came close to blockading Annapolis Royal's harbor. Philipps's outmaneuvered government subdued them with great difficulty—killing four chiefs in the process.

After the Indian wars, Philipps's absentee regime deteriorated; one of his lieutenant governors even committed suicide. The garrison's Huguenot engineer, who assumed power, thereupon prudently ceased to pursue the oath issue. The Huguenot, Paul Mascarene, one of the few English governing officials who could communicate with the Acadian residents in their own language, is perhaps best remembered for his indirect contribution to strengthened Acadian resistance. From the time he arrived in the colony as a major, he had been the liaison for the elected "delegates" that Philipps had demanded from each of the Acadian villages. These limited representatives were presumably there only to receive and implement formal government instructions—though they would periodically submit to their governors independent-minded and infuriating petitions of the "late Queen Anne of happy memory" variety. By 1748, there were forty-eight deputies, a fragmented proto-legislature agitated at every moment by the French government's missionary priests.

Meanwhile, these non-Puritan Acadian settlers continued—in Philipps's own words—to "multiply exceedingly . . . like Noah's progeny." The first serious attempts at English colonization, to counterbalance the Acadian population explosion from 1680 to 1755, did not begin until late—after Philipps's successor took office in 1749. The new governor, Edward Cornwallis, from a prominent English family and something of a military playboy, became Philipps's successor by buying out his gubernatorial commission. Cornwallis declared the dreary Atlantic fishing village of Halifax to be his new capital, and eventually brought in almost two thousand new settlers to join him.

Cornwallis deplored the condition of Philipps's remnant garrison at the barren, rocky citadel of Halifax, a garrison which had an insufficient number of uniforms and greatcoats with which to greet his arrival party in the approved manner. Cornwallis angrily wrote back to London demanding that Philipps be fined for his negligence, but as in most of his other attempts to be governor, the ineffectual Cornwallis proved to be only an armchair belligerent. Although his name was given to the valley of the main river through the meadow that was Grand Pré, Edward Cornwallis is perhaps most memorable as the governor who brought into the councils of colonial government the devious English officer who eventually rid the invaders of their troublesome Acadians. The real power in the Cornwallis administration, he seized control of the vulnerable colonial council at Halifax, which the quickly wearied Cornwallis had left behind. In succeeding moves, that ambitious junior officer eventually managed to become, first, lieutenant governor, then acting governor, and, finally, governor in his own right. His name: Charles Lawrence.

Of the 18,000 Acadian inhabitants of the colony at the time of the Expulsion, almost half would lose their lives as a result of Governor Lawrence's treachery. And Lawrence was hated not only by his French-speaking subjects; he was excessively harsh with German members of the force Cornwallis had brought ashore at Halifax. One member of the inner circle at the garrison describes Lawrence as using "wicked and perfidious procedures."

Major Lawrence first started attending the Nova Scotia colonial council's meetings when Cornwallis was setting about one of his comic-opera attempts to readminister the English oath. While Cornwallis fumed, his ambitious officers, led by Lawrence, set about building a road, the beginnings of provincial Route 1, from Halifax through the central Nova Scotia highland to Pisiquid. At the end of the road, Cornwallis had directed that a Fort Edward should be erected in his honor. Farther down the Minas coast, at Grand Pré, a small blockhouse would also be built—to counteract any previous confusion on the part of those living away from Annapolis Royal about who was in control of the upper reaches of the Fundy.

In 1750, Lawrence, described by another one of the men around him as a "low, crafty tyrant and accomplished flatterer," persuaded the volatile Cornwallis to let him—as newly brevetted Colonel Lawrence—lead an attack on the French fort of Beauséjour. Lawrence, more accomplished at backroom politics than at open warfare, was easily repulsed. And because of his "arrogant and scornful attitude," again in the words of a contemporary, he was even more easily humiliated. He returned to the decimated Beauséjour area the following fall, but the best he could do was occupy the site of the burned-out church in the former village center of Beaubassin and construct his own self-honoring Fort Lawrence. Lawrence was back, glaring across the Missaguash River at Fort Beauséjour, where his principal French antagonist was encamped.

The governor-to-be's nemesis was a French priest who had arrived in Beaubassin the same year Lawrence had first joined the Cornwallis council. Abbé Jean Louis Joseph Le Loutre ("the Otter") hated the English so much that he once personally led an Indian raiding party against Annapolis Royal. Using extravagant amounts of French money, he constructed a considerable number of dikes in various areas of present-day New Brunswick behind Fort Beauséjour. He used all manner of threats and entreaties to move the Acadian settlers into areas he had thus secured. It appears that Le Loutre may even have been responsible for the burning of his own church at Beaubassin —with the help of some friendly Indians—to force compliance with his strategy by the settlers, and to accomplish their removal before

Lawrence's next military attack. After he became vicar-general of Acadia for the Bishop of Quebec, Le Loutre began intercepting English messages and supplies, and in other ways assuming command of all French military activities in the area, with the approval of the governor of French Canada. If anyone balked at his orders, Le Loutre would threaten excommunication.

The French branch of the Roman Catholic Church had long behaved as a sort of spiritual secret police force, a propaganda and mind-control agency for the French monarchy—ever since the fifteenth century, when Francis I coerced the Pope into allowing French kings to appoint all French bishops. After much intrigue, the Jesuits finally succeeding in having the Bishop of Quebec appointed separately by the Pope from Rome, but the French monarchy made certain all shepherds of colonial flocks had their political allegiances in order. Quebec's second bishop, for example, the first prelate ever to visit Acadia, had been the king's personal chaplain prior to his assignment to the see of New France.

Catholic missionary priests, therefore, wielded a form of secular political power in New France that the Puritan ministers in New England were never to equal. Governor Richard Philipps bitterly averred that the priests "presided as governors." And indeed, especially during times of French possession of Acadia, the priests were often the closest thing the colony ever knew or needed of modern government—they kept all birth, marriage, death, and related census records. These services were financed by collective "tithes" for the priests' living expenses and for construction of church buildings—which also served as community meeting halls whenever military officials, French or English, convened the inhabitants to hear their latest orders and demands for oaths. The priests also did 'what little teaching the colony was provided with, always little enough to ensure that the relatively well-educated priests would retain the prerogative of writing all letters on behalf of the villagers.

Le Loutre's real power, however, unlike that of the other French priests, was based on the Indians—for he had been trained in France principally to be a missionary to them. After Lawrence's failure to capture Fort Beauséjour, and as the general situation continued to worsen, English colonial documents begin referring derisively to Le Loutre as "Moses." The Halifax council placed a bounty on his head, offering to pay for either the priest or his scalp. And though often criticized himself for his "pride and vanity," he served the Indians' political interests well: in correspondence with Halifax, Le Loutre demanded English recognition of Indian claims to about half the Nova Scotian land mass. The English thought he was crazy. Le Loutre, in turn, told the Indians that the English killed Jesus.

But Charles Lawrence eventually gained the upper hand. In the power vacuum left by Cornwallis's departure, Lawrence first seized the presidency of the council—and within ten months was named lieutenant governor as he set out to avenge his earlier defeat at Le Loutre's Fort Beauséjour. Lawrence's first official act in power was to send a letter to the Board of Trade—the central company for His Majesty's American plantations—despairing of local political conditions in terms that would easily prepare for his subsequent moves. Lawrence's tone was so harsh that the board uneasily wrote back that "great caution ought to be used to avoid giving any alarm" to what both sides now freely referred to as the "French neutrals," the Acadians.

In the fall of 1754, Lawrence —dissatisfied with the board's response—wrote accusing the Acadians of taking food to possibly "hostile forces" gathered behind Beaubassin, forces gathered at the urging of the hated Le Loutre. Lawrence enclosed an opinion written at his specific direction by the colonial court's chief justice, also a member of Lawrence's colonial council, declaring that any settlers abandoning their lands to help the "enemy" would be fleeing from their oaths and therefore sacrificing their rights to return to that land. This maneuver enabled Lawrence to seize their land if they fled from battle, which most of them did.

The board hastily replied that "we cannot form a proper judgment or give a final opinion" on the Acadian question at that time. Lawrence left them room for none. In the spring he set out to capture Fort Beauséjour and used that seizure to justify the eventual expulsion of all Acadian settlers from the Fundy basin. First, he brought in two

Two views of the Acadian past: Champlain's reconstructed Port Royal Habitation (top), *and the reconstructed church of St. Charles de Grand Pré* CANADIAN CONSULATE-GENERAL, NEW YORK thousand troops from Boston to Chignecto, and sent out instructions that food shipments across the bay were to be strictly prohibited—with seizure ordered for any contraband discovered. By the middle of June 1755, he had succeeded in starving out and capturing the fort, and wrote triumphantly to the board that he had given his officers "orders to drive them [the Acadians] out of the country." The English government was so startled by this news that the Secretary of State himself replied that such harshness might provoke insurrection, and that "it cannot, therefore, be too much recommended to you, to use the greatest caution and prudence."

But that letter didn't get to Lawrence until it was too late. Half of Acadia would be, by that time, already dispersed.

Lawrence spent the summer before the Expulsion conspiring with two visiting English admirals, hawks who had anticipated the Seven Years' War, and who egged him on. Lawrence ordered twenty-four Yankee cargo vessels to be sent from Boston to carry the Acadians away and redeployed his triumphant force from Fort Beauséjour—renamed Fort Cumberland—to the various settlements he would eventually depopulate, strip, and burn.

In the first of a series of covert orders to these redeployed detachments, Lawrence instructed his field commanders to arrest the Acadians and seize their property. "It will be necessary to keep this measure as secret as possible," wrote Lawrence, urging his men to devise some "stratagem to get the men, both young and old—especially the heads of families—into your power, and detain them until the transports arrive, so as they may be shipped off as soon as the boats arrive, to various American colonies." And, for good measure, he added: "Then ship the women and children afterwards to different destinations far from each other." In a later set of instructions, Lawrence stressed: "You must use the most vigorous measures not only to compel the settlers to board the ships, but also to deprive those who might escape of all means of subsistence, by burning their homes and destroying in the region all that might enable them to exist" during the winter months to come.

Lawrence's documents reveal that he hired the boats at a flat fee per head of Acadian deportees, and upon taking up his cargo, each

captain received from Lawrence's troops a letter to the governor of
the colony at the ship's destination. Those letters offered no apologies
for any inconvenience that might be caused to any of the other English
colonies made party to this unilateral action, because Lawrence
preemptively insisted that the prisoner/refugees "can be useful." In
particular, he noted that, at little expense, they "can render services
and in time become good subjects."

Lawrence's roundup campaign went relatively smoothly, but not
entirely without incident. After the fall of Fort Beauséjour in June,
and the delivery of initial orders to his men in July, Lawrence spent
August arresting all the priests and loading the ships with prisoners
from the farms around Beaubassin. The men of the Acadian villages
had their firearms and boats seized, and when they sent delegates to
Halifax in protest, Lawrence imprisoned all who would not take an
immediate and unconditional oath.

As August slipped into September, he tightened his grip. The male
residents of Pisiquid were summoned to Fort Edward for a meeting
and summarily imprisoned behind the stockade. An English boat sent
to Cobequid did not arrive until just after that village's residents had
heard what was going on up the bay and had fled across the Chignecto
isthmus to the sea and escaped to Île St. Jean, where eventual deportation awaited them. While setting the village afire, however, the English soldiers at Cobequid accidently ignited their own boat. Meanwhile, in Annapolis Royal there was an armed uprising against the
invaders, but its details are not clear from the surviving documents.

The closest thing to a direct military engagement between Lawrence's army and the defenseless Acadians occurred on the Petitcodiac
River behind the newly renamed Fort Cumberland, where an English
raiding party was systematically setting fire to two hundred apparently
abandoned houses and barns. A small force of men led by Joseph
"Beausoleil" Broussard came out of the woods wielding axes, hoes,
and hammers as the English torches finally reached their church. At
the conclusion of the encounter, twenty-nine English soldiers lay
dead.

Broussard survived and later, in Louisiana, helped lead another
strategic engagement on behalf of his people. Some historians believe

Broussard walked and canoed his way to Louisiana along the vast arc of French settlements through the St. Lawrence and Mississippi River Valleys, but ninth-generation family informants say he came by boat across the sea. We can't trace such routes with any certainty, for most information about who ended up where and how has been lost.

We are standing in an odd-shaped wooden room twenty-four feet wide—enough space for four full-sized adults to lie head to toe without touching one another. The room is almost double that distance in length. Remove the floor timbers and three additional feet of ballast rocks stored beneath, and you can make the room fifteen feet high. Take out the wall behind, and you can add another dozen feet.

For there are a lot of feet to fit within this room, which has an estimated maximum storage capacity of 150 tons of cargo. Make that cargo human, and count it in at two persons per ton of capacity—which Governor Lawrence ordered his field commanders to do—and imagine three hundred people crowded into this space for up to three months. Given the existing floor area, this would be the result: while one half attempt to lie down shoulder to shoulder, the other half would be required to stand shoulder to shoulder. Build in three layers of decks, which, minus the thickness of their support timbers, gives you just over four feet of height in each compartment, and everyone in the room would be able to lie down together all at the same time, with perhaps a few clothes or other personal possessions—although no one but the smallest child has room to stand. Place a lock on the sole hatch entrance to this space, and you have a floating prison with no windows for light or ventilation, no plumbing, no heat when it is cold (except for the huddled bodies), and a musty odor of damp wood to remind you that the bottomless ocean is no farther from you than the width of a clenched fist.

Governor Lawrence ordered his deportation vessels—most of them with cargo holds far smaller than that of the schooner just described—filled with over five thousand prisoners during the fall months of 1755. Lawrence's scheme could not begin, however, until his troops were deployed from Fort Beauséjour to the various Acadian settlements—and on August 18, the first 313 men arrived at the Minas Basin under the command of Colonel John Winslow. Only at Grand Pré are the day-to-day loading operations clear, because Winslow kept a truly remarkable diary—one of the few to survive from the Expulsion period. Winslow encamped at the church of St. Charles de Grand Pré, temporarily storing his arms in the sanctuary, his men in tents outside in the public square, and himself in the presbytery. A wooden stockade was erected around the church. "These activities," he wrote Governor Lawrence, "have not caused them the least worry, for they have seen the proof that the soldiers will spend the winter with them."

The residents of Grand Pré had little time to think about the soldiers, for they were busy bringing in their harvest. As the month drew to a close, however, three foreign boats arrived in their harbor without warning. "The inhabitants have noticed them and have inquired as to their destination; but I have already interviewed the captains," writes Winslow, "and have given them instruction to tell the inhabitants that the boats were sent for me to accommodate troops to be sent wherever I might assign them."

The first Tuesday in September, Winslow composed a summons, posted the next day, ordering all the men in the area over ten years of age to attend a meeting in the church to hear "what we are ordered to communicate." And at 3 P.M. on Friday, September 5, over four hundred men showed up. Because Winslow did not speak French, his orders had to be translated, and the collaborationist Huguenot merchant who performed that task was made a judge in the post-Expulsion regime. Winslow wore a wig.

And this is what he read to the assembly: "Gentlemen, I have received from His Excellency, Governor Lawrence, the King's instructions, which I have in my hand. By his orders you are called together to hear His Majesty's final resolution concerning the French inhabitants of this Province of Nova Scotia, who for more than half a century have had more indulgence granted them than any of his subjects in any part of his dominions. What use you have made of it, you yourselves best know.

"The duty I am now upon, though necessary, is very disagreeable to my natural make and temper, as I know it must be grievous to you, who are of the same species. But it is not my business to dwell on the orders I have received, but to obey them, and therefore, without hesitation, I shall deliver to you His Majesty's instructions and commands, which are, that your lands and tenements and cattle and livestock of all kinds are forfeited to the crown, with all your effects, except money and household goods, and that you yourselves are to be removed from this Province.

"The peremptory orders of His Majesty are, that the French inhabitants of these Districts be removed, and through His Majesty's goodness, I am directed to allow you your money and as many of your household goods as you can take without overloading the vessels you go in. I shall do everything in my power that all these goods be secured to you and that you not be molested in carrying them away, and also that whole families shall go in the same vessel: so that this removal, which I am sensible must give you a great deal of trouble, may be made as easy as His Majesty's service will admit; and I hope that in whatever part of the world your lot may fall, you may be faithful subjects, and a peaceable and happy people.

"I must inform you that it is His Majesty's pleasure that you remain in the security under the inspection and direction of the troops that I have the honor to command."[1]

Winslow's troops were, by this point, stationed between the church and the stockade, armed. The doors and windows of the church were barred shut. Of course, Lawrence had received no such orders from any king, and Winslow knew at the time of his performance that he had been ordered to *separate* the families.

The church of St. Charles de Grand Pré—a stone replica stands at one end of the tiny park commemorating the long-ago village—was approximately a hundred feet long by forty feet wide, just enough room for everyone to lie down on and under the pews for the night. That night, Winslow's troops began their forays into the village, and they continued doing so, compelling him eventually to issue an order "that an end must be put to distressing" the women and children left defenseless outside the walls of this makeshift prison. Under pressure, he finally allowed small groups of prisoners to exercise in the yard, and permitted twenty a day to go out to make final arrangements with their wives and children. Failure to return was discouraged by Winslow's promise of punishment for all offenses, punishment "to be visited upon the next of kin, if the offender being out of the way, or in default of kindred, upon the next neighbor." Several men did, in fact, escape, but were ultimately prevailed upon to return. The eleven transports expected did not arrive. Only five did, thus delaying Winslow's plans and ultimately causing him to overload the boats even more. Provisions for the voyage were skimpy—bread, flour, and water only—and late in arriving.

When the time came for departure, Winslow ordered all the young men drawn into lines. "Ordered ye prisoners to march," he wrote that evening in his journal. "They all answered they would not go without their fathers. I told them that was a word I did not understand, for that the King's command was to me absolute and should be absolutely obeyed. And that I did not love to use harsh means, but that the time did not admit of parleys or delays, and then ordered the whole troops to fix their bayonets and advance towards the French, and bid the four right hand files of the prisoners consisting of 24 men, one of whom I took hold (who opposed the marching) and bid march: he obeyed and the rest followed, though slowly, and went on praying and singing and crying, being met by the women and children all the way with great lamentations upon their knees, praying, etc."

Outnumbered almost ten to one, Winslow's heavily armed troops were nonetheless able to complete the loading in late October. Of those aboard the twenty-four vessels from the various Fundy settlements, half would die by the first of the year from smallpox or lack of sufficient clothing for an Atlantic voyage in the middle of winter.

The largest group—one-fourth of those who survived the expedition—went no farther than Massachusetts, where, in Boston, families were further broken down and dispersed all over the colony. The Massachusetts prisoners, under virtual house arrest, were forbidden to leave their assigned areas under penalty of imprisonment. The Massachusetts ranks were swelled by six ships originally bound for South Carolina that put in at Boston because their water supplies were polluted.

Groups from Grand Pré and Annapolis Royal totaling seven hundred were sent farther down the coast to Connecticut, but most of them eventually escaped to the area around Montreal (some 10 percent of the population of the province of Quebec is of Acadian ancestry). Still another group from Annapolis Royal, which spent the entire month of December at sea, en route to New York, arrived there with its cargo described as "poor, naked and destitute." Most of the New York prisoners were later dispatched to the French West Indies, and those who survived that ordeal eventually came to Louisiana.

In Pennsylvania, three of the expedition's vessels were held in the Philadelphia harbor—the Acadians were said to have insufficient socks, shirts, and blankets—and the smallpox killed off half of them. In three of these states—Massachusetts, New York, and Pennsylvania, the lands of the 1776 rebellion's patriotic, liberty-loving forefathers —all the Acadians under twenty-one were separated from parents and guardians and indentured to labor-hungry Yankee farms.

In Catholic Maryland, four vessels of refugees were welcomed a bit more warmly than anywhere else in English America, and they were not very well watched. As a result, one group of young men set sail for the West Indies, while others headed through the forest either to Canada or to Louisiana. The governor of Virginia, however, would not agree to accept his allocated boats of refugees, and more died aboard the crowded ships in the Williamsburg harbor before being dispatched to camps in four English ports. There they languished until 1763, when word of their plight reached the French ambassador. Louis XV refused to sign the treaty ending the Seven Years' War— a result, in part, of the Acadian dispersal—until the English government agreed to deliver the survivors of these camps into his personal care. The Virginia group was then repatriated to various French coastal seaports, where other straggling refugees—ultimately three to four thousand—were periodically deposited by the English navy until the end of the war.

Only one in ten of the Carolina refugees survived. Those in Georgia were sold into slavery, not merely pressed into indentured servitude. Yet small groups from both areas managed to escape in small craft, edging the colonial shore northward until captured off the waters of New York and Massachusetts. From there, many walked back to Nova Scotia's Baie Sainte-Marie, to establish what is now known as the French Shore. The South Carolina survivors ended up in the West Indies or in Louisiana. The Georgia survivors who successfully escaped north made it no farther than Île St. Jean, where, after the fall of Louisbourg, nine ships took them away again. Along with the former residents of Cobequid and other refugees, they were deported to Europe. But only seven ships and one lifeboat with twenty-seven men aboard made it to shore.

Only one group of deportees successfully escaped—232 people crammed aboard the 139-ton *Pembroke,* whose crew was overpowered by its captives en route. Setting sail across the Bay of Fundy from Annapolis Royal, they arrived at the St. John River in the winter snow five days before Christmas. In separate raids four and five years later, the English rounded up those who had survived and had remained behind in the St. John area, and imprisoned them at Halifax. Halifax also was the detention center for settlers snatched in raids along the upper coast of New Brunswick, where many of the Acadians had fled on foot—once again seeking refuge with the Indians. In 1771, the English government claimed there were only 1,249 Acadians left in all the Maritime Provinces—but today their descendants make up almost a third of the population of Maritime Canada, and almost exactly half the population of New Brunswick. Those captured and sent to Halifax, however, were eventually deported to Santo Domingo, from where they made it to Louisiana, or to Louisiana directly. Scattered Acadian escapes to Uruguay, Nicaragua, Honduras, and the Falkland Islands have also been reported, and there are also Acadian descendants to be found in southeast Texas, coastal Alabama, France, and New England.

All those who ended up in the West Indies were put to work constructing French government fortifications in preparation for the slave rebellions that would follow the French Revolution. In this work, they were described as "crawling under the bushes, to screen themselves from the sun," perishing miserably. The rigid class structure of Santo Domingo—24,000 whites, divided equally between the plantation-owning *grands blancs* and the small farmer-urban bourgeoisie *petits blancs,* plus 20,000 mulattoes and 400,000 black slaves—was inhospitable in more ways than the climate, so almost all these survivors made their way to Louisiana.

Most of the descendants of those who were shipped to French ports also ended up in Louisiana—though there are Acadians to be found in the Grand' Ligne region of France. The ones who left France had been there for twenty-eight years and had participated in seven unsuccessful resettlement expeditions, until they were finally removed to Louisiana. A French druggist from St.-Malo who had made his fortune in New Orleans and returned to France, at his own expense, to promote importation of the remaining refugees as colonists, precipitated the largest mass migration of European-based settlers to the New World in United States colonial history, in 1785–86 (see Appendix).

And so, in successive waves, thrown up this time on the shores of distant Louisiana, the survivors began to regroup, drawn south by the knowledge that relatives from the Acadian extended family joyously awaited a reunion. Cajunism had been shaken, but would prove it could not be destroyed.

And Governor Charles Lawrence? After a banquet in Halifax, stuffed and drunk and lurching through the night, he contracted pneumonia, took to bed and died within the week. He had ordered up the banquet to celebrate the fall of New France at Quebec.

Trouble in the Sweet Promised Land

Road through the swamp, 1890s
GEORGES FRANÇOIS MUGNIER, COLLECTIONS OF THE LOUISIANA STATE MUSEUM

From far out in the Gulf of Mexico, even if you're high up in the air, the coast of Louisiana is difficult to pick out until you're practically upon it. Unlike the rocky coastal areas of Maritime Canada, or France, or the American West Coast, there are no hills or mountains anywhere near the water's edge to warn you that land is rising up out of the water. From an indigo black in its deepest sections, the Gulf lightens along the continental shelf to a green yellowed with the brown silt of the nearing delta shore. The landfall itself, especially when seen from a helicopter's-eye view three thousand feet up, seems, in relation to the open water, only slightly more brown or solid, haphazardly patched together with irregular expanses of green-brown marsh grass.

Out in the open Gulf, clouds will splotch and scatter shadows across the water in rhythmical patterns that myriad tidal ponds repeat and imitate among the marsh-grass clumps of shore. When the wind and tides are balanced perfectly, only the glistening edge of beige-brown sands clearly demarcates the dividing line between land and water—subject, invariably, to daily change.

This indecisive coastal marsh seems, as you fly closer into it, to float like a pad of lilies anchored in place by the most fragile and tenuous of roots. Farther inland, that growth begins to layer and thicken, an occasional row of mangrove shrubs here and low trees there. Parallel to the glistening shoreline, but inland from it, outcroppings of earlier, abandoned beach edges sprout oak trees in narrow but convincingly anchored strips of land the Cajuns called *cheniers* (*chêne,* oak). The chenier land deposits poke up out of the salt marsh tides just enough to encourage fresh-water plants like trees to grow across them. Even farther inland, these chenier formations—like the handmade dikes of ancient Acadia—gradually block out most of the salt water. Fresh-water marshes, and then whole swamps of towering cypress trees, begin to rise in the distance.

The cheniers, and indeed all the land mass and vegetation of southern Louisiana rise out of a vast delta fan of mud spewed from the Mississippi River. And almost all of Louisiana's new Acadia, the French Triangle—literally a triangle, stretched between Texas and New Orleans as far inland as Alexandria—has been built up by the Mississippi River in relatively recent times. The silt from which these soft, rockless lands were formed was washed down from the thirty-one states and two Canadian provinces which make up the Mississippi River's continental rivershed. Most of it came from the river into the Gulf via what Louisiana calls its bayous—the tracks of the offshoots or distributaries of the Mississippi through the delta. As the river's annual floods rage through these pathways into the Gulf's deep and calmly resilient pool, the water particles gradually drop their loads of silt and slow down, to forget the length of the river for the depth of the sea. The silt swirls through the bayous and bays and sometimes sticks to the existing land mass, or drops out in the Gulf, where later and larger particles rise up to form new land in conflict with the tides. The confusion over what is land and what is water extends most dramatically to the mouth of the Mississippi's main branch, fully a hundred miles out into the tropics off the southeastern Gulf shores of Mississippi–Alabama–Florida. From its mouth a hundred miles offshore, the Mississippi River's brown broth of dirt-laden fresh water (still writhing with fresh-water fish species) stretches yet another hundred miles into the Gulf, depositing hundreds of additional acres of mud flats each year. These deposits gradually acquire their own beaches and marsh grasses and mangroves and oak trees that then raise more land out of the water to join the expanding Louisiana shore.

The fresh-water plume of the river is powerful, rich, and full—full not only of America's best topsoil but also of organic nutrients from the sewage and industrial wastes of half the continent. In addition to the heat generated by the gradual decomposition of these wastes, the water carries the heat of cooling towers from the industrial plants of the lower Mississippi River Valley, especially the American "Ruhr Valley" corridor between Baton Rouge and New Orleans. This added heat and chemical differential between river and Gulf is subtle, but a factor strong enough in an arena of titanic natural forces to pluck an occasional heat-seeking hurricane out of the open water and onto shore. In 1965, "Betsy" came up the Mississippi River's delta like a fly on an old brown lizard's tongue.

The thousands of distributaries that built this delta are like geological capillaries, the veins of an enormous fan-shaped organism that breathes with the rain of the continent and the tides of the Gulf. From high in the air above it, and especially from the satellites that photograph the country's daily cloud cover for the evening TV weather forecasts, Louisiana's riverine delta stands out like a large animal's webbed foot: the living foot of a continent-size swamp lizard, or perhaps the print of a continent-sized duck.

The duck-footed metaphor fits Louisiana easily here, for once a year almost all of North America's duck population, and half its other migratory bird species as well, flee south in and around the Louisiana delta, the mid-point of their instinctual, north-south flyway. "The ducks can be a real problem," muses helicopter pilot Ron Chapman, a Vietnam veteran who now works a commercial, taxi-model cousin of that conflict's principal battle machine for Louisiana-based Petroleum Helicopters, Inc. PHI owns the world's largest private fleet of helicopters, mechanical *maringouins* (mosquitoes) that live out in the oil- and wildlife-rich marshes and open waters of Louisiana's Gulf shore. And low-flying pilots must always beware of ducks. "They'll sometimes come in and cover some of those small lakes completely," Chapman says of the flocks below us, dipping toward the liquid land with a stomach-lurching flick of his steering stick. "Have to watch out for them, 'cause they can cause a 'copter to crash."

Sensible and prudent ducks, however, will generally fly their formations much closer to the growth-encrusted ground, leaving the oil-industry helicopters alone. And as their formations roll through the air over Louisiana's delta webfoot, the ducks are especially attracted to clearings in the cypress and tupelo gum swamps that spring up farther inland, the fresh-water swamps and marshes protected from the Gulf's hurricane rages by the cheniers. For these fresh-water clearings and the cypress-filled backswamps adjacent to them are occasionally pockmarked with shallow pools full of duckweed—the world's smallest flowering plant, and a Louisiana subtropical delicacy you can easily swoop down to dip up out of the water with your very own bill.

baton
rouge

amite

river

french
settleme

ft. bute

bayou manchac

galveztown

louisiana
highway one

st. gabriel

donald-
sonville

plattenville

st. jacque
de cabanoce

bayou lafourche

thibodaux

acadian
coast

0   5   10   15 mi.

Skirting the treetops, scouring this fertile land in search of food, we wing into one such duck clearing just behind the crook of the levee of the Mississippi River. A grove of pecan trees surrounding the clearing is screeching with smaller birds, and autumn's carpet of fallen nuts and leaves spreads over a nineteenth-century graveyard built in part of the clearing and now virtually forgotten behind the river road's brush-lined fence. There are several graves among the nuts and leaves, and the largest grave in the clearing is a stepped and flat-topped and delicately ornamented pedestal. There is a looped, wrought-iron fence forming a small, square, black crown atop the sun-bleached white grave. Across the pedestal and within the crown, an open Bible lies carved in stone, with two crossed swords in bas relief laid across it. The swords also extend across a commemorative tablet alongside the Bible, covered with more nuts and leaves. Just a whisk or two of a webbed foot clears it: Paul, the receding leaves reveal; Octave, they continue; Hébert.

Paul Octave Hébert, Louisiana's second Cajun governor: a most unusual American in that he was a direct descendant of both Louis Gaston Hébert, a member of the original 1604 expedition that founded Acadia, and Paul Gaston Hébert, who burned his house in Annapolis Royal shortly before the Expulsion, when he refused to take the English oath. Paul Octave Hébert, fifteenth Louisiana governor of the Anglo-American period, from 1853 to 1856, was a major force behind the state's antebellum golden age, and the founder of both the state's first public library and what is now Louisiana State University. He lies buried and forgotten here at the northern end of what was once known as Louisiana's Acadian Coast, now known as the American Ruhr Valley, where much of the wealth of the antebellum South's boom economy was centered.

The Acadian Coast stretches eight leviathan loops of the Mississippi from Hébert's grave southeast toward New Orleans, and it was here—in the years following the first Expulsion—that the Cajun people were allowed by the government of France to regroup and rebuild their dream of a bountiful New World Acadia. By the time Hébert ascended to power—coincidentally, the centennial of Le Grand Dérangement—predominantly French-speaking Louisiana had grown to be the wealthiest and most freewheeling region in North America, its Creole capital at New Orleans the undisputed Queen City of the South. Louisiana *was* Dixieland, the literal land of French-language ten-dollar banknotes, or *dix* notes, seemingly spawned directly from the state's rich, living alluvial soil.

This new refuge of Louisiana lay even farther away from the original Acadia than Acadia had been from France, and yet trouble from the English-speaking Puritans of the English-speaking Atlantic seacoast continued to stalk the new homeland. The Louisiana Purchase in 1803 and statehood in 1812 swept the Acadian Coast into irreversible change, and by the time of Hébert's governorship, the Cajuns found themselves scattered and dispersed again, though this time all across southern Louisiana, by a slower second Expulsion that most historians have forgotten.

From the bountiful soil of their first settlements on the Mississippi River's Acadian Coast, located about midway between New Orleans and Baton Rouge, the Cajun refugees were chased by *les Américains* farther into Louisiana's jungle wilderness—chased down into the bayous and across the great Atchafalaya Basin (a refuge for Civil War draft-dodgers) to the vast Cajun prairie beyond, with its promise of a new Grand Pré. The Acadian Coast they left behind is littered still with the telltale tracks of this later Expulsion, and the Cajuns' ongoing search for freedom and safety. Where that search first began in Louisiana was at the town and church of the Acadian Coast that the Cajuns named St. Jacques de Cabanocey—Cabanocey being an Indian word meaning "clearing where the ducks land."

The Acadian flight to Louisiana began in earnest with Salvador and Jean Diogène Mouton, uncle and nephew, who are said to have arrived in the St. Jacques de Cabanocey area in 1754. There were other members of the family in their original party, but all of them died early or left lines that vanished early, as did the few older members of the family who had remained behind in Acadia, where there are now no Moutons left. Salvador's son Jean founded Lafayette and opened up the Cajun prairie, originating the town-centered *chapeau* branch of the family. Other members of the family migrated closer to the bayou-laced coast and formed the *capuchon* (or more rural *chapeau*) branch. But over the years their descendants have gradually intermarried, with one another and with all the other major families of the French Triangle, to form an extended family of about six thousand. "That's the six thousand who carry the surname," figures Franklin Mouton, the thirty-three-year-old great-great-great-great-great-great-grandson of Salvador, who has taken six years to research the family tree. Another six thousand Moutons carried their blood into other families with other names. "We've married into every Cajun family in Louisiana, except perhaps one or two," figures Franklin, who has hand-lettered a chart of the family for private publication. It consists of 204 8″ x 14″ pages. "And the only thing I could paste it together on," says Franklin, meaning the pieces of his paper tree, "would be an airport runway."

The original Acadian flight to Louisiana was by boat, and by foot overland. The Moutons, according to local legend, walked their way along the Great Lakes to the upper reaches of the Mississippi River, where they walked and rafted the rest of the way down to Louisiana. It was a comparatively well-known and well-charted path through the center of the continent by 1754, however—known to the people of French Canada since 1682, when a former Quebec seminarian named La Salle set out to chart it. La Salle entrusted a written message for future explorers to an Indian tribe in Louisiana—much as the Acadian founders had left their original habitation in the care of Micmac Chief Membertou with a promise to return. Seventeen years later, the exploring brothers Iberville and Bienville, setting out from the French Gulf settlement of Mobile to find La Salle's river, retrieved his message and confirmed both his remarkable discovery and the claims of the King of France to this wondrous inland territory.

. Iberville and Bienville entered Louisiana's Mississippi River delta on Mardi Gras 1699 and by March 5 made it upstream as far as the present-day port city of Baton Rouge before turning back. At Bayou Manchac, which lies across the river from the site of Cajun governor Paul Octave Hébert's eventual grave, Iberville headed back for Biloxi via the bayou's short-cut to Lake Pontchartrain—a route the Indians called "manchac" for its "back entrance" to the river. Bienville, however, elected to continue back down the river, exploring other distributaries farther down its stem. In one of Louisiana's legendary tales of French cheek, Bienville is said to have encountered two English boats also exploring their way around the delta, and to have assured them that they had found the wrong river. The Mississippi River lay elsewhere, Bienville lied, and this *French* river, he grandly gestured, was heavily guarded farther upstream by (nonexistent) French forts. The English gullibly retreated. And the turn of the river where that conversation reputedly took place, just barely in view of the Superdome and New Orleans' new sunbelt skyline, is to this day called English Turn.

Keeping the Anglo-Americans at bay in the lower Mississippi Valley was the one overriding obsession of the colorful politics of colonial Louisiana's first hundred years. And though Bienville had lied about the valley's French forts, by 1752, half a century later, there would be two dozen of them scattered in a broad arc from Quebec through Illinois and Louisiana to the Gulf. Explorer-traders, the so-called *coureurs de bois,* were regular visitors to Louisiana across this mid-continent trade and communications corridor as early as 1708. And New Orleans was established as the new territory's provincial capital and magic destination point one decade later.

At the time of the Moutons' arrival, the Indian tribes who populated the lower Mississippi Valley still lived peacefully in relatively sophisticated farming communities, centered on villages with temple mounds and protective palisades, within which they played Maya-like ball games with stones called chunkeys. The Natchez tribes, presided over by their own version of a sun king (to the absolute astonishment of French visitors), held the area of the Lower Valley in the vicinity of the modern Mississippi city of the same name. The "red stick" of Baton Rouge farther south served as the dividing line between the Houmas and the Bayougoulas, whose settlements stretched down into the upper edges of what would later grow into the Acadian Coast. Farther south still, German settlers, brought over earlier in the century, had formed a German Coast on the immediate northern outskirts of New Orleans—so that left only the area around St. Jacques de Cabanocey (now St. James Parish) open for new settlers. In 1757, French authorities legitimized the refugees' spontaneous settlement with authorization for a separate chapel, but even so, colonial authorities were apparently not prepared for the influx to come. Stragglers came out of the woods daily, and cargo ships full of Acadian refugees would appear in the New Orleans harbor without warning.

In 1764, these informal ad hoc arrangements faced an unexpected crisis: Louisiana was ceded to Spain. Though Spain did not take charge of the colony until two years later, the refugees once again found themselves under a foreign flag, with a foreign government; five more years of turmoil ensued before the Cajuns were reassured that they had landed in Louisiana to stay.

The worst thing Spain did to Louisiana at that time was also one of the few actions Spain took at all: sending in a new governor. At the

Sunrise on Black Lake, 1956.
Typical Louisiana swamp scene
ELEMORE MORGAN, SR.

time of the Treaty of Utrecht in 1713, the Spanish throne was occupied by Bourbon cousins of the holders of the French throne; the French secretly transferred Louisiana to their Spanish cousins in order to concentrate on court intrigues elsewhere. The Spanish had their hands full with Cuba, Mexico, and South America, and took Louisiana reluctantly, to keep it out of the hands of the English, who had demanded and received all of West Florida (now Louisiana's "L," north of Lake Pontchartrain, including Baton Rouge). The dour Antonio de Ulloa was sent in as the first Spanish governor. Though Ulloa was a respected Spanish scholar, a naturalist, he was a wretchedly taciturn governor by flamboyant Creole standards.

The Spanish were nevertheless better record-keepers than the French, and in Ulloa's first year we catch the first glimpse of the demographic details of an Acadian refugee ship landing on Louisiana's shores. Ulloa awoke one morning to find that several dozen Cajun families, totaling 210 individuals, had arrived in his harbor from the Minas Basin of Acadia via Santo Domingo and wished to be reunited with their relatives on the Acadian Coast.

Only half of these families had both a mother and a father, Spanish records show, and seven had miscellaneous orphans with them. Eleven families were headed by widowers, four of them with other orphans to care for, and seven were headed by widows. The remaining individuals, all single, were not given land grants until they had married into the colony.

Ulloa sent them up the Acadian Coast beyond St. Jacques to the Mississippi River's intersection with Iberville's Bayou Manchac, where he ordered the construction of a fort and community to be called St. Gabriel de Manchac. The unmarried men among the refugees were assigned to build the fort and garrison it, while lengthy instructions—totaling some twenty-nine paragraphs—detailed the setup of lands and provisions and the rules for the outpost. The town of St. Gabriel stands by the Mississippi River today, in a parish named after Iberville, and the Gulf Utilities Company's giant Willowglen electrical generating station has replaced the old fort. A huge tower stands in the middle of the generating station, and hands a strand of red and white hot lines across the Mississippi to another tower, near the site of Governor Hébert's grave—thus marking with industrial sculpture what was once the northern edge of a thirty-five-mile refugee settlement, the Acadian Coast gently curving back and forth southward to St. Jacques de Cabanocey. By the end of the eighteenth century, some four thousand Acadians from around the world would stream into Louisiana through this Acadian Coast trough, and at that time they comprised two-thirds of all the Acadians who still survived.

The value of Ulloa's contribution was not so clearly appreciated in his time. New Orleans' Creole merchants were particularly annoyed by his restrictions on their trading with France. Moreover, he never had enough money on hand to keep the colony solvent, and once even tried—in vain—to buy out French currency with a Spanish substitute at only 75 percent of its original value. So, in 1768, the New Orleans bourgeoisie, through its representatives on the colonial council, organized an armed revolt—the first one recorded in the Americas against a European power, preceding the skirmishes commemorated by the nation's Bicentennial by a full, if uncelebrated, eight years. The city Creoles were aided in their conspiracy by a volunteer militia of nine hundred rebels recruited from upriver rural areas. Men marched into the poorly defended city from their farms on the nearby German Coast—where Ulloa's government had failed to produce payment for crops delivered. And they came from still farther upriver on the Acadian Coast—where a note had been nailed to the St. Jacques church door warning (falsely) that Ulloa planned to disperse the Acadians north beyond St. Gabriel, perhaps as far as Missouri. Ulloa, completely surprised, had fewer than a hundred men at his disposal with which to meet this challenge. So he retreated to his ship in the New Orleans harbor, as the liberation army celebrated the colony's newly won independence without ever having to fire a shot. Cannon at the city gates had been spiked in advance to prevent Ulloa from offering armed resistance. Legend has it that during the ensuing festivities someone cut loose the rope linking Ulloa's boat to shore; in any event, he soon drifted into obscure retreat in Havana and never returned to Louisiana.

The Spanish government was not at all amused by this display, and the uneasy French government refused to take Louisiana back—even at the entreaty of the colony's aging French co-founder, Bienville. Under the command of an Irish mercenary named Don Alexander O'Reilly, a Spanish armada arrived in the harbor of the Mississippi River Valley's independent guardian city-state within the year, and the ringleaders of the revolt were summarily executed. O'Reilly astutely forgave all the other participants, however, and loosened trade restrictions with France, thereby regaining the colonists' allegiance.

Governor O'Reilly also laid the groundwork for Louisiana's first really efficient colonial regime, including an ingenious settlement program that encouraged the Acadians to develop a new homeland and strengthened the colony to resist possible Anglo-American incursions from the inland north. Spanish planners conceived their move much like a football team's flying wedge: in addition to the main stem of the colony along the thirty-five-mile Acadian Coast, there would be an arrowhead formed by settlements along each of two of the Mississippi River's most strategic bayou distributaries, Manchac to the southeast and Lafourche to the southwest.

From St. Gabriel's protective fort, the refugees were deployed down the bayou to a second settlement at Galveztown (abandoned completely just a few years after the Louisiana Purchase) and a third one at French Settlement (an isolated but still-thriving fishing community, where a rich architectural treasure trove still survives from the settlement's earlier days).

To finish off the other side of their arrowhead of strategic hamlets, the Creole administrators in New Orleans located yet another settlement at Lafourche des Chetimachas—a fork in the river to the west (Bayou Lafourche) inhabited by Chetimacha Indians at the time. Ascension Parish there was the site of the second church to be established for the émigré Acadians after St. Jacques de Cabanocey. Its operations began in 1772, not far from the riverside footpath that eventually became Louisiana's Highway 1.

After the American Revolutionary War, in the largest single European transmigration effort in American colonial history, seven boats brought 1,674 additional Acadian refugees from various French seaports to Louisiana, and the vast majority of them were settled along the Lafourche, Louisiana's other major link from the Mississippi to the Gulf. Down the bayou from the first settlement at the river intersection (now Donaldsonville), a second major new settlement was established at Valenzuela (now Plattenville), where another Acadian parish was formed. Eglise Assomption, as its stained-glass still proclaims, sits back from Bayou Lafourche and Highway 1. The church faces a small, grassy square marked off by a Royal Street—just like the Vieux Carré in New Orleans, though Assomption's graveyard now contains more residents than the surrounding town.

The arrowhead strategy turned out to be a brilliant maneuver for holding the colony while Creole Louisiana's French and Spanish rulers intermarried and consolidated their administration. All through the eighteenth century, Louisiana colonial officials were confident they could successfully resist the Anglos, and were delighted to receive the

Acadian refugees as colonists and as playing pieces in their North American chess game. For one thing, the Cajuns knew how to build dikes—and the forest-covered, flood-enriched soil banks along the Mississippi and its distributaries could not be reclaimed for agriculture and permanent settlement (and military defense) without dikes. Also, the Cajuns were known to have their own personal reasons for detesting the Anglos, and could be counted on for political loyalty to the regime in New Orleans. And they were capable of keeping themselves reasonably well fed and occupied, without posing additional financial burdens to the colony beyond initial settling and expenses. Perhaps most important, the Cajuns could ship their surplus crops and fish downriver from their new homeland to the rapidly growing colonial administrative center at New Orleans, where much of the struggle for what remained unsettled of North America would be waged.

The next major armed encounter took place during the 1776 revolution of England's Atlantic colonies. Upon learning of the revolution, Spanish Governor Bernardo de Gálvez decided to lead sympathetic expeditions from New Orleans to recapture the former Spanish province of West Florida—a critical British possession extending from Baton Rouge eastward, north of Lake Pontchartrain to the Mississippi coast and Mobile and the rest of Florida. The English had built their own Fort Bute across from Fort St. Gabriel on Bayou Manchac—the de facto boundary between Louisiana and West Florida—no doubt reminding the Cajuns of the way Fort Lawrence had been erected across from Fort Beauséjour on the Missaguash only a few years before. Because of Fort Bute, the English had staked out potentially unrestricted military access to the Mississippi River Valley and the west via Bayou Manchac and the Amite River, which connected to a second English fort at Baton Rouge. Fully half of the Gálvez regiment consisted of volunteer Cajuns, and they won every skirmish with the poorly defended forts at Manchac, Baton Rouge, Mobile, and Pensacola, liberating West Florida from English rule. Had not Gálvez and the Cajuns made this move, the English might have opened a third front in the Revolutionary War and invaded the new republic from its western flank, via the Mississippi River.

The perspicacity of Spain's colonial flying wedge and Gálvez's

"The Temple," pirate Jean Lafitte's base camp, situated on an Indian burial mound in the Barataria estuary   GEORGIA DEJEAN

move to secure the continent's south coast from English military intervention was not widely recognized until the War of 1812, when the English attempted to retake the United States with exactly that strategy. The war broke out, coincidentally, the year Louisiana became the first American state admitted to the union from west of the Mississippi River—signaling Mother England that her former colony was on its way to becoming a major world power. With the fall of Louisiana into Anglo-American hands—through Thomas Jefferson's unconstitutional purchase—the United States of America was suddenly launched on its Manifest Destiny. In the final battle of the war that secured the future of that destiny, the Battle of New Orleans—fought, unbeknownst to its combatants, after the treaty had been signed—the English made a last attempt to storm their way up one of the world's richest river valleys and reclaim the continent. There, at New Orleans to stop them, was Andrew Jackson, later the first American President from the newly annexed valley. He was also a principal political influence on the populist style of Louisiana's two antebellum Cajun governors, Paul Octave Hébert and Alexander Mouton, Salvador Mouton's grandson.

Jackson met the English with a ragtag militia of Creole gentlemen, slaves, Kentucky flatboatmen, Indians, and Cajuns. Perhaps his most important ally in the battle was Jean Lafitte, the New Orleans gentleman pirate-smuggler whose upriver Cajun co-conspirators were an indispensable element of a spectacularly successful smuggling operation in late colonial and early American years. Lafitte's communal working camp, on the island of Grand Terre, where the Barataria estuary meets the Gulf, guarded inland access to an administrative center known as the Temple—because it was built around an ancient Indian burial mound. The Temple was easily accessible to the Acadian Coast via the Barataria estuary's western boundary, the nearby Bayou Lafourche, which Lafitte and his men effectively controlled. So easily accessible, in fact, that the smuggling trade along the Lafourche and the Acadian Coast could not be permanently interrupted until the new American government sent in troops in 1812 to occupy the confluence of the bayou with the Mississippi River. With an estimated four hundred to five hundred men, Lafitte traversed this trading area with ease, occasionally even daring to enter the city. When the first American governor offered $500 for his head, Lafitte impishly printed and distributed handbills offering $500 to whosoever would kidnap and deliver the governor to *him.* Even though the Cajuns hated, and had even fought against, the English settlements upriver from their coast, they also freely smuggled and traded with them with Lafitte's aid, just like in the good old days along the shores of the Bay of Fundy.

Despite the colony's lively divergence, sometimes verging on division, the Battle of New Orleans compelled all classes of Louisiana society to join forces—no matter how briefly—to keep the English invaders at bay. It was perhaps French Louisiana's finest hour, for Louisiana colonial society was yet to reckon with the fact that their land was permanently in the hands of an English-speaking government. There had even been a brief plot to free Napoleon from Elba and bring him to New Orleans as the base for a new empire. So, in such a heady atmosphere, full capitulation to the new American masters did not occur until years later—not until after the Civil War, in fact, when Louisiana devised its first all-English constitution. And the key to understanding this phenomenon of cultural resistance for half a century after the Louisiana Purchase, and beyond, lies in the story of the adaptations the Cajuns learned to make in their new homeland.

Upon arriving in Louisiana in 1754, Salvador and Jean Diogène Mouton and their families were thrust into the company of highly advanced Indians who, as in Nova Scotia, lived near the lands the Acadians settled. As in the early 1600's, when the colonists learned the secrets of their first homeland from the Canadian Indians, the Louisiana Cajuns set about learning local survival techniques. But the environment was entirely different from what the Cajuns had known before: here the temperate months doubled the spring and summer growing season well into November or sometimes December. The ribbon form of their Louisiana farms had been predetermined by a French royal decree of 1716 which limited each farm grant to no more than two to four arpents (192 feet) of river or bayou frontage per household. Almost all of these grants, however, extended a generous forty arpents back off the river or bayou's natural levee ridge—almost a mile and a half back out through the bottomland hardwood forests to the cypress fresh-water swamps and bayous of the wilderness—thus making each farm a microcosm of the overall environment.

These ribbon-farm settlements still are common along the French-settled areas of the St. Lawrence River Valley in Canada. They were at one time common around the French arc fortresses of the Mississippi watershed at St. Louis, Vincennes, Prairie du Chien, Green Bay, and Detroit. Ribbon farms also appear in areas of New Brunswick settled by Acadians after the Expulsion, and also in the post-Expulsion French Shore of Nova Scotia—but the Fundy region's geography today is such that we do not know for certain if the original Acadians lived on farms of that same shape.

Ribbon farms for Louisiana were not dictated just by this tradition. Practicality demanded small frontages, so each landowner would be able to build his own protective levee—a practice, known as *corvée*, that was a prerequisite for receiving the land grant. Earlier and larger

House, Bayou Lafourche, 1939. Typical scene on a Cajun ribbon farm, with livestock-trampled pond, pieux *fences, tin roof, cistern, and batten shutters* FONVILLE WINANS

land grants before 1716 had gone, in many cases, to absentee owners or plantation enterprises that were not always capable of building and maintaining vast expanses of regulation levees. A series of ribbon farms promised to solve this problem within one generation.

The immigrants could build levees along the river's natural ridge with minimal effort, and the linkage of levees farmstead-to-farmstead would protect an enormous, well-drained strip along the river edge. Immediately behind the levee, land could be cleared to provide lumber for houses and barns—and the clearing could proceed a few arpents back to provide abundant rich land for growing crops. In areas still farther back, where drainage was not good enough for crops, livestock could be turned loose to forage on underbrush. From the swamps and marshes back farther still, the Cajuns could hunt wild game for food and fur. There was Spanish moss in the trees for reinforcing mud chimneys and stuffing mattresses and livestock collars. There was palmetto for making baskets and hats and trapping huts—as well as for constructing the first season's first house. Wheat does not grow well in Louisiana, but the Indians taught the Cajuns to plant corn. Rice had come into the colony with the founding of New Orleans. Indigo was grown for export, mainly on large plantation land grants made before the Cajuns arrived, but domestic indigo gardens were sufficient for home-dyed weaving. Except for ammunition, a few initial farming and construction implements, some livestock, and some cooking utensils, the Cajun immigrants could take to the Acadian Coast almost completely independent of the Creoles in New Orleans. And what they needed to import could be obtained from Jean Lafitte's organization in return for food surpluses.

By the second generation, the Acadian Coast pattern of settlement had been greatly strengthened, and the old ways had a fuller chance to revive. Children in Louisiana inherit estate shares equally, so the children of the first Acadian immigrants would split their parents' ribbon farms longitudinally, each heir obtaining an equal frontage slice of the farmstead an identical forty arpents deep into the swamp. Levee maintenance was eased considerably through the communal efforts of the extended family in the second generation. Expansion into the underbrush-free, former livestock areas was always possible when needed for additional planting.

Left to their own devices, the Cajuns might well have gone on to populate all of the Lower Mississippi River Valley, the same way they had filled the upper reaches of the Bay of Fundy in the half century before the Expulsion—the same way they populated the lower reaches of the Mississippi's Bayou Lafourche fork after the second Expulsion. As families multiplied and subdivided their farms, and as churches moved in, and also stores and schools, village clusters formed at eight-to-ten-mile intervals along early-settled bayous such as the La-fourche and the Teche. The bayous continue to this day to play a historic transportation and communication role, and in some contemporary villages such as Pierre Part, billboards for local businesses like Griffith's Food Store are located on the bank between the bayou and highway, to service traffic on both avenues of travel. Geographer Lauren Post claims that these settlements attained such density that a message could be passed along Bayou Lafourche by voice from front porch to front porch for a distance of forty miles.

But the Cajuns were not allowed to pursue their development of the Acadian Coast, or to work out their own destiny unmolested.

The roots of the Cajuns' second Expulsion go back to 1751, a few years before the original Expulsion, when the Jesuits brought sugar-cane from Santo Domingo to their plantation outside New Orleans. Sugarcane was first grown in Louisiana as a curiosity, with cane sections sold in markets—as they still are today—for chewing, like a primitive chewing gum of sorts. The Jesuits had staked out their Louisiana holdings when they arrived with Iberville and Bienville in 1699, bringing with them the colony's first orange trees. Citrus still grows in the lower reaches of delta-footed Plaquemines and Ter-rebonne Parishes. When the ever-tinkering Jesuits brought sugarcane to Louisiana, they had just taken control of the Church in the colony, their local superior, a Father Baudoin, having wrested the title of vicar-general for the Bishop of Quebec from the grasp of other religious orders in New Orleans. Their victory, however, was short-lived. The same Creole mercantilist renegades of the 1768 rebellion threw the Jesuits out of the colony in 1763, but kept their cane.

By 1763, the destiny of cane was set. The Jesuit fathers not only kept sugar on their plantation but also kept slaves. One hundred forty slaves when the sugar arrived, colonial records show. Later in the century, when indigo crops were wiped out by a caterpillar infestation, the Jesuits' sugar became the subject of an intense agricultural debate. Slave rebellions in the West Indies were disrupting supplies of sugar the year Louisiana first attempted to refine a commercial grade of cane. In the middle of the indigo crisis, a French Creole planter named Etienne de Boré bought a supply of cane from the Spanish Creole owner of that first mill, and planted the colony's first commercial-scale crop under the moss-draped oaks of what is now New Orleans' Audubon Park. The Louisiana sugar boom was on.

Acadian farmers could grow cane, and some did, and many still do. But sugar production, unlike indigo or the subsistence agriculture of the Acadian Coast farms, works most efficiently on large tracts. Slaves were needed both to plant and to harvest the cane and to maintain the long expanses of levee protecting the river or bayou edges of the plantations—plantations carved out of raw territory or consolidated from hundreds of smaller Cajun farms. One 1859 map shows that only splinter Cajun holdings along the Acadian Coast survived the consolidation process. Those lands were often held by the widow so-and-so and were surrounded by larger and expanding holdings under Anglo names.

Indians didn't make good slaves, so Indian slavery was abolished as far back as 1719. African slaves were imported to Louisiana by Yankee traders throughout the eighteenth century, and especially after 1803, possibly by some of the same men and boats that had helped Lawrence deport the Acadians from Nova Scotia. In the seven years following the Louisiana Purchase, the sugar boom caused the territory's slave population to double. By 1820, there were more black slaves than white residents in the three civil parishes that made up the original Acadian Coast. The Cajuns, however, rarely owned more than one or two slaves per family, if that many. And the Cajuns, accustomed to three hundred years of independent farming, refused to work as serfs on some Creole or Anglo-American sugar plantation. The planters, in turn, regarded these Cajun yeoman farmers as a potentially disruptive force among the slave population.

In the sugar boom which began on the eve of the American purchase and which was accelerated by it and by the coming of the steam engine for mills and boats, the Cajuns were found to occupy some of the best potential sugar land in Louisiana. It was high and well drained, alongside the region's principal river transportation corridor, and secured from flooding by the Cajuns' competent system of dikes.

Weighing cane, sugar plantation, 1890s GEORGE FRANÇOIS MUGNIER, COLLECTIONS OF
THE LOUISIANA STATE MUSEUM

Among the first Anglo-Americans to move in on the Acadian
Coast was one William Donaldson, who purchased the intersection of
the Mississippi River and Bayou Lafourche from the widow of one
Pierre Landry for $12,000. Donaldson hired Barthelemy Lafon, New
Orleans' most prominent engineer of the day, to lay out the town of
Donaldsonville, in blocks that were then placed on the open market.
On Mississippi Street, facing the river, Lafon laid out a small, formal
crescent that stands there to this day. A few blocks back from the river,
along an axis from the crescent, a public plaza was opened up—and
it, too, survives as the green between the town's public school and its
courthouse. Still farther back from the river, Lafon planned a third
public space, a proposed Place l'Acadie. But the Acadian plaza is now
just a memory on an old map. From the hundreds of Cajun farmsteads
settled before the turn of the century, the heart of the Acadian Coast
had shrunk, by the middle of the nineteenth century, to twenty-eight
huge plantations on the river's right bank descending, and thirty-nine
on the left bank.

. . . .

Parlange is the oldest operating sugar plantation in Louisiana still owned and lived in by its colonial family, and it is blessed with one of the oldest surviving plantation manor houses in the New World. The Parlange family trace their land grant back to the early 1700's and the construction of the manor house back to 1750, five years before the Acadian deportation. We see it standing today, a token of what the Acadians saw when they first came to Louisiana. It stands behind its fence, its pigeonniers, its stately alley of oaks, and stares back across Louisiana Highway 1 at the world with a truly magnificent presence. It is a Creole château, a palace of wood—its encircling, columned gallery topped by that massive, distinctive Louisiana roof Creole planters adapted from the West Indies. Parlange is self-consciously aristocratic, and represents the ultimate in Louisiana material aspirations and accomplishment in the mid-eighteenth century, an obvious lure for the more acquisitive-minded immigrants to the rich new colony. But Parlange is also unmistakably French provincial, from the French-dominated Creole province of Louisiana that offered refuge to Canadian French refugees after 1755 and to Santo Domingo planters and slaves and free blacks after 1791.

Virginie Trahan was one of the most unusual of the French Triangle refugees. Born of immigrant parents who settled in Avoyelles Parish, she came to Parlange to live with one of her cousins, the son of the man who had built the house, and eventually married him. He was several years her senior and soon died, so she singlehandedly reorganized the plantation's operations. And she married again, this time a French army officer she met in Paris while searching for a new husband. He was named Parlange, and their great-grandson runs the place today.

Parlange began as an indigo plantation. Wild, scruffy weed patches of it still grow there around gullies and roadside ditches on the plantation's back lot, where tenant farmers and pecan orchards divide up the land. Most of Parlange is planted in sugarcane, however, grown much as it always was.

The best cane, seed cane, is set aside to be chopped into short sticks and then buried sideways under four inches of soil. At each

"Parlange Plantation House." Its Creole grandeur is balanced but languorously asymmetrical in plan, unlike the rigidly symmetrical Anglo-American plantation manors   FRED PACKARD, COLLECTION OF LAFAYETTE NATURAL HISTORY MUSEUM

joint, or eye, a new stalk will sprout. New cane crops are planted every year just before the fall harvest of the previous year's crop. Because the cane is planted before the fall harvest, land must be set aside for it from the previous season, or cleared of the other spring or summer crops that can also be grown in Louisiana's sunny, subtropical clime. As Lousiana's warm fall unfolds, the cane eyes will sprout a growth of stalks that sometimes reach two feet high by the first freeze in December. Those stalks will brown and die and help mulch the later growth of "suckers" that stay safely underground until the following spring thaw. Sucker stalks enjoy the luxury of growing all the way through the balmy days of Louisiana's spring, summer, and fall seasons. Each additional day, until the first freeze, is a time of rising sucrose content, the raw base of refined sugar. About one tablespoon of refined sugar is produced by each full-grown stalk. When the freeze comes, the cane remaining in the field will rot if it is not harvested immediately; the gamble of sugar-growing is to wait as· long as possible for the richest sucrose harvest, while working off your acreage gradually, so as not to leave a full field to the freeze. And the gamble does not stretch over just one year. Harvested cane will sprout a second year's crop, called "first stubble," and if the seed cane is of good quality, a rich third year's crop as well. Sugarcane is temperamental, however, requiring well-drained land to withstand Louisiana's torrential summer monsoons. And cane is not resistant to disease; new varieties must be constantly developed, to combat infections with exotic names like mosaic or ratoon-stunting disease—a virus transmitted by insects. The only prudent way to manage such a volatile crop is to have huge acreages of it that can be divided up among several varieties of different longevity or stubble.

Slaves once planted the cane crop entirely by hand. Nowadays a long, narrow wagon with a shoveling mechanism spreads out the cane, for burial by human labor. At harvesting time, fields are still set afire to burn off the underbrush and dead lower stalks, a practice that originated in Cuba to kill off poisonous snakes before they could kill off the slaves. Flame control is maintained with an army of field workers, each wielding two hands full of "green tops"—the green, wet tops of the stalks, which would be discarded during the harvest anyway.

In the old days, the cane was harvested by machete. But, nowadays, dinosaur-sized machines roam up and down the rows, cutting the cane that is then stacked in heaps for later pickup. These machines, and the even more bizarre, mandible-mouthed cane loaders that accompany them, are manufactured in the Louisiana Cajun communities of Thibodaux and Jeanerette. And though they may be seen in the other cane-growing areas of the world, to which they are exported, they are rarely found in this country outside their native habitat. Mechanical insects, they have brought an astonishing degree of mechanization to the land of sugar. But the marvel of sugar mechanization is to be found not in the fields but in the mills, where the Industrial Revolution first began in the South.

The newest and largest of those mills in Louisiana is the Cajun Co-op, situated just outside the state's sugar capital of New Iberia, in

"The Mirror of Long Ago," 1947. *The glass over Virginie Trahan's portrait reflects the furnishings of the large drawing room at Parlange—a world apart from the rude simplicity encountered by the Cajun refugees who arrived in Louisiana as this home was being built*
CLARENCE JOHN LAUGHLIN, © 1962

a chunk of sugar country alongside the lower Bayou Teche. New Iberia sponsors the annual sugar festival—the state's largest, in attendance—and is so sugar crazy that one local radio station even goes by the call letters KANE. The Co-op mill is huge and shiny, yet not all that different on the inside from one of the oldest surviving Louisiana sugar mills, the Columbia Sugar Company, on what is now Katy Plantation, outside the wealthy Bayou Teche community of Franklin. At both mills, cane is gathered in huge bins, where it is washed of its mud and sent by conveyor to a set of crushing rollers. Three rollers geared together form a "mill," and most plants use five mills in a row to squeeze out the raw sugar juice from the leftover cane scrap, called *bagasse*.

Sugar is an industry guaranteed to appeal to the French-provincial sensibility of the eighteenth and nineteenth centuries, because of the milling operation's intrinsic thriftiness. The bagasse is dried and burned, to cook down the cane juice into various weights of syrup and raw, granulated sugar. Cane syrup was once cooked off in huge iron kettles, but today the bagasse—stoked with Louisiana natural gas—heats boiler-cookers. The steam cooks the sugar in vacuum vessels under pressure, at a temperature low enough so that the sugar won't scorch. That same steam also runs the turbines that run the conveyor belts and grind the gears of the mill and pump the liquid into cooling vats. At Columbia, the machinery looks as if it could run a steamboat as easily as it can a sugar mill. Indeed, it was the arrival of these fledglings of industrialism that made large-scale sugar planting highly profitable for anyone with the capital to invest in the land and slaves and machinery necessary.

The whole apparatus, particularly in Louisiana, is virtually self-sufficient. The mill at Columbia backs right onto Bayou Teche, from which it obtains fresh water for its boilers and also has barge transportation available for its finished product. The refining process involves the use of lime for clarification, and clam or oyster shells from nearby bayous and offshore reefs assure a continuous supply. All the low-grade molasses is saved, to be mixed in with livestock feed. And the impurities—small fiber pieces, mud that didn't wash off—are kept and collected, enriched with sucrose, and used as fertilizer in the cane fields. Because of the current fuel crisis, there is even talk of Louisiana mills banding together to build an agrifuel plant, producing fuel alcohol—Cuba and Brazil are doing it already—to make the entire planting and milling cycle energy-independent.

The cost of operating mills has always been high, however, and has reached the point where few sugar plantations still run their own. Katy Plantation has one of the last few private mills left, and Parlange has none. The Cajun Co-op, with 204 farmer-members, is part of a statewide, nine-mill organization of sugar co-ops that jointly market their crops through Louisiana Sugar Cane Products, Inc. The Co-op members are not all large landowners; in fact, many work farms that also raise cattle and soybeans and truck vegetables. To join the Cajun Co-op, you don't have to be Cajun, though most of its members are; hence, the name. You must pledge a 10,000-ton production as initiation fee, mills officials say, which has a market value of approximately $40,000 and represents the production of approximately 400 acres. Farmers in the five-parish area served by the Cajun Co-op produce an average of 5,000 tons annually, one Co-op official estimates, so Co-op members are the most prosperous independent sugar growers left.

Most of Louisiana's sugar lands are owned by large plantations (like Cinclare, which owns most of West Baton Rouge Parish) or corporate farmers (like Southdown Sugars, part of a south-coast conglomerate that also owns oil wells, cement companies, and breweries), and each year the total number of mills and sugar farmers drops. Even with a small farm, you have to be relatively prosperous to play the sugar game—and most of the Cajuns of the Acadian Coast weren't too keen on the hassle. Most of the ones who stayed with sugar eventually became assimilated into the river plantation and city culture of the Creoles, and those who abandoned the sugar lands became more isolated still.

The Cajuns of the second Expulsion had begun a slow but inevitable specialization away from the mixed farming-fishing culture they had known in Canada and in their early years in Louisiana. The ones who migrated the shortest distance, usually down Bayou Lafourche and its many distributaries, turned principally to fishing for their livelihood, keeping only gardens where once they had tended full-scale farms. The Cajuns who migrated the farthest ended up, by the middle of the nineteenth century, as farmers, entirely removed from fishing—out on the new frontier of the Cajun prairie. Sugar changed them all.

There is yet another untold tale of French Louisiana's antebellum days, a small matter touching on buried treasure.

The booty amassed by Jean Lafitte and his Cajun cohorts in colonial days is said to be buried all over the French Triangle, including one major cache on the plantation near Lafayette settled by Louis Arceneaux, presumably the model for Gabriel in Longfellow's *Evangeline.* After his pardon by the American government and his retirement from privateering, Jean Lafitte, it seems, selectively used his hidden treasure to finance several political ventures in keeping with his earlier convictions. Lafitte was a bright man and has the distinction of being the last New World Frenchman successfully to resist both the English and the Anglo-American government on the North American continent. Born in France, he assimilated into the Creole culture of New Orleans with grace and ease, and apparently found something of his own roots in his experiences with the Acadians and their brave and sometimes brilliant attempts to reestablish what would otherwise have been forever lost.

Though there is speculation in some quarters that Lafitte died disconsolate in Texas, those who claim to be his heirs say he migrated to Missouri and adopted a new name and life style to get away from his earlier notoriety. But his interest in politics continued, especially the skirmishes between the continent's rapidly growing Anglo-American republic and the Spanish colonial territory of Mexico. In one early struggle, Mexico became a republic and—under the presidency of a former slave—abolished slavery on the very doorstep of the slave-holding South. The Anglo-Texans were incensed and so declared their independence from Mexico. Just outside Houston, the Texas city that now bears his name, the Texas Anglos' commander, Sam Houston, routed the Mexican general of Alamo fame, Santa Ana, and saw to it that slavery was restored.

But the Anglos could not, in that war, win all of what is now modern Texas, and they hungered for a southern Pacific extension through what is now New Mexico, Arizona, and California. Zachary Taylor, a Virginia-born Anglo planter and later U.S. President, who settled near Baton Rouge after the Louisiana Purchase, led their war to seize this land from Mexico.

Taylor set out to wage his war in 1846, while Jean Lafitte—aged sixty-four—looked on with horror and dismay, especially since Taylor was embarking on his misadventures from Lafitte's own New Orleans. One year later, Lafitte left on a journey to Germany, where he sought out two young men, German radicals in desperate need of money to complete publication of their controversial political theories. These two beneficiaries of colonial Louisiana's smuggling largesse, as told in a letter written in Lafitte's own hand, were Karl Marx and Friedrich Engels.

3

Cajuns on the Bayou

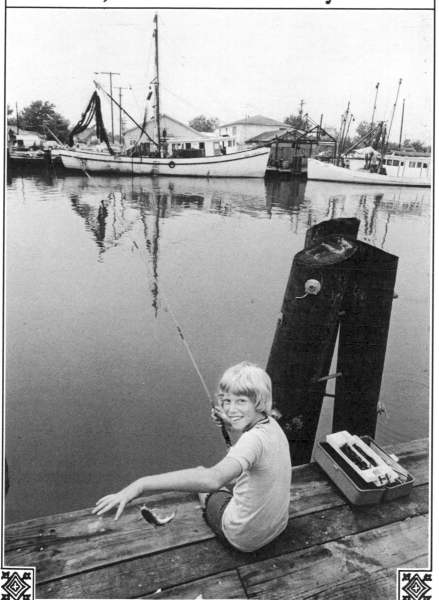

*Dockside in Delcambre, with butterfly nets
on the shrimp boats in background*   DAVID RICHMOND

James Daisy fishes oysters for nine months of the year. And the rest of the year he traps muskrats. Fifty-year-old Daisy—a Cajun with, as he laughs the loudest, an Irish last name—lives in a remote settlement of Terrebonne Parish, a fertile, "good earth" section of Louisiana's subtropical delta fan that is larger than the entire state of Rhode Island. He leases a thousand acres of Terrebonne's brackish public lake water bottoms to raise oysters, plus another four hundred acres in partnership with his brother, who lives next door. Together with his son and a nephew, plus three other men, Daisy's oyster crew works two boats eight hours a day, five days a week, in the temperate cycle's best months, March through November.

"If you need help from anybody, you got it," he says of the life he lives in the tranquil community of Bayou du Large, where almost everyone is related to everyone else. "You don't have to dig down into your pockets to pay for it." If you build a boat, all you need to offer your neighbors is "a case of beer or a pot of coffee to come help you launch it." Saying so, he gestures across the kitchen of a modern, ranch-style house to the world outside beyond a large window over the stove. There's a pot of hot, thick black Cajun coffee steaming on the stove under the window, and also a large pot of chicken-gumbo soup Daisy made that morning. You sit at his kitchen table and he offers you a cigarette in an unmistakably Gallic manner.

Appearances take sudden twists and turns down on the bayou. The ranch house is "modern," but it still collects rooftop rainwater in a cistern, for drinking and bathing. From the kitchen window, beyond the carport driveway and across the street, you can see the sluggish brown bayou, still the main avenue of local work, where James Daisy usually docks his boats. Daisy's close-knit, extended family—he married his third cousin—rise every morning at three, and by four join the boats of their neighbors and cousins heading for the oyster beds. As the dredged-up oysters are pulled on board the boats, which dip down sharply in the middle for drainage, Daisy and his crew look for small ones and toss them back overboard, so that the beds will be replenished. The harvested larger ones are split apart with axes and loaded into big burlap sacks that are tagged and stacked up on the low deck. Here they will be washed and cooled by the water of the remaining day's dredges. "On cool days we'll stay out until dark comes," he says, but on warm days or full days they come back early to feed the refrigerated trucks that seek out Bayou du Large oysters from as far away as Florida.

"It costs me $700 a day," he says of this business, estimating he pays his crews $1 each for the seven hundred or so sacks he averages daily from his water-bottom oyster "farm." Those same sacks are sold for $8 apiece to the trucks parked along the bayou. James Daisy doesn't even need to work a full eight months to live well, much less work twelve hours a day, so why does he do it? And with his considerable oyster income, why does he spend the rest of the year trapping on the side? "Well," he pauses in a curl of smoke, looking out the window again, "out there's where I *live.*"

During the trapping season, he does his living away from the bayouside ranch house in a small trapper's shack he built for himself; it has a cistern, butane lanterns, and a wood heater for burning scrap lumber, sometimes driftwood. The shack sits six feet off the marsh on 18-foot pilings lined up in rows, the way his ancestors once reinforced the structures of their Fundy dikes and fishing piers. Daisy did his own pile driving, using a portable gasoline-powered "wash-out pump" to churn a hole in the soft marsh mud down to a more solid layer of sand. His toothpick-legged shack is surrounded by "three or four sections of marshland," he estimates (one section equals one square mile), which he leases trapping rights to for $300 a year. The trapping lease is next to his oyster lease, but his sector is distinguishable from all the rest of Louisiana's patchwork-quilt coastal marsh only by a few personalized marker stakes upended throughout the various stretches of land and water. "We don't use any compasses around here," Daisy brags with a big grin, knowing how to snag any credulous listener with a salty sea tale or two. "If we get lost in the fog," he grins again, moving in for the kill, "we just stop and *listen.*"

When trapping, James Daisy starts out at daybreak in hip boots to negotiate the marsh grass and any stray water moccasins. He also wears a "red coat"—an ungainly cross between an oversize, sleeveless vest and a fireman's raincoat, with a huge, sewn-in pocket that circles around behind from two side-slit openings. Pocket for the 'rats.

The traps are an ugly steel, and you drop them off in gloves, so the muskrats won't smell the hands that set them. Drop them off in a muskrat "run," usually near some water where you know one will ultimately come running to wash some food, a fastidious and annually fatal flaw. "Sometimes they'll struggle for a while and get muddy— then you have to wash them off, too." Each trap has a chain with a ring set back in the grass and anchored into the ground with a cane pole. You set out two hundred or three hundred traps at a time, and you make several runs through your area each day. If you don't get to your muskrats first, a hungry mink or 'gator might.

Minks are a diminishing fur product in Louisiana these days, and have been far outnumbered by the nutrias that were imported from South America as a curiosity—much like the sugarcane. About six times as many nutrias as muskrats are caught in Louisiana annually, though the nutrias have only been in the marsh since a hurricane blew open a collection of pens on Avery Island, where they were kept as pets by the McIlhenny family of Tabasco sauce fame. Huge colonies of them inhabit those sections of the marsh still fresh-water enough to grow three-cornered grass, their favorite Louisiana food. In years when supplies of that grass and their other vegetarian preferences are low, nutria will come in to chew on the sugarcane. In Terrebonne Parish, the exploding nutria population has apparently also helped bring back the once-endangered alligator.

But nutria-carcass disposal is fast becoming a problem the muskrat trappers never had to worry about before. It used to be that nutria carcasses were sold to the government to provide meat for growing laboratory cultures. Some are still gathered up off-season and sent to the fish-meal plants in the coastal fishing village of Cameron, where they are ground up to feed minks on inland farms. Since nutrias are skinned right there in the marshes, the government won't let the trappers sell the resulting meat for human food—though nutria meat is not unlike rabbit, and makes its own thoroughly rich and mysterious

la-
fourche

bayou blue

houma

bayou lafourche

intracoastal waterway

houma navigational canal

bayou grand caillou

chauvin

bayou petit caillou

du-
lac

bayou terrebonne

pointe
au chien
wildlife area

bayou pointe au chien

golden
meadow

cocodrie

gumbo. The only options for disposal are to leave the carcasses stacked at the trapping shack, compounding short-term skinning odors with a seemingly permanent pile of stench, or to dump them into the bayou, running the risk of polluting the oyster beds. So James Daisy sticks with his muskrats.

One other irritating nutria problem: in recent years, the marsh has become infested with an unusual cocklebur that gets embedded in the nutria's fur and can cause wounds that become terminally infected. The carcass rots and fertilizes a whole new plant of them. Seemingly innocent ecological transformations like nutrias and cockleburs have assaulted the marsh balance continuously over the past century, and the result has often been a net loss of resources. Terrebonne old-timers can recall the days when the sugar lands and orange groves extended far below Houma, the Terrebonne Parish seat, but salt-water intrusion has wiped them out in some areas. That intrusion has come principally from widening bayous into navigation canals, and from dredging an interconnected network of drilling and pipeline canals for the oil industry, both of which have made the area more vulnerable to everything from simple high tides to hurricane storm surge. On some days, the canals also bring salt water into the water supply of Houma, which draws its water from bayous twenty-five miles inland from the Gulf. Industrial and private marsh buggies, a Louisiana cross-breed of tractor parts and tank treads, roll blithely over muskrat tunnels, crushing them underground. They also scar the marshland, which is as fragile as the tundra of the north that it so closely resembles. Levee building for land reclamation and title-claiming purposes in the marsh has engendered all kinds of disruptions and conflicts, including one brief armed struggle remembered in Terrebonne as the Trappers' War.

Much of the land south of Houma that once supported a large population of fur-bearing animals can accommodate only a small number of them now, because excessive salt-water intrusion from careless manmade changes has killed off the three-cornered grass several kinds of marsh animals eat. All along Terrebonne's bayous, intrusion-prone drainage canals were dredged during the administration of Governor Sam Houston Jones. The canals were dredged back into the marsh parallel to the natural water bodies, permitting well-drained sugar and orange fields to be developed in the narrow strips of land between the bayous and canals. But subsequent salt-water intrusion into those ditches by way of the oil industry's navigation channels and pipeline canals has limited what little cane still survives along Bayou du Large to the very highest and closest edges of the road.

The deterioration is subtle, slow, and steady. It has not yet resulted in an immediate threat to Daisy's livelihood or independence, but he seems to sense that some changes for the worse will never be reversed. "There are so many outsiders now—oil people, mainly—that you have to watch where you put things down."

Daisy tried working for an oil company once, back in 1942. He has only a seventh-grade education and thought he'd try his hand at being a roughneck. The try lasted one day. He went back to the marshes, and has fished and trapped ever since then. He lives as close to the sea as the land will allow, and he knows the interdependence of both well enough to know where to find his own place. When the oysters are most plentiful, he tends his oysters; when the muskrats are most plentiful, he traps his muskrats; and when the shrimp are having a good year, he may even catch a few shrimp. Like the shrimp that annually flee to the open sea through the bayous and shallow bays of Louisiana, James Daisy, too, thinks he will always be able to escape.

The Mississippi River begat Bayou Lafourche, which in turn begat Bayou Terrebonne, which in turn begat Bayou du Large, which in turn helped beget Caillou Lake and Caillou Bay on the edge of the Gulf of Mexico. At Donaldsonville, Bayou Lafourche was cut off from the Mississippi by a flood-control levee in 1903. In Thibodaux, Bayou Terrebonne was cut off from Bayou Lafourche by the construction of Canal Street over what had once been a navigable waterway. In Houma, Bayou du Large is cut off from Bayou Terrebonne by a wormy ring of oil-worker subdivisions for the big shots and trailer courts for the little ones.

Fresh-water supplies that formerly entered these lower bayous from the Mississippi and kept the marsh water mixture balanced must

Seed oysters and shrimp in locks, Empire, 1939
FONVILLE WINANS

now come a different way. Most of that replenishing water comes from the Gulf Intracoastal Waterway (GIWW), a barge canal from the Mexican border to Florida that helps tie together most of the industrial growth of America's south coast. Fresh-water supplies from the Mississippi, entering the GIWW through two branches in New Orleans, are the principal reason all the lower Terrebonne bayous have not become entirely salty from Gulf intrusion. Below Houma, this once-unified system of distributaries still branches off from Bayou Terrebonne to beget the parish's duck-footed land mass. To the west toward Morgan City at the St. Mary Parish border, with its huge offshore drilling-rig fabrication yards, there is Bayou Black. Closer in, there is Bayou du Large, where James Daisy lives; then Bayous Grand and Petit Caillou, the big shrimp centers of Terrebonne, led by the village of Chauvin with its packing factories and bilingual frozen-shrimp boxes and its absolutely unequaled fall fishing festival; and finally Bayou Pointe au Chien with its Indians. Bayou Lafourche, the water-bearing main street through neighboring Lafourche Parish, also picks up fresh water from the GIWW. And Lafourche now supplements its supply with Mississippi water from a small pump over the levee at Donaldsonville—a pump belatedly installed in 1955 for the benefit of sugar plantations along upper Lafourche Parish. Bayou Lafourche reaches down from Donaldsonville past Terrebonne Parish to the old haunts of Jean Lafitte along the Gulf's increasingly uncertain edge.

Escape routes to the Gulf, all these related and resilient bayous form a living, fanlike tissue that is dying but not yet dead—a tissue that experiences its most fecund revival during the annual migration cycles of shrimp, the Cajuns' most important fishery catch. Shrimp are the mine canaries of the marsh. They enter the bays and bayous from the depths of the open Gulf, coming in as larvae. Swept in by the tide, the larvae cluster around the reedy underbrush of the marsh, where they eat detritus—tiny pieces of decaying organic material from plants. Some of the bits and pieces are found in the Mississippi's rich spring flood gumbo, stirred up from across half the continent, while some of the other bits and pieces are decayed grasses from the Terrebonne marsh. By August, the shrimps' fan-shaped tails have grown to a size and power sufficient to permit them to migrate out into the Gulf again, seeking its relative warmth and depth in the face of the brisk fall settling over the marsh. By November, when the temperatures begin to drop most dramatically, and all the alligators have opted for a loglike limbo (their own tails fattened up for the hibernation period), the shrimp begin to hightail it out of Louisiana's bayous in such overwhelming profusion that boats from Florida, Mississippi, and Texas flock to Louisiana waters with open nets. The Cajun bayous birth forth a quarter of all domestic American fish, mostly shrimp in glistening boat-hold piles, scratching each other's shells in a dying hiss.

Though the shrimp were there in abundance when the Cajuns arrived in Louisiana, almost a hundred years elapsed from the founding of St. Jacques de Cabanocey to the establishment of commercial shrimping. The Cajuns had to move farther down the bayou before they could become shrimpers. There they noticed that the Indians around them would dip the shrimp right out of the bayous, drying them in the sun the way the Cajuns' ancestors had once dried their Atlantic cod catch on Canada's rocky Maritime beaches. The Indians' dried shrimp were harvested entirely for local consumption, however, until Chinese and Filipino immigrant laborers were brought in to found Manila Village and develop a small but important export business from Terrebonne Parish to the Orient. The dried shrimp are called "sea bob," an English corruption of the Cajuns' *six barbes,* or "six beards," because of their distinctive whiskers. In Jimmy Carter's Presidency, these dried shrimp are also increasingly described as "Cajun peanuts."

Fresh shrimp, crabs, and oysters, on the other hand, spoil easily without refrigeration—so early Cajun shellfishing was entirely a subsistence occupation, shared by the immediate family in the way James Daisy and Louisiana's other Cajun and Indian commercial fishermen still prefer. Those Cajuns who lived close enough to a small town might make a little extra money from bringing fresh shellfish— wrapped in Spanish moss or palmetto leaves to keep them cool—in from the countryside on small pirogues. Commercial production was not possible until shrimp canning began, shortly after the Civil War, and refrigeration of fresh shrimp on gasoline-powered iceboats did not begin until early in the twentieth century. Shrimp freezing in its current form began after World War II, finally bringing Louisiana's Cajun shrimp abundance into America's fast-food restaurants and TV dinners.

In the old days, you could dip just about any old thing into the bayou and come up with shrimp. In sections of the giant inland Atchafalaya Basin swamp, Louisiana's Everglades, the "swampers" would use corn bait inside burlap bags. Hungrier fishermen soon learned to use haul seines, possibly adapted from the nets used to catch the curious, long-snouted paddlefish that once flourished along the Acadian Coast of the Mississippi River. Really hungry haul seiners would head out away from the bayous to the shallow brackish bays that indent the Louisiana coast. Using a small rowboat, the crew of two would set out a half-inch mesh net about 120 feet long by 10 feet wide. One man, in the rowboat, would circle out and back slowly around to his partner, on the lugger, trapping the schools of fleeing shrimp inside. In the most shallow bays, especially during a low tide, you could even stand out in the water and gather in the shrimp by hand. After 1875, shrimp-canning factories were built on barges that anchored in these low-lying bayous and bays, where they could buy the lugger's catch boatside, packing it quickly into cans with a special lining to help circumvent the spoilage problem. Only half a million pounds of shrimp were harvested commercially in 1880, notes Thomas Aquinas Becnel in his 1962 history of the industry, but within seven years, advances in shrimp-harvesting methodology had caused that figure to increase thirteenfold.

Commercial shrimping was only a seasonal occupation. It could be profitable for the coastal Cajuns, and was also comparatively safe. The principal danger to a shrimper was most likely the same stiff northerly winds blowing in over temperate waters that forced the shrimp to flee the marshes in the first place. Too stiff a breeze and your lugger might end up blown out into the open seas. Compasses not necessary here, remember: just stop to look at what's going on around you, and listen.

In its slow, gradual development, commercial fishing in Louisiana on a scale comparable to that of the fishery industry of Maritime

Acadians hauling boats, a scene on the Bayou Lafourche, late nineteenth century ALFRED R. WAUD, HISTORIC NEW ORLEANS COLLECTION

Canada did not begin in earnest until 1917, when the U.S. Bureau of Fisheries introduced a new form of trawling net from North Carolina, first to Florida and then to Louisiana. The nets, sometimes as long as the seines, would be anchored behind a gasoline-powered boat and dragged through shallow water, scooping up an unparalleled harvest of shrimp through a pair of open "doors" in the trawl one person high. The new trawls required fewer men per pound of catch; they opened up fishing grounds in the open Gulf that had never been accessible before; and they allowed the shrimp industry to transcend its previous seasonal limitations, permitting year-round deep Gulf shrimping. The eventual development of the *papillon,* or "butterfly," trawling net also permitted night fishing along the water's surface, where the shrimp rise in the dark. The momentum from these new trawling technologies, and an explosion in the number of ice and canning factories in the bayous, caused the shrimp harvest to double from 16 to 32 million pounds in just one year, from 1919 to 1920.

There had been 300 seines and only 4 trawls, notes researcher Becnel, when the North Carolina experiment began—but two decades later, there were 2,313 trawls and only 35 seines left. Cajuns soon dominated America's burgeoning shrimp industry, sometimes in boats they built for themselves, but now more usually in boats they own in partnership with the nearest bank, and often as employees of vertically integrated shrimp companies that own both boats and factories, with their own brand name.

During the 1930's, while the rest of the country languished economically, several of Louisiana's Cajun coastal villages became virtual shrimp boom towns. During one period of the thirties, the state legislature passed a series of laws to keep Louisiana shrimp in Louisiana shrimpers' nets—but the U.S. Supreme Court systematically knocked them down. The economic tug-of-war for control of the catch of Louisiana's waters sometimes turned to violence, as in 1938, when labor troubles broke out between a shrimpers' union and the canneries over prices. During World War II, when shrimp was rationed and an ice shortage developed, one group of irate shrimpers—in the best upstart manner of Jean Laffite—went so far as to sail into New Orleans and seize the Louisiana Ice Service Plant to keep their catch from spoiling. In the post-World War II period, shrimp harvests continued to boom without precedent, and Louisiana moved into the nation's number-one shrimp-harvesting position, edging out Texas for the first time.

The gradual growth of the shrimp industry, the gradual destruction of the wetlands, and new pressures from all sides have at last, however, brought about a crisis whose exact extent cannot now be fully known. The entire Gulf of Mexico region is becoming concerned over the way the total shrimp harvest in Louisiana has first peaked and then slightly declined. The Gulf of Mexico Regional Fisheries Management Council is considering a so-called limited entry rule that would restrict the number of available licenses for each state's commercial shrimp fleet, while fisheries scientists try to restimulate the Mississippi River delta's productivity. And looming ever larger in the coastal population's most fearful future fantasies is the proposed construction of LOOP—the Louisiana Offshore Oil Port—a so-called superport for unloading supertankers full of imported foreign oil.

LOOP's unloading dock would be located twenty miles offshore, due south of the line between Terrebonne and Lafourche Parishes, the two most productive fisheries jurisdictions in the state. Louisiana oyster fishermen like James Daisy serve a full fifth of the national market, and they could be wiped out by any large Gulf oil spill carried into Louisiana's already severely strained wetlands. The Louisiana Shrimp Association, a fishermen's group, is concerned that LOOP's spills, debris, and maze of underground pipes could both destroy their trawls and kill off the shrimp. LOOP would consist of a central pumping station and several floating unloading terminals with flexible pipes interconnected along the Gulf floor in 120 feet of water—all of it connected to shore by a 48-inch pipe. On shore, LOOP would require more pipelines and storage facilities of still undetermined size and location (possibly salt domes), destroying additional acres of wetlands, and introducing new industrial and urbanizing disruptions also not predictable in advance. LOOP is to Louisiana what the Alaska Pipeline is to Alaska, except for the fact that the pipeline couldn't possibly destroy Alaska the way LOOP might destroy Louisiana.

Meanwhile, life in the shrimp villages goes on. South of Houma and east of Bayou du Large along Bayou Petit Caillou, life goes on particularly well in Chauvin. Chauvin is a town where men like Curman Chauvin still build their own boats without the aid of blueprints. Curman's great-great-grandfather—a landlubbing hunter fleeing south—founded the village as a base for harvesting the feathers of the marsh's once-common red-breasted herons. Chauvin was, at that time, the only place along that stretch of Bayou Petit Caillou where the land would still remain above water when the spring floods came. Over the intervening years, Chauvin has grown to support another one of the bayou country's closely interrelated Cajun communities, this one of eighteen hundred families whose principal occupation is shrimping. The shrimp boom was given significant recognition for the first time in the thirties, when a Cajun named D. J. Theriot persuaded the Catholic bishop to bless the fleet at Chauvin. Bishops now annually swarm with the shrimp, blessing the fleets of all the assorted coastal shrimp villages—Delcambre, the farthest west; Morgan City, with a home fleet of over a thousand boats and the self-proclaimed title, "shrimp capital of the world"; Golden Meadow of the populous lower Bayou Lafourche; and the Barataria region of Jefferson Parish, a coastal suburb of New Orleans. But the shrimp boom is nowhere so thoroughly a Cajun phenomenon as it is at Chauvin, where the annual "Lagniappe on the Bayou" celebration is fast catching up to the attendance records of the state's largest Cajun festival contender, New Iberia's Sugar Festival.

Chauvin's Lagniappe—a Cajun-Spanish word for "a little extra free something," like the thirteenth cookie in a baker's dozen, or the shrimp harvest of the Louisiana Gulf—takes place in an open court now enclosed by modern buildings alongside the bayou. Entrance is past the dramatic new sanctuary of St. Joseph's Church, with its roof like an inverted boat hull. Originally, St. Joseph's was the principal beneficiary of the festival's considerable financial accumulation, which enabled it to subsidize the parochial elementary school, built directly behind the church. But St. Joseph's spiritual parish eventually gave the building to Terrebonne's civil parish, which expanded the facilities and added a public marine vocational-technical school. The third major facility built in the complex, a public recreation center, houses the massive bingo game that is Lagniappe's best-attended function. Gambling is also the featured attraction of the Cajun "village" constructed each year in the paved court between these more permanent structures. A palmetto-thatched plywood and cardboard playland, the Lagniappe village covers the equivalent of about four New Orleans city blocks and can hold almost 100,000 high, happy, dancing people. The fair is surrounded by enormous parking lots, for the traffic jam on two-lane Louisiana Highway 56 from Houma sometimes stretches a full eight miles back up the bayou to Presque Isle. The Lagniappe is also surrounded by an extensive campground, the whitewashed raised tombs of the Chauvin graveyard, and a traveling carney midway with its landmarking ferris wheels and its take-home Kewpie dolls.

Other than the gambling, the drinking, the crafts, the music, and the crowds, Lagniappe's prime attraction is its shrimp-based food— all of it prepared by village volunteers. Most of it has been partially or wholly prepared in their homes. One shrimp specialty, which the

Pirogue boathouse built onto a cypress tree, Pierre Part   DAVID RICHMOND

Chauvinistes call a *boulette*—a sort of spicy croquette—is prepared in mass quantity two weeks before the festival in the cafeterias of all the bayou's public schools. Some ten thousand boulettes are prepared annually, deep-fried and then frozen in boxes donated by the local shrimp factories. During the three-day weekend festival, the boulettes are brought to the Lagniappe village for steaming in outdoor kitchens. The communal preparation of the boulettes in the schools is a remarkable example of the blur between public and private sectors in this close-knit community. The cooperative effort with which the women fashion their boulettes is matched by the way that the men gather the sixteen thousand pounds of shrimp that the revelers will consume. On an appointed Saturday in the fall, the men join forces to go into the Gulf and bring in one colossal communal catch, which is peeled at the shrimp factories—again, by volunteer weekend labor—and refrigerated there until it can be prepared. Crabs and turtles caught in shrimp trawls during the regular prefestival runs are also carefully set aside and used to add to the endless tubs of gumbo and the Lagniappe's famous turtle *sauce piquante.*

This eight-year-old example of enterprising Cajunism grossed a quarter of a million dollars in 1976, and its founders have used it to clear up the church-building debt and, lately, to make improvements to both the Terrebonne Parish recreation center and the state's marine school. Casting their nets a little farther each year, the festival organizers say they one day hope to move the entire event back into the marsh a few hundred yards from its present site. Barely visible from the bayou, their proposed new Lagniappe site stands by an untouched swamp alongside one of those back-marsh drainage canals from the era of Governor Jones. There, in a permanent setting they can more carefully control than the sprawling fair site they use at present, the Chauvinistes say they want to reconstruct an entire late-nineteenth-century Cajun fishing village as a year-round celebration and entertainment center.

While the oyster fishermen of Bayou du Large and the shrimpers of Chauvin and Bayou Petit Caillou are both prosperous and politically active, the future seems to be less optimistically perceived by their neighbors and cousins in the surrounding fishing villages of Pointe au Chien and Isle Jean Charles (nearer to Bayou Lafourche) or Dulac (on Bayou Grand Caillou). These villages have families named Boudreaux, Trahan, Landry, and Rodrigue—all common Cajun names—but they also incorporate an influx of surnames, such as Fazzio and Robinson and Fitch and Smith, from various other ethnic stocks. The most telling surname to be found here is Dardar, telling because it happens to be an Indian name. The residents of Pointe au Chien, Isle Jean Charles, and Dulac are mostly Indians, numbering three thousand of Louisiana's largest surviving tribe, the Houmas.

While the Houmas, whose name means "red," live mainly along these lower Terrebonne bayous, they—like their Cajun cousins—have left their mark all over the rest of the state. They are responsible for the name of the state capital, Baton Rouge—so called for the ceremonial red pole the French explorers found demarcating the Houmas' hunting grounds from those of the neighboring Bayougoula tribe.

The Houmas, the Bayougoulas, the Tangipahoas, the Okelousas, and the Acolapissas—all neighboring and interrelated tribes engaged in fishing and some agriculture in the lower reaches of seventeenth-century Louisiana—are members of the Muskhogean linguistic group, from which we get the Indian word *bay-uk* or "bayou." There is tantalizing archaeological evidence to suggest that they are directly related to the Mayas of Central America.

Few of their descendants survived into the twentieth century, however, because of European diseases and a devastating series of Indian wars provoked by English and French rivalries in the lower Mississippi Valley in the eighteenth century. During this turmoil, the Houmas moved first south from their Baton Rouge homeland to New Orleans, and then back halfway up the river again to Bayou Lafourche, before finally embarking, in the memorable year of 1776, for the relatively greater obscurity and isolation of lower Terrebonne Parish. This Houma migration—a mini-Expulsion of its own—was sparked by one particularly disruptive Anglo-inspired episode, when the Tunica tribe north of Baton Rouge were chased off their lands by English Indian allies. The Houmas took them in, but the ungrateful refugees rose up and massacred large numbers of their hosts—so the frightened and betrayed Houmas fled south. Safe and open lands were not available in the New Orleans area either, so the Houmas migrated back to the Mississippi's juncture with Bayou Lafourche—just as the Acadian Coast began to be developed. Both Indians and Cajuns would eventually be driven from this region by the sugar planters. Though the Houmas departed first, they remained long enough to leave their mark here too, lending their name to one of Louisiana's most magnificent antebellum sugar manors, Houmas House, one-time residence of the period's foremost Anglo sugar baron, John Burnside.

From Bayou Lafourche, the Houmas migrated south to Bayou Terrebonne, where they established a village that is now the thriving oil center of Houma. But it was not until 1964 that Indian children of the Houma tribe could come back up the bayou to attend integrated public schools in the town bearing their own name. For bountiful Terrebonne Parish was—and still is—a community of peculiar and particular social and ethnic stratification. The Houmas are of mixed

Manilla Village harbor scene and general store, 1939. Seat of Louisiana's dried-shrimp industry, the village was originally the home of Oriental immigrants who have

blood: Indian, as well as Cajun, English, and sometimes African. The whites would not admit their Indian cousins into white public schools, even after the school desegregation ruling of 1954, until compelled to do so by the federal government. The Indians had in turn kept their distance from the Terrebonne blacks in much the same way that the mixed-blood Creole *gens de couleur* ("free men of color") of New Orleans had kept their distance from the darker blacks. The Indians are therefore virtually alone, without any political allies.

Locally, the Houma Indians are also known as Sabines, after the forcibly intermarried women of Roman antiquity. As with the métis, mixed-blood Acadian Indians of Canada, white fathers in Louisiana would often abandon illegitimate children to be raised by Indian mothers. Illegitimacy, seen from the cultural perspective of French or Spanish colonial Louisiana, was never much of a problem; but from the perspective of the Anglo-dominated, white-controlled government that ruled Louisiana after the Civil War, illegitimacy created myriad legal and social barriers for the Houmas, especially with re-

now been absorbed into the multiracial Sabine population of Terrebonne Parish   FONVILLE
WINANS

gard to inherited land claims and the oil or fishing rights attached
thereto. One renowned Houma family, with the Scotch-Irish surname
of Fitch, is said to have intermarried not only with blacks but also with
some of Terrebonne's population of Oriental shrimp driers—a mul-
ticontinental multiracialism that, because it is the most mixed and most
isolated, is also the most feared. Signs at some local bars and restaurants proclaim NO FITCHES ALLOWED—because some individually
notorious members of the Fitch family have become, in self-fulfilling
social prophecy, the baddest boys on. their block or bayou.

These Indian-African-Cajuns still speak a vibrant French, a French
gently laced with traces of the Muskhogean tongue that survives in
their midst only in scattered words. Their physical isolation is more
pronounced than that of any other community in Louisiana—for, until
1952, Isle Jean Charles remained literally an island unto itself, entirely
inaccessible except by boat. And the road built in 1952 by the state
highway department still floods occasionally, when the high tide is
accompanied by a strong south wind. The Houma Indians fished and

trapped in this region, unnoticed and unmolested in their isolation until the oil companies and the state's Wildlife and Fisheries Commission suddenly came along after World War II to challenge their rights to the lands and water bottoms surrounding their villages. The illegitimacy issue put the Indians at an initial legal disadvantage for defending their property rights, and their French-speaking illiteracy was certainly no help.

Down each of Terrebonne's bayous, therefore, at different speeds and with different degrees, twentieth-century troubles have inexorably advanced. Oil wells and workers have streamed into the marshes around Bayou du Large, prompting oystermen like James Daisy to be more circumspect about securing their equipment. Down Bayou Little Caillou, beyond Chauvin at the village of Cocodrie, where the road finally stops, Texaco—the oil giant of Terrebonne—has built an enormous clamshell parking lot to service its rig workers, who are scattered farther out on platforms in shrimp-rich Terrebonne Bay. Where the road to Isle Jean Charles connects back to Bayou Pointe au Chien, an enormous natural-gas pumping station illuminates the nighttime marsh with its Faustian glow. And at the end of the road along Bayou Pointe au Chien, the largest of the Indian settlements, not only has the marsh been taken over, but armed agents of the outsiders are now posted to patrol the area and make arrests.

The armed agents work for the Louisiana Wildlife and Fisheries Commission, which has set aside the Houmas' fishing grounds as the Pointe au Chien wildlife refuge. The "refuge," in turn, has been given to the weekend sportsmen who purchase almost one million hunting and fishing licenses from the commission every year; these weekend "sports" come streaming into the bayous and marshes that the new roads and oil activities have opened up. A substantial number of them are Anglo-American immigrants working for the oil companies, seeking what one visiting Canadian sociologist termed "escape from the WASP-like way of life." They hunt the marshes for deer and disrupt the trappers' carefully laid traps. They fish offshore for virtually inedible sports fish like tarpon, drawn increasingly into Louisiana waters by smaller fish feeding at the algae-covered "artificial reefs" created by the oil industry's three thousand offshore rigs and production platforms. (These artificial reefs have dramatically disrupted the food chain by supporting net-shredding immigrant pests like barracuda.) For the Indian commercial fishermen, the "sports" have proven to be most bothersome in the Pointe au Chien refuge that now literally surrounds their largest settlement and lays siege to their only livelihood. Wildlife and Fisheries Commission agents allow the weekend interlopers virtually unlimited fishing privileges, while confiscating the nets and boats of Indian fishermen, who, the government contends, threaten to deplete the sportsmen's recreational supplies. There have been gun battles between sports fishermen and Indians, and there have even been armed confrontations between Indians and game agents trying to run them out of their confiscated territory. There are now a series of federal lawsuits underway to protect what the Indians consider their ancient rights to an independent livelihood.

The turmoil along Bayou Pointe au Chien is, ironically enough, not unlike a similar episode in the Kouchibouguac National Park in New Brunswick that erupted in the mid-seventies. That 87-square-mile area, also with a mixed Acadian-Indian heritage, once supported a community of 1,100 people in 235 families in eight villages of fishermen and trappers. To "preserve" the park, government agents —in the New Brunswick situation, members of the Royal Canadian Mounted Police—finally attacked the villages with smoke bombs at dawn, bulldozed the captured residents' houses, and took resistance leader Jacques "Jackie" Vaudtour and his four sons to court the following day in leg irons.

Louisiana has not yet reached the point of hunting down and arresting all its coastal fishermen and seizing their boats, houses, and land—but oil has seized their lands already and has begun arresting the annual fisheries harvest upon which these people and a sizable number of other Americans ultimately depend. Should Louisiana's independent-minded fishermen and trappers decide to take matters into their own hands—which is what they have historically done, anyway, even before there ever was an America or an oil industry to threaten them—arrests may well become inevitable. It has been only two hundred years since Le Grand Dérangement, let us remember, and in both New Brunswick and Louisiana the echoes of forced dispersal continue to be heard. If we just stop and listen.

4

The First Cowboy, and Other Prairie Tales

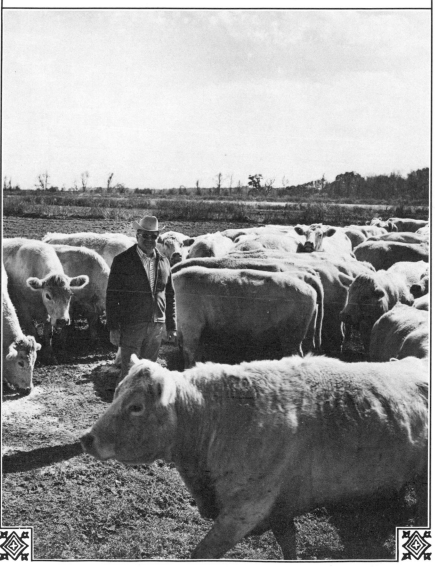

*Beausoleil Broussard's legacy: descendant Charles Broussard
surrounded by his prize Charolais herd*
ANTOINETTE DUCREST

New Orleans' Art Deco Union Passenger Terminal occupies the entrance to a small but strategic urban valley spread out between the Louisiana Superdome and a forty-five-story office tower. The tower is called the Plaza Tower, for it overlooks a Deco-baroque plaza in the center of the valley, where more period-piece artifacts—statues of the explorers Iberville and Bienville—stand vigilant forever. The plaza, its Plaza Tower, and the New Orleans Union Passenger Terminal mark the site of what was once a turning basin for a shipping canal built through the city during the nineteenth century by immigrant Irish labor. But the turning basin has long since been filled in to create the plaza; the canal has now become the terminal's railroad tracks and the expressway alongside them, which heads toward Metairie and the city's other northwestern suburbs. The Union Passenger Terminal, in imitation of the turning basin it replaces, collects buses from the expressway and trains from the railroad tracks, and then dispatches them all over the continent. Especially to and from the Golden West, for New Orleans serves as the origin and destination point of the legendary Sunset Limited passenger train.

Down from its legend to only three days a week, the Limited regularly leaves New Orleans for Louisiana's bayou country, tracing its route along the Gulf edge of the French Triangle, on its way to Texas, New Mexico, and Arizona, with a Pacific Sunset destination of Los Angeles. Before the Civil War, the rails which now carry the Limited all the way to California extended westward only as far as Morgan City, at that time a sawmill town where the massive cypress swamps of the Atchafalaya Basin meet the Gulf of Mexico. After the Civil War, construction of the railroad resumed until 1881, when the newly organized Southern Pacific Railroad Company laid claim to the sunbelt's first open route to the West.

Until 1935, all westbound trains left New Orleans from Algiers, a Victorian gingerbread suburb on the river's West Bank descending. Located across from the heart of the old East Bank main section of the city, Algiers grew prosperous from ferrying freight cars back and forth across the river. In 1935, the year of his assassination, Huey P. Long's memorial bridge, just upstream of the city, provided a link over this last water barrier: the longest, highest railroad bridge ever built across the largest, widest river in the country. Today, from the shadows of the Plaza Tower—the city's second tallest building, and its symbolic gatepost to the West—all Pacific-bound rail departures from east of the Mississippi River must climb the long incline of the Long Bridge, there gathering the momentum to hurtle the rest of their way west.

When Charles Dudley Warner made the trip west from New Orleans for *Harper's New Monthly Magazine* in the late 1880's, he found the region on the immediate far side of the river "little attractive except to water-fowl, snakes and alligators." Known as the Barataria Basin, the area was marked "by an occasional rice plantation, an abandoned indigo field, an interminable stretch of cypress swamps, thickets of Spanish-bayonets, black waters, rank and rampant vegetation, vines and water plants." Bounded by the Gulf to the south, the Mississippi River to the east, and Bayou Lafourche to the west, this sizable patch of Louisiana's web-footed delta—the staging area for the first phases of Acadian resettlement in the state—is still the richest estuary in the country. But the eighty miles you have to travel through the Barataria Basin and beyond to Morgan City—past the bayous of James Daisy and Percy Dardar and Jean Lafitte—count as only half the distance you must travel to find your way to the Cajun prairie, where the West begins.

From Bayou Lafourche westward to Bayou Teche, all of Louisiana drains into one or another branch of the rivers that make up the Atchafalaya Basin, in land area the state's largest estuary, and its most formidable. The Atchafalaya Basin is the home of the crawfish and most of the rest of the state's fresh-water fishing industry. The Atchafalaya gives "this region a great deal more water than it needs," demurred Warner, as he peered nervously out of his railroad coach window. And all that water also carves up St. Mary Parish beyond Morgan City into myriad marshy islands scattered along the track until you reach the relatively higher grounds of the Bayou Teche. The Teche, an Indian name for "snake," wanders toward the Gulf "with a great deal of uncertainty of purpose," continued Warner, "but mainly southeasterly, and parallel with the Atchafalaya . . . Steamers of good size navigate it as far as New Iberia, some forty or fifty miles, and the railway follows it to the latter place, within sight of its fringe of live oaks and cottonwoods."

South and west of the Bayou Teche lies the Cajun prairie, which extends the French Triangle as far west as the Calcasieu River and the industrial port of Lake Charles. That prairie, "a vast plain cut by innumerable small bayous and streams," had become, by the time of Warner's *fin de siècle* visit, the "principal home of the Nova Scotia Acadians."

You could hinge the French Triangle right down the middle, with New Orleans and the bayou country on the right and the Cajun prairie on the left. The prairie half, Louisiana's rice bowl, is a plain so rich that it supports a population almost equal to that of the entire province of Nova Scotia on a land area less than half its size. Soybeans, cattle, some sugarcane, and a host of other agricultural products come from the Cajun prairie's rich soil—but rice is the richest product of them all, endowing Louisiana with the nation's largest acreage of rice cultivation and fully one-fourth of the nation's annual crop.

All through the Cajun prairie, the rice lies shallow by the railroad tracks, threaded in curvilinear rows within walled and flooded ponds. The rice mills rise out of the prairie like the cathedral spires of Gothic France—each one marking the site of an approaching town, and each one built close enough over and around the tracks to be grasped from an open coach window as you clatter on through. Built of cement and long expanses of corrugated tin, the towers benevolently dust the surrounding land and tracks with a light, sweet incense. As you pick up speed on the straight-track prairie section that shoots due west just outside Lafayette, the spires of the last rice settlement barely recede before the spires of the next one soar into view, and everywhere you turn, there is rice all the way to the horizon.

The largest aggregation of rice mills along the railroad tracks is to be found at Crowley, the self-proclaimed rice capital of Louisiana, and the site of the state's annual Cajun rice festival and parade. From a train depot among the Crowley mills, we disembark and pick our way

louisiana's french triangle

bird's eye view

1- alexandria
2- lake charles
3- lafayette
4- baton rouge
5- new orleans

of mexico

aplan

cameron

southern

lake charles

pacific

port arthur

railroad

la.

tex.

s.

e. w.

n.

along the platform to Louisiana Highway 13—also the main commercial boulevard through downtown Crowley—which reaches back through town to a small centerpiece plaza graced with an Art Deco courthouse from which the surrounding parish is administered. ACADIA PARISH is carved in stone in large letters across the building's flattened façade. The broad, sculpted stone steps at its base connect the courthouse to a banner-draped reviewing stand erected in the Highway 13 boulevard's median strip for the day's grand occasion. The rice-parade platform and bandstand command the thronged view from the courthouse down the few congested blocks back to where the train pulls slowly out of sight, having deposited a few more curious faces into the parade. Both sides of the street are filled with people whooping it up and milling around an endless progression of floats. The scene is reminiscent of high noon on Disneyland's Main Street, except for the fact that Cinderella never spoke Cajun French or lived in an Art Deco castle emblazoned with the word *Acadia*.

Cinderella never threw bags of rice from her carriage to the crowds of a Disneyland parade, either, as does Nancy Tabb Marcantel, the Cinderella of this parade. Ms. Marcantel, a Cajun Joan Baez, sings out greetings between throws and the crowd sings back, between catches, as the rice parade rolls on. It's a parade with the usual tinsel floats and high-school bands playing stadium-volume versions of the latest disco hits, and purty wimmin wearing next to nothing, of course, just like any other small-town American parade. But here and there you will also find such things as a float for the winner of the morning's accordion-playing contest; a calliope wagon sponsored by the Cajuns' own Evangeline Maid bread bakers; a playhouse-size Cajun cottage perched insouciantly on one float to advertise an Acadian summer camp for pre-school kids, where the usual arts and crafts are supplemented with fishing and pirogue racing. Louisiana's white-suited Cajun Congressman, John Breaux, a Crowley home-town boy, waves by in an open convertible. And still to come are all those legions of Cajun cowboys.

Cajun cowboys? They bring up the rear of the parade, cavalries of them, riding their extravagantly decked-out horses. Resplendent cowboys, these, fitted out in Louis XIV brocades and rhinestone collars. Mike Moreau leads one of the batallions, riding a silver saddle. His horse has had red ribbons tied gaily in its mane; his cowboy shirt is a riot of bangles; and his close-cropped, Gallic gray mustache is shaded by a big red Stetson. As the parade passes on the modern Cajun prairie, all the cowboys pause to tip their hats with a soft, gracious, "Howdy, *cher!*"

The cattle industry of the Golden West is the cornerstone of both the diet of Anglo-America and its romantic remembrances of the nineteenth century—and yet it was originally an Acadian enterprise. The modern American cattle industry started on the Cajun prairie almost a full century before Anglo-Americans even began their emigrations to Texas. Louisiana's cattle industry goes back at least to 1739, the date the first cattle brand was recorded in the state's French "brand book." The brand book continued to be the legal register for Louisiana cattle until 1954, and until then was kept at St. Martinville, originally the military Poste des Attakapas—a French-Indian trading post that grew into the first major settlement on the Teche, thereby opening up the Cajun prairie. Attakapas—the name given to that early trading-post fort, the surrounding prairie, and the most prominent of Louisiana's Cajun historical societies—comes from a tribe of supposedly cannibalistic Indians ("Attakapas" is the Choctaw word for "man-eater"). Frightened of the Attakapas, the Creoles did not venture out of their half of the French Triangle to trade or settle in the area west of the Atchafalaya Basin and the Bayou Teche. Thus, the southwestern prairies were left isolated, attracting dispossessed Cajun leaders who were attempting to keep their communities insular and intact after the first and second Expulsions.

There are only scattered brand-book entries until the 1760's, when the Acadian immigration to Louisiana began in earnest and the state's cattle industry began to expand. A Bernard in 1761 and a Broussard in 1762 are the first two Cajun entries in the brand book, preceding by three years the first organized party of 231 settlers headed for the Cajun prairie. Their arrival in the St. Martinville area

St. Martin of Tours Church, St. Martinville   DAVID RICHMOND

eventually led to the construction of the colony's fifth Cajun parish church, St. Martin de Tours, which now considers itself the Mother Church of the Louisiana Acadians.

The picturesque village of St. Martinville that grew up around the Poste des Attakapas is really where the West begins, but it is not your typical Wild West cow town. St. Martin's Church occupies center-stage of a substantial, oak-filled town square. The square is surrounded by common-walled, townhouse-style, commercial structures with their sidewalk-spanning galeries and their bilingual merchandise signs. A once-prosperous steamboat port along the Teche, a port abandoned to relative obscurity when the railroad ran six miles to the

west and on through Lafayette, St. Martinville attracted a steady
stream of French-speaking immigrants during its heyday in the 1700's
and 1800's. In addition to the Cajuns, that flow included dispossessed
royalists after the French Revolution, and, later, some of Napoleon's
followers, causing St. Martinville to style itself "Le Petit Paris" of the
West. One somewhat curious consequence of this is that almost everyone you'll ever meet from St. Martinville self-consciously claims to be
descended from royalty—a conceit that belies the more important
Acadian origins of the town. St. Martinville also lays claim to the most
famous Cajun immigrant of them all, Emmaline LaBiche, the model
for Longfellow's Evangeline and, later, for one of Dolores del Rio's
most celebrated movie roles. Evangeline's statue, authentic in historical detail down to her wooden shoes, stands in the abandoned graveyard behind St. Martin's Church and looks forlornly back toward the
Teche and an enormous old black-oak tree. That still-standing Chêne
Evangeline, according to local legend, is at the spot where she finally
met her Gabriel—after he had given her up for lost and married
another woman.

Among the other important early Acadian arrivals to St. Martinville was Joseph "Beausoleil" Broussard. He had once been an elected
delegate to Governor Lawrence's council from the Beaubassin region,
where he was later to lead the resistance movement in the Petitcodiac
River area when Lawrence's soldiers came scorch-earthing through.
On April 24, 1765, in his new Louisiana homeland, Broussard participated in an unusual contract between several of the prairie settlers
and Captain Antoine Bernard d'Hauterive, French colonial official
and entrepreneur. Captain d'Hauterive agreed to lend Broussard and
each of his community's participating settler families eight cows and
one stud bull for a period of six years—at the end of which the Cajuns
would return nine cattle plus half the offspring produced in the intervening years. Pierre Arceneaux, also originally from Beaubassin, and
one of the signatories to the agreement, settled outside the prairie
village of Carencro—the home of Evangeline's supposedly real-life
Gabriel, Louis Arceneaux. Pierre died in 1793, leaving behind him
an estate of 400 cattle raised from his d'Hauterive stake. For the
Cajuns, who had left over 100,000 head of livestock behind them in

Canada, d'Hauterive's contract was a seminal element in their social and economic recovery.

Louisiana's colonial-era cattle were mainly Spanish longhorns, imported from Cuba and Mexico and deployed on Cajun ranches called *vacheries*. The brand book was an essential legal instrument on the Cajun prairie because of the comparatively casual way the vacheries were run; often they were poorly fenced and the cattle ran *au large,* or wild. The *pieux* fences of the prairie ranches and farmsteads were built to keep the cattle out, not in, and featured stepladder entrances (reproduced at the LSU Rural Life Museum's village outside Baton Rouge) to keep cattle or other critters from crashing any gates en route to the tasty treats in maman's herb and vegetable garden.

Cattle are not raised that way in France, nor were they raised that way in Acadia—so the Cajun *vachers* apparently learned their Louisiana cattle-raising techniques from the Indians and from Spanish *vaqueros*. Le Page du Pratz, who published the earliest account of Louisiana, in 1758, reports that free-ranging cattle of unknown origin were being raised by the Avoyelles Indians, and the Indian cattle seemed to flourish.

The Indian cattle-raising area observed by du Pratz also proved later to be a critical crossing area for herds headed from the Cajun prairie to the slaughterhouses of the lucrative New Orleans market. Most prairie trails led to Breaux Bridge, a herd-gathering town that developed on the Teche north of St. Martinville. From there, the cattle were driven up the Teche levee to the bayou's headwaters juncture with the Atchafalaya River. Farther north, the Red River's log "raft" of spring debris provided passage across Atchafalaya waters to the east bank of the Mississippi. The cattle would be driven around the top edge of the Atchafalaya Basin and down the Mississippi to Baton Rouge for loading on southbound cattle boats.

South of St. Martinville, in the other direction, prairie cattle would be driven down the Teche levee to Berwick, which lies across the Atchafalaya Basin's Gulf terminus from Morgan City, where more cattle boats waited. The cattle's S-shaped journey to New Orleans by the southern route included a trip down the Teche to Berwick, then up the Atchafalaya and through Bayou Plaquemines to the Mississippi

River, and down again past the original Acadian Coast. After the destruction of the Red River raft in the years immediately following the Civil War, a move necessitated by steamboat development of Louisiana's Red River Valley, cattle traveling the northward route could go no farther east by land than the town of Washington. So, from that once-prosperous port, the head of navigation for Bayou Courtableau, the cattle would follow a somewhat larger S-shaped route—down the Courtableau directly into the Atchafalaya Basin, then up through Bayou Plaquemines and out into the Mississippi.

Ponderous proof of the prairie's isolation, these complicated routes through the wilderness were, nonetheless, extraordinarily profitable. Old newspaper accounts report that the port of Washington, now a sleepy architectural treasure trove and arts center, shipped as many as 15,000 head of cattle each year to New Orleans—many of them driven over the Cajun prairie from as far away as Texas. The coming of the Southern Pacific Railroad in the 1880's reduced the prairie's isolation from New Orleans and cut the waterborne cattle business back to nothing, as the general decline of the steamboats set in all over the South.

The modern-day cattle industry of Louisiana is still dominated by Cajuns, however, and by the prairie of southwest Louisiana. Beef cattle predominate, but a cooperatively owned Cajun creamery in Abbeville, named for the prairie's Vermilion River, provides most of the region's dairy products as well. Louisiana's modern version of the brand book reveals that there are quite a few more Broussards registered (340) than there are Smiths (205)—and also more Héberts, Trahans, and Guillorys than Smiths. Most of their modern Cajun cattle ride to market in the train, or in trucks, just like those of their other American kin—though some of rancher Charles Broussard's prize French Charolais and Brahman breeding cattle receive more special treatment. From his 3,000-acre rice and cattle spread at Forked Island, southwest Abbeville, Broussard ships his stud bulls to customers in South America and other far-flung locales via a special livestock airport facility at the Acadiana Regional Airport in nearby New Iberia.

The modern-day Cajun cowboy usually saves his best horse for the festival parades and rides on the range in his pickup—typically a pickup equipped with a CB radio and a sticker for KXKW, Lafayette's Cajun country-and-Western station. Rancher Charles Broussard rides the range of one of the most modern Louisiana cattle operations of them all, a particular point of pride since he's also a ninth-generation descendant of "Beausoleil" Broussard. Like his restless ancestor, Charles Broussard once made a strategic contract that vastly accelerated the growth and modernization of the cattle industry—this time the world cattle industry. His tale is a typically Cajun one.

In the early 1950's, Charles Broussard and his father imported an experimental French Charolais herd from Mexico and created an international incident that is still talked about today on the Cajun prairie. The Broussards at that time owned ranches in Florida and Mexico, as well as their Forked Island spread, and in Mexico they had become acquainted with a neighboring French émigré rancher who raised cattle as a hobby. The Broussards' neighbor had a herd of sixty-four Charolais he had purchased from the daughter of Mexico's late French ambassador, the hobbyist who had imported the cattle to the New World in the first place. Everyone in the American cattle industry had since been trying to buy the herd, Broussard says, including a major national meat packer, and politically connected Louisiana oil barons such as W. T. Burton and Judge Leander Perez. But the Broussards were the herdowner's neighbors, and besides, they were French-speaking Cajuns, so they were eventually entrusted with the future care of the herd—which Broussard now admits they acquired for a song.

In further developments, the sixty-four cattle were to become the object of a $8.75 million cash bid by Swift and Company because of their phenomenal ratio of weight-to-feed gain. It seems that a skinny, white, docile, and dumb-looking Charolais steer will gain a pound of beef for every 6¼ pounds of feed you give it; Black Angus cattle, by contrast, require 8¼ pounds of feed per pound of beef, Broussard says. The true value of their Charolais herd was only belatedly recognized by the Mexican government, which—fearful of losing a potential national asset—attempted to slap an excessive export fee on the Broussard family's shipment. The cattle subsequently came across the border without paying the tax, an episode since described in a variety of conflicting versions, to Charles Broussard's continuing dismay. But the worst part was yet to come: the two-year quarantine imposed on their new herd by federal and state agriculture departments while the Mexican government seized their family's foreign ranch and rival cattle breeders and the meat-packing industry maneuvered to get their hands on the sixty-four impounded Charolais. Texas cattle interests put up the money to buy off Louisiana regulatory officials, Charles Broussard charges, telling how he finally had to bring his congressman to a hearing and threaten court action to get his two-year quarantine lifted.

Since then he's kept a more wary eye on Louisiana political developments. In fact, Broussard's Flying J Ranch—the flagship of his Forked Island holdings, so named because a "J" with wings turns into a Cajun fleur-de-lis—has been the scene of many a notable Louisiana political barbecue, including the one that launched Cajun governor Edwin Edwards's successful bid for the statehouse in 1969. Broussard also helped found The International Relations Association of Acadiana (TIRAA), the private-sector economic-development group that funds various "French Renaissance" activities in various areas of the French Triangle (which business interests have dubbed Acadian-Louisiana, or Acadiana).

Through his TIRAA connections and his friendship with Governor Edwards, Broussard chaired the official Louisiana delegation that headed north to Acadian New Brunswick in the summer of 1977. The group was sent to Caraquet, site of the Williamsburg of Cajunism, the reconstructed Village Historique Acadien, for its opening dedication. Reminiscing about those days, Broussard brings out a record album by a Canadian group named for his ancestor, an unusual souvenir of his visit. And he tells of the bomb threats his delegation received from Francophobe Brunswickers. The old animosities of Acadian Canada remains the same, it seems, but in Cajun Louisiana the promise of the classic Grand Pré has been redeemed: Broussard pegs the worldwide distribution of his Cajun Charolais herd at somewhere over one million.

.   .   .

The early Louisiana prairie—where the first Cajun cattle and, originally, buffalo ran free—was once full of long, waving stands of wild prairie grass. When the Acadians first came to settle, they found that there were several interconnected prairie areas, divided like ponds by stands of distantly visible trees. Subtle, rolling gradations in the terrain made the grass seem like the surface of the sea the Cajuns had left behind them in Canada. The line between the prairies and the trees seemed very much like the shore; that's how prairie villages like Robert's Cove and Church Point acquired their names. As one drives into Church Point today, the town steeple stands against the trees like a lighthouse.

But as the wild buffalo eventually gave way to cattle, so the wild prairie grass eventually gave way to another, more domesticated variety, civilization's most highly prized and cultivated cereal grass: rice.

Even in the years before the construction of the Southern Pacific Railroad would usher in a boom in rice farming and an explosion in population, every prairie Cajun farm had its casual patch of precious rice. The Cajuns followed "a sort of Oriental system of hand culture in the raising of rice—they planted it in places that one could scarcely have plowed," noted Professor Lauren Post, the foremost authority on the life style of the Cajun prairie. Rice was simply thrown into the nearest pond, and what came up the Cajuns would call "providence rice," cutting it later by hand. Along coulee ditches, small bayous, or the small ponds adjacent to them, there was never any problem with the flooding rice needs to grow. Sometimes these rice ponds would start as a small "dig" to provide a water trough for livestock, but the trampling of cows and hogs would deepen and enlarge it, until it could be made suitable for rice cultivation and fenced off.

The Cajuns' success with subsistence rice cultivation enabled them once again to be self-sufficient in foodstuffs. Surplus cattle could be sold to La Ville, as New Orleans is still known on the Cajun prairie, for whatever outside necessities had to be purchased. The continuing, stubborn, neo-medievalism of their non-surplus economy was reflected in land-distribution patterns: most of the pre-railroad farmer and vacher holdings tended to form around the prairie's bayous in the

Rice field, near Crowley, 1953   ELEMORE MORGAN, SR.

same ribbon pattern found along the Mississippi River and Bayous
Lafourche and Teche. The wild-grass prairies beyond were both unsettled and unclaimed; as late as 1850, half a century into the American period, one-third of the state had not even been surveyed.

The completion of the Southern Pacific Line in 1880, resident
Cajun proficiency at rice cultivation, and an influx of immigrants—
mainly from overexpanded wheat-planting areas of the Midwest—
combined, however, to change all that and launch another major
outside challenge to the Cajun people's cultural resiliency. Ironically
enough, it would be mainly British capital that financed Louisiana's
newest land boom; London-based North American Land and Timber,
for example, swallowed up 1.5 million acres of land in what is now
four Cajun prairie parishes, paying twelve cents an acre for marshland
and as little as seventy-five cents an acre for prairie.

The Anglo-Saxon rice immigrants lured to Louisiana from the
Midwest were mainly of British and German stock; between 1880 and

1900, they caused the population of the Cajun prairie to double. They brought their wheat-growing machinery with them and adapted it to mechanized rice planting on a scale that still astounds: in 1886, the Southern Pacific shipped two million pounds of rice from the prairie to New Orleans, but six years later those shipments had increased a hundredfold.

While the Anglo-Saxons made the prairie more prosperous, they also made it less interesting than visitors like Warner and Frederick Law Olmstead had remembered it. The immigrants tended to settle closer to the railroad—they even named one of their new railroad towns Iowa—and all the original French place names along the rails have now been lost. Not only new towns were created, but new political subdivisions, beginning with Acadia Parish, established in 1882. The Acadia Parish seat at Crowley is laid out along the railroad with a rigid rectangular grid of letter streets in one direction and number streets in the other—a complete Midwestern town plan transplanted intact to its new Cajun soil.

But these railroad towns eventually grew to be predominantly Cajun-populated and French-speaking, as Crowley is today. Cajun ranchers and farmers picked up their new neighbors' tools and moved closer to town themselves, sometimes marrying and moving in. New Iberia, which now has one of the highest proportions of Cajun surnames in its phone book of any Attakapas region community, didn't include one Cajun name in its 1880 census, the year the railroad first came through.

The melding of blood and culture was also facilitated by a series of economic crises beginning with a drought in the 1890's. Overextended cultivation led to an unexpected depletion of bayou water supplies—the very condition which had led many of the Anglo-Saxon rice immigrants to leave the Midwest for Louisiana in the first place. Canal irrigation and well-pump companies were organized, the first near Crowley. Many of the Cajuns who decided to join the "modern" rice industry had their first start as sharecroppers on lands owned by these water companies. Seed and water were furnished in return for one-fourth of the final crop—and rice farms could be run as family operations, without the need for large numbers of slaves or hired labor. Unlike the plantations of the sugar boom, the new farms of the rice boom did not drive the Cajuns from their Louisiana prairie homeland but merely taught them how better to use it.

The turning point may well have been the year 1892, when the rice prairie declared its economic independence from the surviving mercantilistic structure of Creole New Orleans, which was trying to consolidate power over the prairie via the railroad. Commodity brokers on the crescent city's North Peters Street waterfront "rice row" attempted to corner the market that year, and ended up losing all their influence on the prairie instead. The Farmers' Cooperative Rice Milling Company was formed to fight the speculators, and the railroad began moving prairie rice west to Lake Charles instead of to New Orleans. Now a thriving petrochemical center and the state's third-largest port, at the southwest tip of the French Triangle, Lake Charles was dredged into a major deep-draft port to the Gulf—and the prairie rice industry built the state's largest mill there, where the railroad meets the water of Lake Charles' Calcasieu River. Large quantities of Louisiana rice are still traveling west these days, most of it no farther than Houston, where Budweiser makes it into beer.

But some of that rice has also gone west past Los Angeles, as far west as Korea, where it has helped feed the alleged Koreagate bribery scandal. In fact, the affair started out in the French Triangle way back in 1959. That's the year Fidel Castro took over Cuba and nationalized sugar plantations and mob-run casinos in Havana—to the rank displeasure of Louisiana's sugar families, who lost a lot of land, and New Orleans' rackets figures, who lost a valuable foreign source of hard currency. The American government's fumbled Cuban policy—President Kennedy's trade embargo of 1962 and the abortive Bay of Pigs invasion—was most notable out on the Cajun prairie for costing southwest Louisiana what was, at that time, its largest and most lucrative single international rice-export market (in one year a total of 400 million pounds). Then one day, in the midst of this crisis, Cajun lawyer Edwin Edwards heard about U.S. Congressman T. Ashton Thompson's fatal car accident. Edwards, who had risen from hot young lawyer around Crowley's Deco-Acadia courthouse to the state senate, ran for Thompson's vacated seat in 1965 and won—landing himself in Congress during one of the Louisiana rice industry's worst hours. When he came to Washington, Edwards brought along another young Crowley lawyer named John Breaux to be his executive assistant. With help from north Louisiana Congressman Otto Passman—the one-time terror of the House Agriculture Committee, whose subcommittee directed foreign sales of surplus rice—Breaux and Edwards began negotiating rice deals, beginning with a whopping 900,000-pound sale of Louisiana rice to Korea in 1972.

Tongsun Park, the notorious Korean rice dealer, says he first met Congressman Edwards in 1970, and that their friendship extended past the 1972 rice deal to the time when Edwards gave up the Seventh Congressional District—Louisiana's rice-bowl seat—to become the state's only modern Cajun governor. Breaux succeeded his boss in Congress. Since then, some of Louisiana's highest public officials are alleged to have received a quarter of a million dollars and other gifts from the Koreans—small potatoes, really, when you consider that the value of the 1972 rice sale to Korea amounted to $155 million alone, and that Korea continues to be one of Louisiana's most important rice-export destinations. Denying most, but not all, of the rumors that follow him everywhere, the irreverent Edwards—movie-star handsome and a brilliant raconteur—delights Louisiana political audiences to this day with an introductory string of Cajun-accented Tongsun Park jokes.

Though the grand prairie of southwest Louisiana is the scene of some of the most profound changes in Acadian cultural and technological history, it still retains a wondrous rural quality that sparkles, in its subtropical setting, with the subtle changes of every season.

The lyrical progression of the seasons has been nowhere better described than in Lauren C. Post's *Cajun Sketches from the Prairies of Southwest Louisiana.** "The seasonal changes in the vegetation and crops, the weather at different times of the year, and the routines of the farmers and cattlemen are far better indicators of the seasons than

ton Rouge, La.: Louisiana State University Press, 1962.

are any instruments," wrote Post. "The weather elements, in the yearly cycle, make four entirely different landscapes," which he proceeds to describe in some detail.

Winter: "Although the winters are short they bring about a dullness in the landscape thought to be characteristic only of climates of far more northerly latitudes. Few trees on the prairie besides live oaks and pines stay green through the winter months. The deciduous trees, of course, shed their leaves, and the annuals leave no trace of green. Long before Christmas the sugar cane stubble and leaves, the corn stalks, cotton stalks, and the rice stubble have lost all suggestion of the verdant aspect they showed in the spring and summer. The contrast is complete, and the same strong contrast is to be found in the old natural pastures and roadside weeds . . . Between the cold spells, the balmy winds from the Gulf blow and ultimately bring rain. The winter is thus a succession of changes between cold north winds and warm south winds, the former bringing clear, cool days and the latter warm, mild conditions with considerable precipitation."

Spring: "With the advance toward spring the fields are plowed, and each additional plowed patch adds to the surface of grays, browns and blacks until about the first of March, when every square foot of land that is to be planted has been turned. The vision across the fields is least impaired by vegetation and, seemingly, there are no greens in the landscape except the live oaks, conifers, and some young grass which is just beginning to grow in the pastures. With the warm days of early spring, budding and growth of leaves bring some of the most abrupt changes of the year, changes that can be exceeded only by a prematurely early frost in the fall. The crops, though planted early, fail for a time to obscure the ground. The flatness of the entire landscape is maintained throughout March. Cotton is planted a little later than corn, and between April tenth and fifteenth, hundreds of farmers are seen putting in their crops. While cotton farmers are busy, rice farmers are also busy making every minute count. Their crop makes a more sudden change in the landscape than does cotton, for as soon as the rice is a few inches high, it is flooded by artificial irrigation. Flooding usually goes on in the month of May, and as the young plants are not entirely submerged, they form a most pleasing mass of green."

Summer: "Summer rains are quite unpredictable, as are those of all seasons. Sometimes dry spells last for weeks on end, causing the corn crop to burn, and at other times rain comes in great or small quantities for forty consecutive days. Usually the rains begin to come with considerable regularity about June 8, which is St. Medard's Day. Sensible temperatures are augmented by the very high relative humidity, and the steamy air of some hot, wet days is perhaps the most impressionable feature of the summers of south Louisiana. Although fanned and tempered by the breezes of the Gulf, it is still too humid for the greatest exertion and comfort. July is usually a month of rest and relaxation for both man and beast. Odd jobs such as fixing fences and cutting wood occupy a great deal of the time of the more industrious, but little that one can do now will help or hinder the making of the crop . . . On the Fourth of July, we most generally have ripe figs, green corn, and watermelons. August then finds cotton picking and rice cutting at their height."

Fall: "Corn is gathered immediately after the cotton is picked, but the cutting of cane never begins until after the middle of October . . . Summer and fall hurricanes sometimes visit the prairies and leave in their wake a number of felled chinaberry trees, but these storms were not feared, and were seldom taken seriously by the inhabitants until Hurricane Audrey struck in 1957. The leaves of the catalpa trees fall in September. The chinaberry trees keep theirs a little longer, and they turn a beautiful yellow with the first frost, which is apt to come in November. In the rice field, the mass of green turns to a rich yellow and does not lose its beauty even when it is in the shock. The cotton fields whiten as soon as the bolls open, but the pickers soon change the scene to one of stalks with only a few fast-turning leaves upon them. Sugar cane holds its color longest, yielding its green only with the first frost, which turns its leaves to a light buff color. The dangers of frost, rain and mud are to be avoided, so the planters speed up the work of cutting so as to finish in December, and thus the last of the crops is harvested. The winter draws on, and the cycle is completed."

5

Texas and the Oiligarchs

*First offshore oil rig, built in 1947 and still operating
45 miles southwest of Morgan City*
KERR-MCGEE OIL COMPANY

Lafayette, the oil center of the French Triangle, and its de facto capital, is spread out across the velvet-smooth Cajun prairie like a giant trey of diamonds.

The highest of the three diamonds walls in the old city, originally founded in 1821 as the village of Vermilionville. The Cathedral of St. John the Evangelist, honoring founder Jean Mouton's namesake, was built on land he donated in the middle of the original township—at one time part of his plantation. The graveyard out back slopes gently down to the Coulee Mine, named for the Fundy tidal basin at Grand Pré. Out front, the steps of the church open into a short, two-block commercial street ending at the parish courthouse. Early settlers diligently filled out the street grid spread into the corners of this first diamond, and spilled out beyond it.

The next diamond down, which almost touches the corner tip of the old downtown, contains the University of Southwestern Louisiana (USL)—founded a few years after the railroad came through. USL trained the railroad's telegraph operators and mechanics, and later the farmers and teachers who would help make the Cajuns masters of their new prairie. In the center of the USL campus stands the Dupré Library, with its third-floor archives section full of French and Spanish colonial documents and microfilms and other records that mark the Acadian passage into the newborn land.

At the southernmost tip of the university's diamond, beside a small park distinguished principally by the fact that a small Civil War battle took place there, USL's glistening new School of Art and Architecture stares out toward the Gulf. Designed by Lafayette's Cajun firm of Barras, Breaux and Champeaux after a national competition, the stark cement structure stands on a small bluff overlooking the shrunken, landscaped bayou winding through the oak-filled park. The architecture building resembles a beached Cajun fishing boat, with its second-floor deck and third-floor, cabinlike overhangs. The park below is full of autumn colors and dancing at the annual Festivals Acadiens—three days of outdoor concerts and other events at the beginning of September that commemorate that other fateful September on the fields of Grand Pré. The Cajuns have become a fully landed people in Louisiana, more secure than they have ever been before in the three and a half centuries of their American history. And yet, as the beached boat of their university fleet looks out over the dancing and through the leaf-shedding trees, it does not command a clear and unobstructed view to the sea over which they came.

Instead, the prairie horizon beyond the park spreads out to reveal the third and newest of Lafayette's civic diamonds, laid out in 1952, the so-called Oil Center that sprang from the bowers of Maurice Heymann's one-time orchard and nursery. Originally planned as a complex of one-story buildings, each adjacent to sufficient parking-lot pads to let the oil moguls motor their autos and helicopters easily in and out, the Oil Center buildings have gone on to spore a generation of second and third floors, and the complex now features hotels and high-rise hospital towers. The Oil Center's dwarf resemblance to Houston or Los Angeles is not altogether unintentional. Over eight hundred oil-related companies maintain their Louisiana regional-exploration offices there. Most of the outsiders are Texans or those aspiring to become like the Texans—Texians, as the bayou Cajuns sometimes contemptuously call them. Adventurers and fortune-seekers, all of them, the Texians know how the cards are stacked these days in oil-soaked Lafayette, and they have streamed into town in such numbers that the population of the metropolitan area now approaches 120,000—four times what it was before oil was discovered offshore in the Cajun fishing waters. The outsiders are still descending on Lafayette, darkening the sky as they wing their way in on Texas International Airlines. The flight pattern is low over the city, crossing straight through the first diamond, and then the second, and finally screaming across the third, to grip the Lafayette airport's tarmac runways a short distance beyond.

The first and most important of the Texas outsiders was W. Scott Heywood, who "brought in" Louisiana's first oil field in the northwest corner of the prairie's Acadia Parish in 1901—also in the fateful month of September. The area attracted Heywood's attention because it had geological outcroppings characteristic of those of the Gulf Coast's first oil field at Spindletop, outside Beaumont, Texas, where Heywood and his brother made their first big splash in oil. Prior to the success of that gamble, Heywood, a native of Columbus, Ohio, had supported himself on a series of misadventures ranging from playing cornet solos at the 1893 Chicago World's Fair to gold prospecting on the West Coast. While on a railroad trip east from Houston along the Southern Pacific's rice line, the versatile Heywood espied the potential Jennings Field alongside Bayou Nezpique, which might be quite literally translated in this context as "nose dive." Louis Clement, the Cajun prairie farmer who leased Heywood the land where the Jennings Field gushed, later recalled, "We heard a noise and saw the oil go out. At first, we thought it was black smoke from the boiler at the well. But it kept on blowing, and we saw the mud blowing out over the derrick." It kept on blowing for 160 feet and within the year had prompted the formation of seventy-six new companies to explore and extract the state's vast, newly discovered underground pool of oil.

That oil is older than any of the landscape above it—for the oil under the marsh is merely another layer of the same organic materials that make up the marsh. Those materials end up compressed underground in high-pressure layers that eventually liquefy. As plant materials are buried and compressed and begin to decay and oxidize, the ash left behind forms particles of clay that are later buried by layers of sand and marsh grass or seabed, or even soils deposited by the annual flood runoff. From this beginning, if they are sufficiently pure, the weight of upper layers will compress the clay particles into solid peat, and ultimately lignite—which, pressed even harder, could turn into diamonds.

The lighter oil and methane-gas particles squeezed out of this solid carbonaceous mass seek escape into the surrounding sands—but they cannot rise through the clay layers unless a natural geological formation or a manmade oil well punctures through into this hot, black underground sea. Salt domes, massive underground salt pimples, sometimes form natural outcroppings along the landscape—especially

Oil rigs and cane field near New Iberia, 1949
ELEMORE MORGAN, SR.

noticeable where the fabled Five Islands (including Tabasco-making Avery Island) rise out of the coastal marsh. As the more lightweight salt is pushed upwards through these underground layers, vast quantities of surrounding oil and gas are collected under them, as if the salt dome were an enormous plug. Farther inland begin the *coteau* formations, where a slight fold in the underground strata occasions an escarpment—a drop of anywhere from ten to fifty feet from the higher prairie, again allowing the underground sea of oil or gas to seep closer

to the surface. It was just such a formation that Heywood saw from
the train.

What later became the lucrative Anse La Butte field between
Breaux Bridge and Lafayette is said to have been oozing away along
its escarpment since at least 1893. Natural-gas seepage farther south
in the swamps, combined with a bolt of lightning in a storm, is said
to have ignited one entire island for a wondrous three months in
1812. Natural gas was known to range across the state as early as

1823, when French engineers drilling for water in Pointe Coupée Parish kept opening up wells of methane gas instead. In those earlier periods, oil and gas were merely something of a nuisance—but nothing compared to what was yet to come.

Since the folks from "Takes-Us" first started organizing a way to pump it out of the ground, the oil produced in Louisiana has totaled over 14 billion barrels. That's enough to coat every square foot of land surface on earth with an oil slick nine inches thick. The industry floating in this black sea has netted Louisiana many troubles, and a bizarre collection of firsts and mosts and leasts. Items like the United States' largest refinery complex, started in 1909 by the corporate predecessor to what is now Exxon at Baton Rouge, which thanks to Louisiana oil has become the nation's fourth largest port by volume (after New York, New Orleans, and Houston). Or the first oil well ever drilled over water, at Caddo Lake near the state's northwest Anglo city of Shreveport, one year later in 1910. The Shreveport first paved the way for the first offshore oil well and drilling platform in the open Gulf, installed off Morgan City in 1947 and still functioning today. Morgan City's offshore-obsessed oil and trailer-park metropolis nowadays claims to be the home of more deep-sea divers and more private helicopters than any other city in the country. The oil-administration center of Lafayette claims to be the home base of more independent oil operators than either Houston or New Orleans. At the other end of the superlatives scale, the minuscule and independent Evangeline Oil Company (seventy-eight stations in the French Triangle) claims its sole refinery operates the world's smallest catalytic cracker—the machine which separates gasoline and kerosene from other raw hydrocarbon products.

Another Louisiana "least" is the benefit all this oil activity has had for the Cajuns—for the oil, and the incredible wealth it has generated, has been literally stolen out from underneath them, both out on the prairie and down on the bayou. And that theft was nowhere more blatant than during the regime of Governor O. K. Allen, Huey Long's handpicked successor and accomplice in the so-called Win or Lose scheme. As subsequently detailed in an investigation by Lafayette *Daily Advertiser* oil editor Paul F. Matthews, and a spectacular high-stakes lawsuit unprecedented even in Louisiana's seamy political history, Win or Lose worked like this:

Allen, in the governor's exclusive capacity, sold lucrative exploration leases on oil-rich, state-owned water bottoms to selected cronies. Principal among them was multimillionaire industrialist W. T. Burton of Lake Charles, who pyramided his slice of the take into the largest bank between Houston and New Orleans and a variety of other thriving enterprises. Burton, in his turn, would hand over his leasehold to an assortment of cooperative oil companies waiting in the wings. The oil companies would give him a lump sum of cash for his trouble, Matthews reports, plus an annual rental for the life of the lease, plus a $1/24$ share "overriding royalty" on all oil and gas produced. After completing these arrangements, Burton would quietly sell three-fourths of this negotiated package, sometimes for no more than $10 per package, to an entity known as the Win or Lose Oil Company. Allen, Burton, and friends saw to it that Win or Lose had the pick of the crop. The most lucrative single Win or Lose package was the so-called Lease 340 in coastal St. Mary Parish—250,000 acres (a land area the size of Los Angeles). Burton picked up Lease 340 from the state for a mere $75,000, Matthews charges, and sold it a few days later to a major oil company for a $20,000 immediate profit, plus $10,000 per year and the $1/24$th override. Because of its size alone, Lease 340 has been the most profitable single oil and gas production area in the entire French Triangle, and it is still producing today.

When the assets of Win or Lose were liquidated in 1951, its list of stockholders caused quite a stir. Included were former Governor Allen's children, Huey Long's personal secretary, former Governor James Noe—Allen's lieutenant governor at the time of these transactions and his eventual successor, who pyramided *his* share of the windfall into a chain of Louisiana broadcast stations, and, of course, Huey Long's children and grandchildren—including his son Russell, U.S. Senator from Louisiana and Big Oil's most powerful paid political apologist on Capitol Hill. Win or Lose had been established with working capital of a mere $200 as a paper corporation that never operated with even so much as its own office—so the true value of its plunder has never been determined. Nonetheless, after the liquidation, former Win or Lose shareholders and their heirs were collectively sued for restitution of revenues to the State of Louisiana. Bringing suit was the eccentric Louis J. Roussel, a feisty and unpredictable Cajun nose-thumber and upstart multimillionaire banker of considerable cunning—and an independent oil operator who started his business career as a New Orleans streetcar conductor. Roussel went to court to make Win or Lose pay back $250 million, but since it was a state court, the suit is still pending.

Though several oil companies were involved in this scam, ultimately most of the major oil producers in Louisiana, the most skillful of them all turned out to be the Texas Company, now Texaco. Texaco eventually became the nation's number-two domestic oil producer, and the largest producer in Louisiana. Texaco's largest Louisiana operations are to be found in Terrebonne Parish, where political oldtimers will flat out declare that the oil under Terrebonne *made* Texaco.

The folks from Takes-Us stalk the oil-rich Cajun swamps, marshes, and prairies of Louisiana with a relentless boldness that, since the days of Huey Long and O. K. Allen, they have perfected and exported to every other oil region across the world. And yet nowhere do they stalk their way as boldly as they do in a borrowed Lafayette cow barn—at a biennial industry trade show, the Louisiana Gulf Coast Oil Exposition (LAGCOE).

As the morning haze clears, the fairgrounds surrounding USL's Blackham Coliseum come less mystifyingly into view. Huge, portable, telescoping oil derricks the height of a twelve-story building have sprung up like a mechanical canebrake and crowd a space shared with amphibious airplane dragonflies trucked in for the occasion, other odd vehicular creatures with tank-tread feet or one-eyed operator cabs, and a maze of sculptural machinery shells glistening in yellow- or red-enameled gloss. A yellow dirigible is tethered over this mechanical jungle, advertising a company that produces drilling mud—a foul and heavy goo of barium sulfate removed in vast quantities from the hills of Wyoming for burial deep in the marshes of Louisiana.

LAGCOE's participating companies and their exhibitions continuously verge on the surreal: one Texas-based company calling itself Gator Hawk, for example, features a trademark of a winged and hardhatted alligator clutching a piece of drilling pipe in his wide, grinning jaws. Gator Hawk supplies equipment to test drilling pipes for structural flaws that might cause expensive or dangerous breaks—and claims to have already inspected enough pipe to encircle the world twice, the kind of claim you'll often find bandied about LAGCOE.

Gushing forth from helicopters, charter buses, and limousines, thousands of clean-scrubbed, crew-cut oil industry ole boys and their beehive-coiffed wives or mistresses arrive here to promenade endlessly past these toymakers. All are decked out in the paper-thin plastic hardhats each major exhibitor vies to give away. It is the carnival of Hades, the petroleum netherworld's midway lined with peculiar pumps and pipes and other infernal paraphernalia for exploiting the riches of this "oil patch," as the Texians have taken to calling their Louisiana annex. They stumble through the three hundred-odd exhibits of LAGCOE, greedily loading up their plastic shopping bags with worthless but symbolic baubles and brochures, and they swill beer from bottomless kegs in garden-party tents floored with several varieties of petro-plastic grass.

Most of the companies and camp followers who come here in the odd years also congregate in the even years at Odessa, Texas, where the Permian Basin petroleum area stages its own biennial companion piece to LAGCOE. When Louisiana pays tribute to Texas, Odessa stages a barbecue; when Texas comes to Louisiana, Lafayette throws what always becomes its most decadent and talked-about Cajun-style cocktail party. The Lafayette bash in 1977 was hosted by J. P. Owens, Sr., one of the most colorful and outspoken resident Texas immigrants, an independent operator who has gone broke several times. In between those times, he has anted up the cash to memorialize himself with projects such as the entire arts center at Southern Methodist University in Dallas. The Owenses' bayou-side Lafayette residence is a quasi-French château with a faked second floor and boxed trees lining the formal entryway out front, and a somewhat incongruous Roman-style atrium inside where uniformed servants dispense plastic champagne glasses full of tequila. The dining area, which occupies one whole glass-walled room overlooking the atrium, centers on a table laden with enough silver bowls of French-fried frogs' legs to restock a medium-size swamp. While an orchestra leads an Arthur Murray party in the ballroom-size front parlor, more adventuresome guests move out to the garage and parking court in back, where an aluminum pirogue full of iced oysters on the half shell and a crawfish racing contest—complete with its bull's-eye table, bets, announcers, and mudbugs imported intact from the semi-annual Breaux Bridge Crawfish Festival—provide the ultimate in Cajun exotica for the wide-eyed guests. Raw oysters, opened before your wary eyes and served cold, wet, salty, and slimy on the still-sandy half shell, are guaranteed to send twittering shock waves through all those Neiman-Marcus gowns.

But the star attraction of the evening in the garage, on the terrace, in the atrium, at the dining table, or on the dance floor is a regal, oil-black-gowned young woman in Medici collar and cape, her velvet and peau-de-soie costume heavily encrusted with gushing rigs hand-worked in pearls and rhinestones. In less formal moments, she is attired more like her ladies-in-waiting, the so-called Oil Drops, who play hostess at LAGCOE functions in their bondage black boots, black vinyl hot pants, and gold plastic hardhats. But for tonight's party it's not just a little tits and ass but the full drag ball. As this portable beauty-pageant entourage maneuvers between the evening's pinches, grabs, and stares, Queen LAGCOE gleams out over it all with her scepter and enormous crown, topped with a gushing oil derrick made of aurora-borealis stones and, yes, of course, real diamonds.

What the LAGCOE fuss is mainly all about is offshore oil. Since that first Morgan City rig in 1947, over three thousand have sprung up in the waters off Louisiana alone, each of them a self-contained industrial plant requiring vast amounts of machinery, maintenance, capital, and labor—a vast captive market for LAGCOE's fairgrounds full of goodies.

The rig cities clustered off the Louisiana coast come in ungainly clumps, sometimes in scorpion or other animal shapes; around South Timbalier block 135, the rigs are lined up in an almost perfect circle one mile in diameter. Some of these structures are two hours or more out by helicopter from fifteen permanent bases operated along eight hundred miles of Gulf coast by Lafayette-headquartered Petroleum Helicopters, Inc., and other bases operated by other companies. PHI modestly claims to operate "a helicopter transportation-communications network without equal in the free world," including similar operations in Alaska, Africa, Bolivia, Ecuador, and Saudi Arabia. Some offshore Louisiana rigs are serviced mainly by boat, but all rigs have built-in topside helipads. PHI even maintains a network of offshore repair bases, fuel depots, and roving copter squads based on cooperative platforms all along the Gulf rim to provide emergency services wherever needed. PHI also supplies the U.S. Weather Bureau with most of its raw data on Gulf weather conditions, because the corporation needs precise weather data. Their pilots will not venture out unless there is a three-mile visibility from five hundred feet. From out in a helicopter high over the open Gulf, shrimp boats become scattered corks. And the rigs look like Tinkertoys until you come close enough to be swallowed up by their sheer gargantuan scale. Like the arthropod creatures of H. G. Wells's *War of the Worlds,* these rig giants stalk menacingly through the marsh and sea, and they keep stalking farther and farther away from the shore. Sometimes they reach such depths that they require subsea support structures that, if assembled on land, would tower above New Orleans' fifty-one-story One Shell Square oil office tower.

Most of the rigs are assembled on land first, in pieces that are barged out into the Gulf and sunk in designated places to be stacked one on top of the other, just like real Tinkertoys. Most of Louisiana's rigs are assembled at two massive outdoor yards near Morgan City, the gritty industrial "manchac," or rear entrance to Louisiana's oil patch. The railroad that once hauled huge cypress logs from Morgan City when it was starting out as a booming, pre-Civil War sawmill town now brings in rusting pipes instead. They're stacked in dusty fields alongside the booming Gulf Intracoastal Waterway, which meets the Atchafalaya Basin at Morgan City. The pipe comes mainly over that waterway from a Houston steel mill, but raw steel sheets barged in flat can be rolled into larger pipe sizes here under a nomadic-looking assortment of tin sheds.

Offshore wells are usually drilled by exploratory, semi-submersible drill ships, a New Orleans invention now used worldwide. A top barge floats while dropping another barge filled with water until it settles on the bottom. A "jacket" is ordered for the drilling hole, with a platform later built over it and an above-the-waterline deck to go on top. Each rig is custom-built, and its pieces are sealed with valves that divers open to lower each successive structural layer into place. Each rig has many wells, all of them angled out slightly from the bottom of the jacket to suck up the widest possible area of oil from the cheapest possible single-site investment. The costs for all this are truly unbelievable, even in the bargain basement, for the drilling bits that chew through the rock layers under all that water are usually diamond-tipped. Production platforms that pump the eventual finds are often left unmanned. Nuclear-powered navigation aides and elaborate, high-tech computer tentacles—connecting a subsea maze of pipelines to shore—control and safeguard the rigs' catch. The same general technology for drilling offshore oil has also been adapted for offshore sulphur mining. And one French-owned firm has set up shop in Morgan City to build its own rigs—so rig building has now become a multimineral, multinational enterprise. Though on land these machines look virtually impregnable, at sea they aren't. In 1964, Hurricane Hilda blew twenty-seven of them over—another one of Louisiana's world records—and several more rigs blow up each year, spreading lethal oil slicks over America's richest coastal fishing grounds and spewing millions of tons of wasted fuel thousands of feet into the smoke-darkened sky. Shell Oil holds the current Gulf disaster record, with 137 days of blazing inferno at its Bay Marchand Platform B, which consumed eleven wells at an estimated cost of $36 million. But Morgan City manages each year to build more rigs than either hurricanes or negligence can destroy, and so the pipelined Gulf floor is slowly being webbed over with hollow steel.

Big Oil runs Louisiana's corruption-plagued government back on shore in Baton Rouge because Big Oil also pays most of its bills—severance taxes alone equaled almost one-third of state government expenditures for 1974–75, and direct sales of oil and gas production from state property equaled another third. But out in the swamps and marshes and prairies there are scattered pockets of Cajun political guerrilla resistance to all of this, most notably in the Terrebonne Parish seat of Houma, where druggist Donald Landry fought his way to an election victory over an oil-patch representative on the parish police jury (the Louisiana equivalent of a county board of commissioners). He beat a man who worked for Avondale, one of the Morgan City-based offshore rig builders backing a controversial $25 million expansion of the Bayous Boeuf, Chêne, and Black between Houma and Morgan City. Landry campaigned hard against turning that delicate bayou system into a stinking industrial ditch—and the expansion was one of the U.S. Army Corps of Engineers projects canceled by President Carter after the 1976 election, until members of Louisiana's Congressional delegation pressured him to reinstate it. Both Landry and the Carter Administration fear the project might turn the entire Houma water supply salty from Gulf tidal intrusions. But, at whatever cost to everyone else, the rig builders say they need their plantside bayou remodeled so that they can expand their facilities and fabricate larger and larger rigs that can be sailed out deeper and deeper into the Gulf and perhaps even one day around the world. They say Landry is crazy. Landry, meanwhile, has dragged the Corps' environmental impact statement for this oil-industry subsidy through one noisy public hearing and courtroom case after another, and at one point even succeeded in persuading the Terrebonne police jury to join in one of his suits. In a state where oil-patch bumper stickers sullenly proclaim OIL FEEDS MY FAMILY, and where the oil industry just last year helped the banks knock off organized labor's power with a "right to work law" before the unions could begin their long-overdue organizing campaign for the offshore labor force, Donald Landry is in some quarters a much-feared and much-loathed man.

Personable and quiet-spoken in person, he learned his love of pharmacy from his father, who once invented an athlete's foot remedy. Pharmacist training gives Landry's attacks on the Corps project a certain scientific precision. He also approaches the problem from thirty-seven years of personal contact with the land he says the Corps and the oil companies are seeking to destroy. As he goes about his business, Landry usually hops on his boat to go into town—and the reason he *must* use his boat, instead of the automobile sitting idle in his carport, tells much of the nature of his struggle. Once upon a time there used to be a steel bridge that extended across the Gulf Intracoastal Waterway to connect Houma's North Main Street to South Main, where Landry's drugstore is located, just one block back from the water. The steel bridge was there until a barge tow on the congested waterway bashed it out. In the interminable period of repair delay, Landry can drive downtown only by way of the circuitous and traffic-clogged collections of tunnel and bridge corridors that link the various islands of Houma, afloat in the coastal marsh like a little Venice. Houma is sliced by the Intracoastal east and west, plus Bayou Terrebonne running north and south near Landry's Main Street pharmacy, and then several more bayou branches and a ship channel to the south. The driving hassles there have become so severe that Landry just hops into his boat instead, and putters over to park behind the old federal post office—now a smart restaurant conversion on the levee between the Houma town square and Bayou Terrebonne. Landry putters to town several times a day, over a black-watered bayou old-timers say was once crystal-clear, to keep track of his police jury business at the Terrebonne Parish courthouse on the other side of the oak-shaded square.

The Bayous Boeuf, Chêne, and Black project that started his political career, and has at least indirectly sent him back to his boat, makes him weary of pharmacy and especially weary of politics, he says, and wistful in an ever so soft-spoken and Cajun way for a life farther down the bayou with some sort of fishing boat. But while he's still here in Houma, the high-handed politics of Big Oil make him furious, and his scientific background makes him a formidable foe of the development alchemy he sees destroying the landscape around him. The Bayous Boeuf, Chêne, and Black project would destroy yet another seven thousand acres of valuable marsh in one fell swoop, and Louisiana is losing over sixteen square miles of coastal marsh every year to Gulf erosion already, even without any new canals to accelerate that process.

Perhaps as much as half the erosion is believed caused by Corps levees along the Mississippi River which have retarded the annual flood siltation cycle that first formed these low-lying delta areas. But the remainder of the erosion is believed caused entirely by the extraction and transportation methods used by the oil industry under and through what marsh is still left. Land subsidence, because of oil and gas extraction, is part of the problem, of course, but even worse are the navigation and pipeline canals crisscrossed through the delicate, tundralike marsh. Older canals have sometimes widened into virtual lakes, and Landry estimates Terrebonne Parish alone is losing over two thousand acres of land every year. Scientists at Louisiana State University estimate that 39 percent of the total coastal-zone destruction can be traced directly to pipeline canals, and note that, once dug, these canals tend to double their width every fourteen years. Unlike threats to tundra permafrost, this damage does not freeze at the edge, but continues to eat away the rest of the marsh. In the fisheries-rich Barataria estuary on the other side of Bayou Lafourche from Terrebonne Parish, an estuary responsible for a full tenth of the nation's annual fisheries harvest, LSU scientists estimate that 10 percent of the land mass has already been irretrievably lost to canals. The Gulf shore of Louisiana is on the verge of ecological collapse, Landry charges, looking up over a kitchen table covered with old newspapers and a gradually diminishing pile of boiled, peeled, and to-be-eaten shrimp. At the current rate, he figures all the shrimp will be gone from Louisiana's estuaries at or before the time the remaining reserves of oil and gas finally run out. Unmolested, on the other hand, and carefully husbanded, the wildlife spawned by Louisiana's marshlands might eventually be able to provide enough fish to feed the entire country—another dream as old as Grand Pré, and a dream that will not yet be relinquished.

Regardless of what happens to Louisiana's people and fish, Big Oil is nonetheless well prepared for making its next move when the local supplies of oil run out. The oiligarchs would be willing to abandon their offshore platforms to hurricanes and refugee colonies of strug-

ROLLAND GOLDEN

gling Cajun fishermen, perhaps. But all those inland pipelines connected to the refinery and industrial complex of the American Ruhr Valley along the former Acadian Coast corridor between Baton Rouge and New Orleans can and must be preserved, their own peculiar sense of ecological thriftiness suddenly demands. And that infrastructure must be fully utilized and expanded in order to keep the rest of the country going. A billion-dollar rescue effort for all that capital investment is in the planning stage now—a deep-water superport for oil imported in mammoth supertankers. Each vessel would stretch out longer than the Empire State Building is high, and be deeper of draft when fully loaded than any domestic American seaport except Seattle can accommodate. Big Oil plans to float its unloading depot twenty miles out into the Gulf, into its rusting forest of rigs and platforms.

If built off the Lafourche and Terrebonne Parish coastline as planned, the Louisiana Offshore Oil Port (LOOP) terminal's onshore pipeline will touch land within sight of Jean Lafitte's old smuggling base on Grand Terre Island. In its own special pipeline canal, LOOP will burrow its way northward along the same Bayou Lafourche those earlier smugglers used, but with vastly more disruptive and antisocial results. For as the LOOP pipeline moves erratically along the bayou it does not go all the way through to Donaldsonville—where a rock nightclub called Lafitte's Landing has been established in an old plantation house—but stops short of this crossing, and veers east through the cane fields south of Donaldsonville to meet the Mississippi via another, more devious route. Veering east through St. James Parish, LOOP's pipeline will be designed to connect with something called the Capline—a pipeline system that makes a thousand-mile push up the Mississippi Valley to refineries in St. Louis, Chicago, and the Ohio Valley, with links to all the nation's other major pipeline systems along the way. Opened in 1967, the Capline is operated by one of LOOP's partners, Shell Oil, for a consortium of other oil companies. The Capline operation already draws together four major pipeline nodes from the Gulf floor, and connects to another pipeline system servicing Shell's New Orleans area refinery and the New Orleans airport downriver. Barges bring more oil in to this octopus, above and beyond what the existing Gulf supplies and pipelines can furnish, and smaller tank-ers have already begun bringing in imported crude, too, now un-loaded at huge docks stretching half a mile up and down the Missis-sippi River levee next to the Capline's central control tower.

Inside that tower, microwave communications link controllers with pumping stations throughout the Midwest, and six color-television monitors flash continuous readouts of transmission data from all those pipes, and also from a huge tank-farm reservoir across the river road stretching back into the riverside cane fields. Pipes arch their way across the road connecting the terminal to its tank farm, which looks like a giant's one-time steel-trunked orchard mowed down into squat but shiny stumps, or *chicots*. And everywhere you turn, everything is surrounded by barbed wire and posted with signs warning you not to dig or smoke. From their electronically secured command post, the pipeline operators seem like imprisoned guards, lulled by Muzak and rows of colored lights until boredom occasionally takes them out onto the balcony for a look at their black-blooded domain. The Capline plantation, for that is literally what it has become, is situated almost midway between New Orleans and Baton Rouge. This is a prime location from which to service the other industrial plantations of the American Ruhr corridor, which is rapidly filling with refineries, chemical plants, and grain elevators all up and down the river where sugar plantations—and before them, Acadian farmsteads—once stood end-lessly green. Oil has usurped the industrial progress and prerogatives of sugar in Louisiana, and also much of its prime land, where living plants once reigned confidently supreme.

The landscape of the Capline plantation, with its few gnarled oaks out front, like the oak alley to a long-lost plantation house now re-placed with the pipeline's stark control tower, is completely cleared except for one small but noticeable, shrub-shrouded intrusion just a few hundred yards from the tower. Peering from the tower's balcony, you can see all too clearly what that intrusion is. It was there before sugar came to the Acadian Coast, and it was there before oil came in, too, and probably will remain there long after the oil is gone: the grounds of the old St. Jacques de Cabanocey Church, with its ancient, stone-marked graveyard, the Louisiana Acadians' first.

6

Reconstructing the Cajun House

Arceneaux house, Longfellow–Evangeline Memorial State Park, St. Martinville. The simple Cajun house grown into a "raised cottage," with exposed brick piers below and unadorned wood columns above   DAVID RICHMOND

Robert's house: it rests in a field of high grass, surrounded by even higher shading trees. The dusk that rises out of the swamp beyond chases the evening's fading light up the trunk of every tree. With little resistance, maybe just a first rustle of the evening breeze, the treetops give up their gleam—but it lingers on in the lighter browns and yellow-greens of the grassy clearing and clings longest to the sides and roof of Robert's graying, cypress-wood house.

Anse La Butte: "cove on the hill," a small hillock trailing off through the swamp trees to an even smaller stream, a tributary of the legendary Bayou Teche. The house perches on one of the highest spots of the cove, and rises out of dusk's breeze-combed grass to float atop a series of masonry piers. Steps rise to a broad, recessed galerie punctured by shuttered windows and doors that open to reveal clusters of candles already lit within. As the aging cypress walls, bleached a gray-white patina no paint could ever match, give up the last rays of light ebbing slowly from the cove, the candles bob ever more brightly.

It is the galerie which gives most early Louisiana country houses their unusual shape and character, opening and closing off a subtle sequence of interior and exterior spaces. The galerie, with its row of irregular columns, establishes an impressive presence against its backdrop of trees—and yet this porch, larger than any interior room, is no mere ornamental accessory or afterthought. The galerie is a weather-protected, outdoor living room, its length lined with clusters of Cajun chairs and small tables or benches. All the downstairs rooms in the front of the house open onto it. And the rooms of the massive overhanging attic, or grenier, open directly onto the galerie, too, via an exterior staircase at one end of the porch that is also an identifying characteristic of the Cajun architectural code. It made no difference how poor or how prosperous a Cajun was—his house always had a galerie for outdoor display, entertainment, and receiving of passers-by.

Robert's house originally belonged to a more prosperous farmer, so it also features a second layer of rooms behind the front ones that are separated from the galerie. The rooms are coupled around a center hall—an intrusion of Anglo-American influence that is absent in Louisiana colonial architecture, Cajun or Creole—dating the construction of his house to some time after the Louisiana Purchase of 1803.

By means of a supplementary back porch, the main house is connected at a right angle to an adjacent outbuilding reserved for separate kitchen facilities. In addition to a modern kitchen, Robert has installed a modern bathroom there, too, all part of a careful remodeling and preservation job he undertook after moving the house, piece by piece, from its original Iberia Parish farmsite to his carefully manicured cove outside the Bayou Teche village of Breaux Bridge. Robert Smith, a New Iberia-born architect who studied his craft at the Cajun University of Southwestern Louisiana, has developed a specialized practice finding, moving, and renovating residential architectural treasures from the Louisiana countryside, and his own house is a living museum of the astonishingly sophisticated life style that was possible in this pre-industrial backwater of our not-so-distant American rural past.

All over the French Triangle, he has found houses with construction techniques borrowed from Creole, Anglo-American, African, and native American Indian sources. Because the Cajuns were the largest population group in south Louisiana from the 1780s on, it is their peasant folk tradition that forms the glue—that plays the tar-baby —for the exotic architectural conglomerations of the Triangle.

That well-rooted, radical, Cajun architectural tradition is a wholly domestic one. Other than houses, the only distinctive Cajun structure is a communal family dancing hall—merely a larger, simpler, and more specialized version of the space arrangements common to every Cajun house. The Cajun house conception is a finite one, but admits a plasticity sufficient to allow it endless variations, additions, and embellishments. As new regimes, new crops, and new prosperities spread through the French Triangle, the Cajun cottage form blossomed into its own architectural genre.

A few of the surviving Cajun houses express sensibilities and

"Anse La Butte," Lafayette architect Robert Smith's restored farmhouse near Breaux Bridge
DAVID RICHMOND

treatments also found quite frequently among the houses of the landed rich in Louisiana and the rest of the South—for, after all, eighteenth- and nineteenth-century societies shared the same limited range of building materials. But the Acadian dwellings share few of the ornaments, functions, or origins of the non-Acadian dwellings of the South. Greek Revival Southern plantation mansions, for example, share their style and purpose and social function with the elaborate commercial and institutional buildings in those urban centers, like New Orleans, that bulwarked the Southern planters' economic and political power base. The evolving Acadian tradition remained rural and proletarian, even in the demi-village structure of ribbon farmsteads along the bayous.

Both the mansions of the plantation South and the townhouses of urban precincts like New Orleans' Garden District feature columns and cornices with neo-classical ornamentation—always carved out of cypress wood in Louisiana, since there is no native stone to speak of.

The Cajun galerie, by contrast, stands functional and *au naturel* against the druidic expanses of Louisiana's cypress and tupelo-gum swamps. Greek Revival ornamentation on columns does not appear in a single known Cajun cottage, even the larger raised cottages of the few Cajun rich. In nineteenth-century Louisiana, Cajun parents went through a curious phase of naming their children for literary figures from the Greek and Roman classics—possibly as a result of the dawning of public education in the state during the terms of office of Cajun governors Alexander Mouton and Paul Octave Hébert—so they were familiar with the bulk details of classical Western culture. But phony and ostentatious neo-classical ornamentation of their own houses would have been unthinkable.

The Cajun galerie column was usually squared off, and often was lightly turned on a lathe for a simple, grooved decoration similar to that found on the tops of Cajun chair posts. But even in the more elaborate two-story raised cottage, a mansion style that the wealthier Cajuns came to share loosely with their Creole and Anglo neighbors, neo-classicism is held at bay, as in the Arceneaux house—now the Acadian House Museum at St. Martinville's Longfellow-Evangeline park. Its first-floor columns are of unadorned brick, not even plastered over—doubtless a simple, direct expansion of the masonry piers commonly used to keep the floors of even the most basic one-room shack up off the wet and sometimes critter-crawling ground. On the second floor of the Arceneaux house, wood columns rise from these pillars to frame the galerie—which has been raised to the second floor here but is still left open and covered by its distinctive overhang roof and grenier attic.

There is no end to the possible explanations for this uniform simplicity over such a wide economic spectrum, from mansion to shack. For one possibility, we must remember that the elaborate carvings of the Garden District mansions were made almost entirely by black slave craftsmen or free men of color, and the Cajuns were, with few exceptions, not owners of slaves or in need of their labor. Moreover, the neo-classical porches of the Anglo-Americans were built mainly for show, to make their houses look more important—not to make them more useful. The porches of the Anglo-Americans fell into disuse and decay—but not so the galeries of the Cajuns, who still sit on their front porches until dusk, swapping stories until the swamps' Golden Lady spiders come out to erect their giant nets for the nightly beetle and mosquito catch. As their ancestors have done for the last two centuries in Louisiana, the Cajuns barely step back inside for the evening meal, leaving their galerie-facing doors and windows wide open and covered with wire screens (stretched fabrics in earlier times) to keep out what mosquitoes the spiders cannot catch. The open spatial configuration for the evening guarantees that each passing breeze will clear the air. Dinner is served on a table of the same wide cypress planks that structure the house, in dishes stored inside a free-standing armoire built of the same material. The table, with candles burning, would in turn be surrounded by the same basic wood chairs used on the galerie or elsewhere around the house.

At Robert's dinner table, the evening fare served in this manner is customarily fish or fowl, or some tasty combination thereof, prepared as a one-dish meal in a large pot with a sauce based on the traditional Cajun browned flour roux, and ladled out into large bowls over scoops of rice. For more formal Creole occasions, a little red wine might be mixed in with the roux; the dish is then served over squares of toast, in wide-rimmed soup plates. Robert has carefully assembled a set of Empire-style Haviland china that no Cajun farmer or trapper would have had the economic means to consider, but at least he has reinforced the prevailing mood of the environment with utensils of more or less the same period as the house and its other furnishings. And while the candles flicker over the evening's quiet conversation, interrupted occasionally by the sounds of bullfrogs or night birds or a light evening rain, it is not so very difficult to imagine and at least partially reexperience how life was lived here once.

While the Cajun house's galerie overhang, exterior staircase, and heavy but unadorned cypress columns are perhaps its most noticeable architectural features, the walls beyond and within narrate a far more revealing tale. Peel off the weather-beaten cypress cladding and you'll find underneath that the walls are made of a stringy and fuzzy mud

(above) *Moss picker's boat, Bayou Pigeon, 1950*   ELEMORE MORGAN, SR.
(below) *Louisiana's last operating moss gin, near Bayou Sorrel*   TURNER BROWNE

the Louisiana French called *bousillage.* The mud is fuzzy because it has
been mixed with Spanish moss—an air-eating relative of the pineapple
that grows in profusion on all Louisiana swamp trees but the willow.
(The willow bends under the weight of the moss, and drops it effortlessly away.) Sometimes the bousillage mixture includes burned, and
thus powdered, clam or oyster shells, in which case the end result is
somewhat similar to cement.

The Acadians had been making mud walls for their houses long
before they came to Louisiana, but never with the name bousillage.
In Canada, architectural mud is called *torchi*—made of earth, marsh-
grass straw, and horsehair. Mud was commonly used for peasant
houses in Europe because of a lack of wood supplies, most of which
were owned by kings and used to build ships for their navies. Back
in France, where this peasant mud-and-timber construction technique
is known as *columbage,* precious timbers were hoarded and filled in
with mud and sticks; a book on the intricacies of this technique was
published in 1719. But the Acadians went on to devise their own
versions in the New World, where wood was more plentiful.

Not just mud walls but mud floors were common in the early
Acadian houses of Canada—though in the nineteenth century in New
Brunswick, underground root cellars roofed with wooden floors became more common. Mud chimneys are reported on mud houses in
Port Royal in 1699, and are also common in early Louisiana Cajun
houses. The Louisiana mud chimneys—there is a fabulous one at the
LSU Rural Life Museum—are made of four saplings erected like the
corner posts of an oil derrick, tapering toward the top. When carefully
built, they are said to be fire-resistant. Post-Expulsion Acadian houses
in New Brunswick, on the other hand, are usually built of stone, as
we must assume a great many pre-Expulsion chimneys were also.

The original Acadian roofs were commonly of hay, or, in more
prosperous times, of shingle—but there was no galerie overhang, and
no front porch. Canadian Acadian houses were not intended to let the
breezes through; they often featured birch-bark insulation over mud-
packed walls or, in later elaborations of primitive style, under shingles. The roofline would always be sharp, to shed snow and to form
the large attics, greniers, where Acadia's winter wheat supplies were

stored. In Louisiana, the grenier usually retained its name but some-times changed its purpose. It could be used as a loom room for the women of the family or as a dormitory for adolescent men children —a *garçonière*. New Brunswick greniers retained their storage func-tions until the 1870's, when they were gradually converted to sleep-ing quarters.

So the refugees brought their attics and mud chimneys and mud walls with them, but found that the other structural elements of their new houses would have to be invented or adapted from other sources. The mud filler made in Louisiana, bousillage, was soon discovered to be vastly superior to Canadian torchi, because of the density and holding power of Spanish moss as reinforcement. The torchi straw grew freely in the diked Canadian marshes, but the bousillage "straw" grew even more freely from thin air—and the Cajuns quickly adopted the local Indian tribes' method of building mud walls out of it.

Indian use of Spanish moss, which the Creoles called *mousse* and the Cajuns called *barbe espagnol* (Spanish beard), was extensive and imaginative, and generated a number of innovative adaptations of which bousillage is only the best known. The Indians also used it right off the trees to make loincloths, toy dolls, torches, swaddling clothes, wraps for patients undergoing sweat baths, and so forth. The coming of the cotton gin to the South saw the parallel development of moss ginning in the French Triangle, and also a substantial nineteenth-century moss-gathering industry whose products stuffed the very best Victorian furniture. Moss fibers could also be spun to produce a ropelike material known as *tarabi* with which to hand-make horse blankets, horse collars, and bridles. Harvesting was accomplished with long hooked poles operated from pirogues—Indian dugout canoes fashioned from fallen cypress logs—or from derricklike structures that were mounted on small barges. Either way, harvested trees were capable of regrowing their crops in three years. A decline in the furniture-stuffing market has left only one operating moss gin, and massive air pollution from automobiles and Louisiana's petrochemical industry is believed to be killing off the delicate, air-eating plant. Spanish moss is not a parasite and causes no harm to anyone—though it sometimes serves as a home for unexpected colonies of small bugs.

In spite of the plant's decline, Cajun geographer Malcolm Comeaux —author of the definitive text on Atchafalaya Basin swamp folk industries—speculates that large-scale national economic difficulties could dramatically alter this downward trend. "If another depression develops," he suggests, many Cajuns living off oil or fishing near existing swamp areas "would undoubtedly fall back on moss for an income."

In earlier days, bousillage preparation entailed a process that can best be described as coprophiliac. First a pit was dug and then refilled with a mixture of the excavated mud, moss, and burned-up shells— a mixture worked with the feet. As in conventional French columbage construction, standing posts are fitted with small, bracing crosspieces called *barreaux,* and the bousillage mixture is drawn out of its mixing hole in long strands to be laid over the barreaux. You start from the bottom, adding more barreaux and mud as you go up. The finished wall is uniformly packed and is often as much as four inches thick. The Creoles commonly covered it with a fine plaster, though their Cajun country cousins sometimes just improvised a wallpaper made of old newspapers. In the attic of another Louisiana colonial house he recently trucked to its new location, designer Smith discovered an exposed, interior bousillage wall on which the swirling handprints that formed it were still visible.

The Louisiana environment presented these mud houses with problems the Cajuns had not encountered in Canada. For one thing, there is Louisiana's incessant rain, which peaks in summer and winter monsoonlike seasons of daily downpour. New Orleans has the highest average annual rainfall of any city in the country; in 1946, the skies over the coastal fishing community of Morgan City opened up to an all-time annual Louisiana rain record of 111.28 inches.

Indian bousillage huts were therefore subject to the constant threat of dissolving, and none of their original buildings survive to this day. But the Cajun builders—with what one observer describes as "a deterioration of Indian methods, and somewhat less than complete adaptation of European forms and methods"—solved that problem with exterior siding, usually of durable and once-abundant cypress. Indian dwellings built directly on the ground were also prone to being washed away by the floods of the delta that provide the spring intermission between monsoons. So the Cajuns learned to raise their walls and floors off the ground, on substantial beams supported, at first, by piers made of cypress stump rounds. These rounds were in common use until brickmaking for piers (and chimneys) became widespread.

The Cajuns could have chosen to build their houses entirely of cypress wood, or followed the Creole custom and built most or all of them of brick, as in the French Quarter. The choice of bousillage walls, protected with cypress weather cladding and raised off the ground, made house building a much more complicated proposition. But their Canadian sojourn had taught them the value of insulation, and it appears that the Cajuns prized their bousillage most for its insulating capability. House interiors were insulated from contact with the sun not only by the walls but by the air space of the attic, and windows and doors could be closed off with simple batten plank shutters; thus the rooms of the Cajun house could be kept refrigerator-cool during the otherwise unbearable middays of July and August. And during the mild winters, bousillage walls reduced the need for firewood. From Bayou Teche westward, the early Cajun farmers planted chinaberry trees in their back yards. Chinaberry grows rapidly and can be pruned of half its bulk at the end of each growing season. Those farmers near enough the Teche or some other bayou to both build bousillage houses and harvest the branches of a chinaberry grove could eliminate the need for supplementary supplies of firewood. This achievement of independence, thrift, and ecological balance seems all the more significant today, when the heavy heating and cooling demands of modern construction consume one-third of our national energy supplies.

Understanding the nature of Louisiana building materials is essential to understanding the evolution of the Cajun architectural style—form following function, in the material sense. It becomes the essential key in this case, because there is still much difficulty sorting out the specific points of that style's transition through time. The earliest days of Cajun architecture in Louisiana are, at best, obscure. Like the Indian bousillage huts that washed away, no positively authenticated houses from the immediate post-Expulsion period have survived. The situation for architectural historians is even worse in Canada, where all pre-Expulsion, and apparently most of the immediate post-Expulsion, houses were burned. One possible pre-Expulsion survivor was found on a farm near Falmouth, Nova Scotia, after World War II and shipped off to the government's Acadian Expulsion commemorative park at Grand Pré. But because of an unfortunate combination of internal bureaucratic disputes and utter stupidity, compounded by the fact that the decision-makers were Anglo-Canadians, it was eventually demolished. Grand Pré guards, surprised at the inquiry about this outrage, will reluctantly take you through the adjacent cow pasture and point out the still-marked earth where the transplanted house's foundation once lay.

Because Louisiana was settled later and was never so systematically burned out, even by the Yankees, the specifics of its earliest building traditions are comparatively easier to find or deduce. We have a fairly clear idea of the architectural and technical milieu into which the Cajuns brought their steep roofs, their mud chimneys, and their wattle-daub walls. The earliest description (1722) of European immigrant housing in Louisiana acidly remarks that New Orleans had "perhaps a hundred scattered huts, a big wooden store, [and] two houses which would not be considered decorative in a French village." We do not know exactly what the "huts" may have been, but we can assume they were made of bousillage, or perhaps of palmetto leaves, or some improvised combination of the two reinforced with the Mississippi River's abundant driftwood. The first settlers at Lafourche des Chetimachas on the Acadian Coast were said to be encamped in "tents." An all-palmetto hut or tent was possible, made from striplings arranged to form a teepeelike structure that would be cross-braced with encircling bands and then draped with the dried, fanlike palmetto fronds. In his 1947 survey, William Knipmeyer included a photograph of what is now believed to be one of the last of the Cajun-made variations of this palmetto-thatched hut, a trapper's shack.

We don't know the exact date of Louisiana's first transition from mud and palmetto huts of some sort to the more extensive use of longer-lasting cypress timbers to support and protect the bousillage mud walls. But the change was probably not long in coming, and in one or another version may even have preceded the arrival of the Cajuns in their new homeland. Early French explorers and settlers in Louisiana were fascinated by cypress, a wood they had never seen before—an ancient tree that could be characterized as the sequoia of the South. To their delight, the French soon discovered that cypress is exceptionally durable—it is not attacked by insects and it will not rot when immersed in either fresh or salt water. Cypress offers builders suitability for every use, from foundation stump piers to the whole roof, including gutters and rain barrels. Cypress is easier to saw and easier to work with simple hand tools than any other wood of the region. Because it is straight-grained, it can easily be split into shingles. Since it does not warp when sawed and used "green," it is suitable for structural applications of almost unlimited scope—there are several nineteenth-century brick "skyscraper" warehouses in New Orleans with cypress posts and beams that anticipate the steel frame inside a modern glass office building. Because it does not warp when dry or rot when wet, cypress is ideal for building boats. And maybe best of all, it is difficult to burn.

Unfortunately, it is also difficult to harvest, because it grows only in standing fresh water. Folk techniques developed after 1725 enabled early French inhabitants to kill the trees in the fall and topple them into the spring's high water for floating removal. By the middle of the eighteenth century, just as the Acadian refugees began to arrive, cypress had become the colony's major export "crop"—even more important as a wild agricultural harvest than plantation cultivation of indigo. This economic prominence would continue until the mid-1790's and the arrival of sugar.

The Acadians were not strangers to building with timber, however, for Nova Scotia had been chockful of it. Colonial governors stationed in pre-Expulsion Acadia had periodically complained that the people preferred diking in marshes to clearing higher fields of timber—the Acadians having had an early respect for trees and an urge to chop them down only when they could be used for local consumption. Not so the English. Acadian areas of New Brunswick, even today, are somewhat bitterly characterized by French-separatist circles as the "lumberyard of England."

Timber was used for the first permanent European-built structure in Atlantic America, the fort of Champlain's Habitation. Timber could be cut into finished planks in nearby Port Royal, using a sawmill known to be in operation as early as 1692. Most early timber houses in French colonial Canada were built *pièce-sur-pièce,* with timber sawed into workable pieces squared, fitted, and stacked—in distinct contrast to the round logs that make up the log cabins in Anglo-American cowboy-and-Indian movies. There is only one known example of presumably Canadian-influenced pièce-sur-pièce architecture surviving in Louisiana's French Triangle. It was found on the grounds of Parlange plantation, in an area frequented by Canadian *coureurs de bois* in the years before the 1755 Expulsion. This hidden jewel at Parlange, in Pointe Coupée Parish, on the *west* side of the Mississippi River, is possibly one of the oldest European-built structures of the Old West —certainly it is earlier than any Anglo-American building in the West. It has been moved down the road from the Parlange manor house and is being restored as the Pointe Coupée Parish historical museum. Sad to consider, however, is this modest plantation building's original purpose, an eerily illuminating legacy from Virginie Trahan and the colonial Creole life style: the oldest surviving American "log cabin" to cross the Mississippi River heading west was a jail for Parlange plantation slaves.

The Acadian refugees, in all likelihood, encountered their first Louisiana cypress in Santo Domingo—a major market for the colonial timber trade. The promise of Louisiana's vast forests of virgin cypress may well have been an inducement for early Acadian remigration to Louisiana from the brewing mess in the French West Indies. A number of Cajuns later driven from their farms by Anglo sugar planters seem to have turned to timbering as a first line of economic defense. The populations of one-time farming villages like Bayou Chêne are said by Malcolm Comeaux to have made total switches to "swamping," as cypress harvesting was once known. Immigrant lumberjacks were certainly attracted by the cypress-harvesting industry, and during the Civil War the cypress-rich Atchafalaya Basin swamp was also a prime refuge for draft dodgers—many of whom were later absorbed into the Cajun culture and extended family. Swamping is now a lost art, for the development of the railroad and machinery to drag the harvested timber up to it—principally the cable-operated overhead skidder and the pullboat—eventually depleted most of the state's commercial-size cypress groves. Swampers, during their day in the sun, developed a unique, cypress-built houseboat architecture that also has disappeared—only one well-preserved and relatively recent example, moored at the municipal Swamp Gardens park in Morgan City, remains. By the beginning of the twentieth century, most of the swampers had become fishermen, or migrated west of the Atchafalaya Basin to the Cajun prairie to become farmers.

Though we know endless minute details of this sort about the various material and social changes going on in Louisiana before and during the time that the Louisiana Cajun house tradition was developed, we are still missing a number of planks in our historical floor or, more accurately, in our galerie. Even knowing that cypress timber has endless design capacities, and that bousillage is a combination of techniques based on known variations in mud-wall construction, and that some of the Acadians' Canadian house roof forms were retained, we still cannot point with any certainty to the specific European or North American source of the form and proportion and design details of that distinctive Cajun galerie. Canadian Acadian houses had absolutely no porches of any kind until Victorian times, and those have nothing whatsoever in common with a Louisiana galerie. The galerie's specific Louisiana form seems to have been invented there, but through none of the known material or technical access routes we have traced. Except perhaps one: the Santo Domingo connection.

The squalid French sugar and slave colony of Santo Domingo was but one of the many destination and humiliation points for the Acadian refugees after Le Grand Dérangement. During their arduous journeys, they were pressed into indentured servitude in most of the thirteen original American colonies, and even sold into slavery in Georgia. And the Cajuns were not much better treated in Santo Domingo, where French colonial rule was much more direct, arrogant, and authoritarian than any they had ever known in the days of the Acadia of "benign neglect." In Santo Domingo,

(left) *Haitian slave cottage, from the era of the Acadians' passage through the West Indies*
A. D. ISELIN

(below) *African-style houses adapted to Louisiana's cypress and* bousillage *construction idiom. Algiers, a suburb of New Orleans, 1890s* GEORGE FRANÇOIS MUGNIER, COLLECTIONS OF THE LOUISIANA STATE MUSEUM

the Cajuns were also brought face to face with the ugly reality of slave agriculture, which tainted all interpersonal relations on the island with class conflicts they had never before experienced. The badly divided white ruling class of the French end of the island was nearly equaled by the number of illegitimate mulatto offspring in the colony—and the slave population was ten times those two groups combined. When the Cajuns first struggled ashore there, they had neither the land nor the money of the *grands blancs* at the peak of the white pyramid, nor the comparatively more "modern" artisan and shopkeeper skills of the mostly urban *petits blancs.* So the colonial bureaucrats—the white community's third force—promptly put the Cajuns to work building extensive new fortifications with which to forestall any takeovers of the island's fabulously profitable enterprise, be they from foreigners abroad or dissidents within. At the time of the Cajun arrival, advanced signs of the impending slave revolt were as clear as the Soweto situation is now. By the time of the French Revolution, white control of Santo Domingo was doomed.

It is likely that Cajun refugees employed in this manner may have been housed, at least temporarily, in some of the plantation slave dwellings of the eighteenth century—buildings that were themselves one step removed from Africa. We have a fairly good idea of what those buildings looked like, for there are variations of them extant today. Some recent researchers have concluded that these slave dwellings may also have a later North American influence in the design of New Orleans' famous shotgun houses—so named because the rooms are lined up one after another, usually with doors arranged so you could stand at the front door and shoot a bullet through the house without hitting anything. Shotguns eventually spread from urban New Orleans into other, mainly Southern rural areas of the continent, these researchers believe. Shotgun houses appear in bayou Cajun settlements in the nineteenth century, so at least some sort of Santo Domingo–Cajun architectural bond is assured.

But the shotgun-transplant theory is an incomplete one. The African formal tradition of the Santo Domingo slave cottages loses too many major elements in its shotgun transition. The building materials of the slave cottages share more in common with Canadian Acadian houses than with shotguns. The slave cottages are built with a wattle-and-daub variation of the same technique used in French columbage, Acadian torchi, and Cajun bousillage—but North American shotgun houses are not usually built that way. Moreover, the roofs of the slave cottages are constructed of crushed sugarcane stalks—producing a thatch similar to that used on Acadian houses of the North but never found in the shotguns of the South. There is a slight variation in roof pitch because the slaves had no need for the Cajuns' large grenier storage areas.

The major difference between the African and North American shotgun forms is found in the outdoor room on the front of the slave cottage. Open on three sides, this porch is covered by the thatched roof and is recessed into it. A colonnade along the front utilizes the same post construction found within the cottage walls—minus the wattle-and-daub infill. In the West Indies, that infill was subjected to constant weather abuse—except where the outdoor room and the front indoor room form a common wall protected by the overhang; as the only protected mud wall, it provides the structure with its only bracing.

The slave cottages were considered in the Santo Domingo of that day to be as temporary and disposable as their inhabitants; cypress would have been limited to use for the dwellings of the whites, or in commercial and military construction. But working with cypress made the Cajuns realize it could be used to strengthen the bracing of the simple slave-cottage structure and protect its exposed exterior walls— giving the final product a measure of permanence. With just a slight expansion of the slave-cottage roof, the Cajuns could accommodate their traditional grenier and, as well, incorporate the African outdoor front room under it into an innovative dwelling more appropriate to their new climate.

We can be reasonably certain that the Cajuns did not borrow the form of their galeries from the Louisiana Creoles or the Santo Domingo *grands blancs,* who built their versions in complete circles around the second floor and always plastered over their bousillage. The houses of the Creole planters stand apart, surrounded by galeries facing out in every direction and thus, by definition, isolated. Only in the bayou village of French Settlement, down the Manchac/Amite River corridor from St. Gabriel and Galveztown and the early Acadian Coast settlements, can we find Cajun galeries with a few peculiar wrap-around attempts—actually, just add-ons to their frontal overhang that extend the galerie wider than the house and just slightly around the front corners, as if the house were attempting to sprout small wings or flippers. But this edging never runs more than a few feet, and stops abruptly, as if it had been abandoned in mid-construction—almost as if it had been a

Cajun caricature of the more pretentious Creole manor's encircling galerie.

Transplanted to the bayou, the reconstructed Cajun house uses its galerie to create a social space unprecedented in the American building tradition. Ribbon-farm settlements along Louisiana bayous placed these structures side-by-side, facing one another across the water. The water becomes the shared, central experience—encircled by outdoor rooms that are looking in rather than facing out. The wilderness beyond the community is blocked off, but within the shared space you encounter an odd reminder of that wilderness, a curious handprint from the Cajuns' sojourn in Santo Domingo. The cypress that forms the structure, sidewall cladding, and roof shingles of each house has been deliberately omitted along the recessed front walls of the galeries. The African heart of the Cajun house beats in the bousillage wall left exposed under the galerie's protective roof overhang. It's not that the Cajuns were too lazy to cover these walls; usually they are whitewashed. But whether exposed or whitewashed, the resulting texture remains the same: a common surface around the community space formed entirely of exposed earth.

The classic one-room Cajun cottage is much like a bullfrog bellowing away in the swamps. *"Ouaouaron,"* the house says its Cajun frog name. *"Ouaouaron"* again, and it puffs out to say it another time, and another.

Each time it croaks like that, the Cajun house moves into another one of its stylistic variations. From one room it puffs up to two, or puffs up to three and becomes more like a shotgun, or puffs up to four clustered rooms under an expanded grenier.

The simplest of these expansions follows a specific room-sequence pattern, with several North American variations. The most primitive possible slave shack in the Santo Domingo idiom or the simplest house in the Canadian Acadian idiom would be one large interior room, but common practice resulted in two. The slave shack featured a waking hours' gathering room in front, near the covered porch, and a communal sleeping area behind. The earliest known post-Expulsion houses

Old woman on front porch, near Vacherie on the Acadian Coast, 1941. Two side-by-side cottages linked into one structure. Note batten shutters, cistern, and exposed bousillage *wall under the* galerie   ELEMORE MORGAN, SR.

in Canada also have two rooms, one for day and one for night. That one-two pattern also appears in a bizarre genre of urban slave dwellings built in New Orleans' colonial-era Creole suburb of Faubourg Marigny, just outside the Vieux Carré, or French Quarter. The Marigny houses were built by white Creole men to house their slave mistresses, who entertained in the front room and stored any resulting mulatto offspring in the rear one. Frederick Law Olmstead wrote that buying a mistress in New Orleans would enable a visiting Yankee businessman to save a considerable sum in hotel bills—perhaps an indication of why there are so many of these buildings still standing. Because this one-two arrangement is found first in the early Santo Domingo slave cottages, folklorist John Vlach believes they influenced the development of the urban New Orleans shotgun—so we might as well acknowledge its Marigny mistress-cottage cousin, as well.

But the urban shotguns and slave-mistress cottages both gave up the distinctive front porch of the Santo Domingo slave houses when they moved to the city. Only in rural areas, and particularly in Louisiana's bayou country, where Cajun shotguns became more common after the Civil War, are the outdoor living porches retained. The classic Cajun cottage, with its one main room, or carré, features the outdoor galerie in front and sometimes a second and smaller room—often a lean-to shed—out back, thus duplicating the exact floor plan of the Santo Domingo slave cottage. That floor plan becomes a shotgun by adding on a third room and dropping the grenier roof—which is exactly what began happening on Cajun bayous after the Civil War. In Canada, and initially on the Acadian Coast, the Cajuns had been both farmers and fishermen, without the specialization in fishing that characterizes the lower bayous. Fishermen don't need grenier attics, and so that form gradually disappeared and the shotgun took its place. *Ouaouaron.*

Out on the prairie, however, the shotgun is a rarity and the classic form continues—developing alternately by replacement or expansion. The most common of these changes is an expansion from one or two rooms to four. The "classic" one- or two-room floor plan, which is almost square, is conveniently expanded by clustering four rooms around a central chimney, made of brick in the later model instead of mud. The grenier roofline is retained, but correspondingly expanded as the family under it grows. Other forms of expansion beyond this first step might link previously separated kitchen buildings to the main living quarters with fill-in construction. The house literally bites onto an adjacent structure and grows. *Ouaouaron.*

The process is most easily visualized through the use of letters of the alphabet. Start with a T. When the additions are made to the middle, the final floor plan looks like a T; when the additions come at one or the other side, the final floor plan looks like an L; when the addition itself has a high grenier roof, placed back-to-back with the original structure, as if duplicating it, the two peaks seen from the side look like an M.

Expansion and replacement are not only activated by larger families and additional prosperity; they also mark the various dates of outside cultural intrusions. In downtown Lafayette, for example, sits founder Jean Mouton's house, now the Lafayette Museum, which illuminates this process most graphically. The original section, a grenier-topped cottage in the classic Cajun style, was built by him around 1800. In the 1820's, his son Alexander, later the first Cajun governor, lived in a slightly expanded version of this house: a new structure of two rooms was added to one side, facing out toward what became a street, and the original cottage behind it was converted into a kitchen. In the 1830's, yet another structure was added: two more rooms, just like the second addition, adjacent to it but separated by a center hallway just like the one at Robert Smith's. In 1849, an entire second floor and hallway staircase were added to the expanded base, and a row of neo-classical columns was erected across the front—not by the Moutons, by this point in the house's history, but by another family, a family of *Américains.*

Still other transitions in the Cajun house occur because of changes in social organization. One more tale about the history of the grenier is particularly revealing, because that attic space eventually acquires both a new use and a new name: the garçonière. Young men in the Cajun family were given considerable autonomy during puberty to help prepare them for moving out of the house one day and setting up their own family. As increased security in the new homeland led to storage of food in outbuildings instead of under the roof of the home, the garçonière evolved as a dormitory for the male brood. A sleeping place by night, it was by day the place where the family's women could keep their looms and work on their weaving projects while the men and children tended the fields. The garçonière, with its separate, exterior entrance from the galerie, also kept the young men from tracking their day's worth of earth through the rest of the house when they returned home at dusk.

The galerie staircase, so steep as to be almost a ladder, remains a distinctive Cajun feature throughout the nineteenth century, and one way of distinguishing the basic Cajun from the basic Creole house: the Creoles put their stairs out back. Like the Cajun houses, modest Creole houses sometimes featured four rooms gathered around a central fireplace—and sometimes even a steep-pitched roof with a galerie. But a recurring and equally distinctive phenomenon in the Creole house is a pair of small rear rooms called *cabinets,* which are attached to the main part of the house in such a way that the rooms form a three-sided enclosure around a *back* porch—also recessed under the roof—that is hidden from the view of the river or the road. The cabinets could be used for storage, cooking, bathing, or countless other purposes. In many versions, they enclose staircases leading to the attic, or form the structural backdrop for an exposed staircase from the open porch to the attic. The cabinets introduce a dramatic interior innovation to the Creole houses, which typically feature three single rooms side by side in front. With the two smaller cabinets in back, the rear porch is often the largest space under the roof, and a common point of access to all rooms, eliminating the necessity to walk through other rooms first.

While the cabinet form is always found in Creole structures, it is sometimes also blended in with houses built in the Cajun idiom. Gert Trahan, a Lafayette antiques dealer, lives and runs her business out of one such house—another of Robert Smith's move-and-remodel jobs. Together, they converted the garçonière into a display room for the shop, and gradually acquired other colonial-era buildings, moved in to form a small complex on a pleasant wooded site east of Lafayette. Gert lives on the ground floor of the main building, and has glassed in the back porch between her cabinets to make a sun-filled television and plant room. One cabinet has been converted to a kitchen and the other to a bathroom just off her bedroom. In completing these renovations, Trahan and Smith decided that her bedroom had been the original parents' bedroom after all, and raise their eyebrows when the discussion turns to its adjacent cabinet. Seems there was only one door going into it, from the parents' room. While the men children were cavorting in the garconière each evening, Trahan and Smith speculate, the young women of the family were locked away in the cabinet so they could neither leave nor be reached, except with parental knowledge and approval.

·   ·   ·

Although the historical transformation of the Louisiana Cajun house remains largely obscured within its walls, Canada's Acadian cousins have succeeded in assembling a chronological display of their post-Expulsion houses into a complete architectural museum—the Village Historique Acadien outside Caraquet, New Brunswick. Louisiana's LSU Rural Life Museum outside Baton Rouge includes a number of excellent architectural fragments and outbuildings in its collection, but the Cajun pieces are scattered through an exhibit devoted to all of Louisiana. The so-called Acadian Village at the Alleman Center in Lafayette contains several buildings of architectural or historical note, such as the birthplace of the late state senator and Hadacol manufacturer, Dudley J. LeBlanc. But the crowded, self-conscious, unauthentically arranged "village" functions mainly as a commercial tourist attraction, linked to an adjacent development called the Jungle Garden —the entire complex having been conceived as an employment scheme for retarded and handicapped residents of the Alleman Center. That's progressive social policy, but not very good architectural history—especially when compared to the remarkable New Brunswick development at Caraquet.

In Caraquet, a 1964 funding agreement from both federal and provincial sources supported a team of scholars who began collecting post-Expulsion buildings from all over New Brunswick for reassembly into a village. The 500-acre settlement is located along a string of Acadian dikes built in the pre-Expulsion manner sometime soon after the Expulsion. The dikes and the river adjacent to it are surrounded with 2,500 acres of reserved forest land to keep any visual evidence of the twentieth century appropriately at bay. You enter the village by auto or bus, but leave your vehicle at the parking lot. After passing through an ultra-modern audio-visual orientation center, you are loaded onto a horse-drawn cart, which takes you over a mile back into the wilderness to the oldest and farthest house. From that point, you walk back to the orientation center, stopping at each cluster of houses and outbuildings, which have been carefully laid out in chronological progression. Nearest the village center, you'll find a small chapel, a schoolhouse, a store, and the original home of the man who served as the real village of Caraquet's English-speaking justice of the peace.

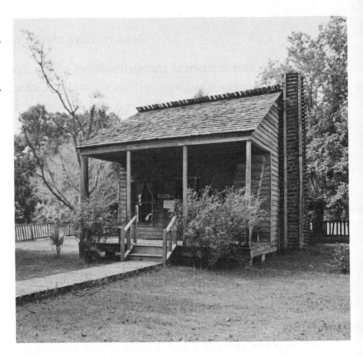

Curiously enough, his house is Georgian, with an Acadian kitchen appended—and you are told that the woman who cooked for him was prohibited from setting foot into the main house.

The first home in the village's progression is built pièce-sur-pièce as one large room with a grenier roof and an interior ladder-stair to its storage loft. As you walk back along the road, the houses grow larger; their furniture and finishing become more elaborate. Included in the progression are Acadian houses showing substantial influence from Irish immigrants or from the distinctive architectural tradition of the nearby province of Quebec. Thus, the Acadian houses of the North are shown to have the same absorption and expansion quality of the Cajun houses that encountered Creole, Anglo, or other influences in colonial Louisiana.

That characteristic Acadian adaptability and inventiveness are seen not only in the Caraquet buildings but also in the overall way the team in charge of the facility went about setting it up. The village is an employment center for the surrounding area. Local people serve as guides, with, for example, a real blacksmith working in the blacksmith shop, repairing iron items actually used in the village. All clothing worn by the employees is based on early designs, done up in the same materials, and sewed on the site. Surplus production is sold to the public through the gift shop at the interpretive center. In each of the houses, the women guides are also responsible for preparing a noon meal—which is eaten by their farmer "husbands," the blacksmith, and other employees. Tourists returning to the interpretive center find a cafeteria serving the same dish they saw prepared in the houses earlier that day; the cafeteria adamantly refuses to sell hamburgers. The village staff expects that their farming operations on the property will soon make them self-sufficient in foodstuffs and other materials—a condition already achieved in maintenance matters like repairing wagons or making shingles.

At two key places along the long walk back, the village team has constructed two contemporary but discreet canteen buildings where beer or soft drinks can be purchased by foot-weary visitors. These facilities are large enough to permit folksinging and dancing in evening hours—a valuable cultural resource for the entire Caraquet region, as well as a built-in student center for the winter-period college-study program planned for the snowbound months when the tourist traffic falls off. Convention-style meetings can be held in the canteens, but massive resort or convention-style hotel construction has been prohibited by the local planning commission. Tourists can be accommodated in one small rooming house and the homes of local residents —for periods of a week, or even more—under the auspices of yet another part of the regional economic-development program.

Though the eighteenth- and nineteenth-century architectural solutions devised by the Acadian refugees of New Brunswick diverge widely from those in Louisiana, the intrinsic Cajun pride in self-sufficiency—and an intimate appreciation of their material surroundings —reverberates through Caraquet. *Ouaouaron.* In much the same way that the bousillage and cypress houses with their chinaberry-tree firewood combined into an energy-balanced whole in Louisiana, so do the various elements of this large-scale cultural experiment in New Brunswick—expanding the Cajun sense of self-sufficiency further still.

For when the oil runs out, or when Canadian tourists stop coming in with their fresh supplies of paper currency, the Cajuns of Caraquet will be the last to suffer. As always, living content unto themselves, they will doubtless gather around their fires, eating and singing and laughing sympathetically at the confusion of the rest of the world.

Another curious aspect of the Cajun architectural tradition of Louisiana is this: most of the old houses that still exist are being lived in. Modernization has brought indoor plumbing to replace outhouses and cisterns, but not everywhere. Corrugated metal roofing, commonly used on rice mills and on farm outbuildings, is frequently a replacement roof material—nailed right over the earlier cypress shingles, preserving them intact. The new metal roof usually fades right into the same color gray as the rest of the structure, and seems not to be a modern addition at all.

In the new suburbs and subdivisions springing up all over Louisiana's French Triangle, you'll notice a disproportionately high percentage of pseudo-French-provincial tract houses, with mansard roofs and other such "French" trimmings. In Lafayette, one real-estate company houses its office in a bad, but still recognizable, imitation-Cajun cottage complete with front galerie and exterior staircase to nowhere. Mansard roofs top shopping centers with names like Galeries La-fayette or Place Norman. In some subdivisions, urbanized Cajuns with French-provincial or other mixed-breed tract houses sometimes add their own fake front-porch stair for old times' sake. One such house even has a name emblazoned on a sign out front: LA MAISON DES CINQ SOEURS. A veterinarian named LaCour built it on Rue Chauvi-niac, in a fussy subdivision on the Vermilion River south of Lafayette. Not only is there a staircase on the galerie, and a sign in the yard, but also signs in the side yard identifying a garden in memory of one of his five daughters.

Most of the modern houses in Louisiana, with their air condition-ing and barbecue pits, have, of course, no kinship with their surround-ings at all, and look depressingly like Everywhere Else. Surprisingly enough, the "modern" houses that perhaps come closest in spirit to the venerable old ones are trailer houses. In oil boom towns like Morgan City, fully half the people live in them—and like the earliest Cajun huts, the trailers are disposable, especially after a hurricane. Like one breed of Cajun houses built on the prairie, they can also be picked up and moved to a new location. During the nineteenth cen-tury, a thriving business was conducted by sawmills on rivers like the Mermentau, constructing complete houses, which would be loaded on long timbers stretched between several wagons. In an old custom known as a *halerie,* neighbors would bring their wagons and oxen to participate in this hauling bee. The teams could move across the flat, unfenced prairies twelve to fifteen miles per day—often moving houses forty or fifty miles from the mill, recalls Lauren Post. And at night, the haulers would make a gumbo, have a party, and sleep inside the house!

Elements of this tradition survive today in Robert Smith's projects, and around Abbeville—where thirty-two-year-old contractor Ray Needham started up a prefabricated fishing-camp construction busi-ness sixteen years ago. Like large numbers of other Cajuns these days, he has an Anglo name and speaks English, but his mother was French (a Dufrene from Bayou des Allemands, a German-Cajun community). He has also joined the Cajun revival in his own way, by designing and marketing a "Cajun" model. The roof is low, but it covers a built-in, recessed porch which is lined with cypress posts. Inside, Needham uses a brand of Masonite siding that looks just like cypress. His houses are set in place on small, pyramid-shaped, precast concrete piers—today's successors to the cypress stumps or brick piers of yesteryear. "I've even toyed with the idea of putting a tin roof on it," he jokes. Though they are only second homes, escape homes, business is brisk. "I'm building five or six more right now, and I just can't get them finished fast enough."

Instead of wooden wagons and oxen, Needham—like architect Smith—resorts these days to flatbed trucks and state-police escorts to get his houses moved. For one recent hauling to Butte La Rose, in the middle of the Atchafalaya Basin not too far from the crawfish restaurant capital of Henderson, Needham and his party started out early in the morning, not long after dawn. By 10 A.M., the hydraulic jacks had lifted the house off its construction site, and by eleven the house was on the road and ready to roll. Needham drove to Opelousas, then back down one of the Atchafalaya spillway's guide levees to the appointed site in a cypress swamp. By dusk that afternoon, the finished house was safely in its new place. *Ouaouaron.*

7

Weaving Together

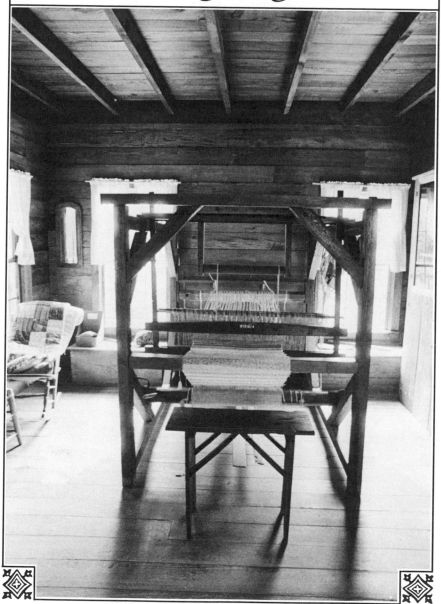

Acadian loom fashioned of cypress, set up in the crafts shop at the Longfellow–Evangeline Memorial State Park, St. Martinville   DAVID RICHMOND

Once upon a time, there lived a farmer in Louisiana's Cajun country who grew to be a wealthy planter. So wealthy that, just outside St. Martinville, he built his home at the end of a carefully measured, two-mile-long alley of oaks and pines—an alley which grew as old and as dignified as he did. When the time came for his daughters to marry, the old man decided that only the most splendid wedding would do.

So he imported a collection of large spiders from France, and released them into the oaks and pines. There, in the alley's looming shadows of black and green, they spun a canopy of webs that the planter sprinkled with gold and silver dust from a special bellows. The wedding party's procession was through the alley, at night, by candle-light.

The specific details of the Cajun spider legend probably are not true, though a pine-and-oak alley with a historical marker recounting one of the versions of this oft-told tale still stands outside St. Martinville—and Louisiana's spiders still weave their exotic, glistening, nighttime swamp pavilions that mysteriously melt away from the posts of the galeries in the light of the morning sun. What *is* true about the legend is its emphasis on the Cajuns' joy in spinning and weaving, the pleasure they still take in creating a whole cloth from tattered strands of homemade yarns, or perhaps palmetto leaves or oak saplings. As with their affectionate remembrances of the wispy products of the lowly spider, the Cajuns have long seen imaginative possibilities in their surroundings that less resourceful visitors or inhabitants might miss.

Among the most precious and mysterious of their treasury's botanical jewels is a yellowish-brown cotton the Cajuns call *coton jaune*. It does not seem to be native to Louisiana, and it can't even be grown in Acadia, so no one knows for sure exactly where it did come from. In some places it is called Nanking cotton, for it is similar to that better-known Chinese variety, though botanists insist it is not the same plant. There is belief in other quarters that it is a mutant cotton that came with those Acadian refugees who passed into Louisiana through the West Indies. Another variation of this story describes it as "slave cotton"; slaves were supposedly permitted to grow and use it so that they would not steal from a plantation's more valuable crop of white cotton. Wherever it came from, Cajun women still grow it, spin it, and spin yarns about it, all in pursuit of an irregular soft thread of a distinctive natural hue. Brown cotton has weaving qualities unlike the flax and wool the Acadian women had always known before—some better qualities, some worse. But the disadvantages never stopped the weaving for one minute; weaving is the principal and most accomplished craft of the Cajuns. Outside of Cajun music and the rich Cajun language, weaving is the oldest, and least modified, surviving folk phenomenon of the culture.

Gladys LeBlanc Clark grows her brown cotton in a small garden across the road from the farmhouse where she lives with her husband, Alexis, in the Cajun village of Judice, southwest of Lafayette. While Alexis pilots huge red machines through his own fields of rice and soybeans, and an adjacent three hundred acres he sharecrops, Gladys spins threads on a small spinning wheel and then weaves them on an even smaller loom. She is joined in these tasks by her mother and two granddaughters, who live with one of her sons in the next farmhouse over. *Dans le vieux temps,* when Acadian weaving was at the height of its glory, when both the spinning wheels and the looms were much larger than the ones Gladys uses now, large parties of usually interrelated women would gather after the noon meal to work what Longfellow called their "gossiping looms." The fields of brown cotton were larger then, too. This year, Gladys will have one meager row to harvest, in part because "worms have eaten most of the leaves." "The same worms," she hastens to add, "that ate the beans," her husband's soybeans. "Too much rain," she scowls across a steaming cup of black Cajun coffee. She's sitting in a spacious country kitchen, the spotless linoleum floor of which spreads through the dining room and right up under the color television console against the far wall in the living room. Her husband sits in front of the evening's TV fare, rocking out of earshot of this entomological inquest, oblivious to this assessment of the vexatious worms. And yet the bean bugs eat just a little bit of brown cotton—while the bureaucrats once tried to chew up the whole enterprise.

"The government tried to stop us from growing it," she relates with an intonation of righteous incredulity. "They thought it might be *diseased,* but we never tried to sell it on the market. We grew it for our own use."

Nor are these most recent bureaucratic troubles anything new to Cajun cotton. French and Spanish colonial officials sought to prohibit weaving in Louisiana altogether, in order to encourage importing and dependency on the mother country—policies which probably succeeded only in encouraging the activities of Jean Lafitte and his Cajun cohorts in contraband. A rich variety of legal textiles could be found in New Orleans shops, and were much sought after by Creole planters. But, as in Acadia, the early Cajuns preferred to make their own clothes and bedding materials, with their own raw goods and their own homespun weaving, thank you, especially out in the virtually inaccessible Attakapas region of the pre-railroad prairie.

Brown cotton remains to this day as semi-wild as its habitat in an earlier and less structured Louisiana. The bolls are spaced farther apart on the brown stalk, and the fibers are shorter than those of their white hybrid commercial cousins. Brown cotton boll fibers are, in fact, mostly white, but are tinged with a rusted edge that, when spun, produces threads in uneven shades of a soft, light brown. On a small spinning wheel—like the one Gladys uses at her grandmother's old rocking chair whenever *she* sits to watch television in the front room —the slower and more controllable spin can produce a yarn more regular and uniform in color and diameter than the bulky yarns produced on the large wheels. Gladys is skillful enough on her small wheel to produce a finished brown cotton thread of a consistency that appears almost machine-made. The threads of the very best old cotton Cajun cloths are always this fine, a point of pride with their makers. But the Cajun textiles most interesting to the contemporary eye are likely to be those rough, antique blankets in which the handmade yarn variations are more vividly apparent.

Variations in yarns and threads are not limited to browns and whites, though Louisiana Cajun textiles usually display only one other color—a delicate shade of blue. The blue comes from indigo, Louisiana's principal plantation crop at the time of the Acadians' arrival. Caterpillars and sugar planters have chased both the indigo and the Cajuns from their colonial-era fields in the years since then. Gladys's grandmother, from whom she learned to spin and weave, used a pale indigo powder that looked like chalk. Grandmère would mix it with water and fireplace ashes, and cook it until it was ready for a test egg. If the immersed shell came out coated, the dye was ready for the cotton. The Acadian Weavers and Spinners Guild of nearby Lafayette, a group of leisure-time, oil housewives who experiment with a broad range of non-traditional techniques and styles, made the astonishing discovery a few years ago that water taken from the bayou made their natural dyes more vivid—a richer yellow-green from ragweed, for example, or a darker brown from onion skins. Gladys runs to a hidden closet and comes back with several of her grandmother's blankets, all with bayou-bred indigo stripes: despite repeated washings—she exclaims as if giving testimony for a television laundry-soap commercial—"they're still blue!"

There were blue dyes used in the old, pre-Louisiana Acadia as well, but few of those early fabrics have survived. Those in the collection of the Musée Acadienne at Moncton, New Brunswick, are believed to have been dyed with blueberries, or a blue stone containing copper sulfate from the geological deposits that gave the populous, pre-Expulsion Minas Basin its name. Red was used only rarely in the early textiles of the Acadian North, and it was derived mainly from cedar bark. Some other authorities speculate that the very earliest Acadian weavers used only black and green dyes. The Canadian combination of cold weather and an abundant population of sheep produced weavings that were mainly of brown and gray wools that were not especially receptive to dyes of any sort. Flax, commonly grown and used in the old Acadia for linens and other fine garments, proved difficult to grow in Louisiana. Because Louisiana's mild winters and insect-infested summers forced the Acadians to abandon the use of wool, only a few old Louisiana pieces incorporating wool yarns survive. The wool is usually woven in as decorative trim, to add yet more variety to fabrics that are otherwise made of nothing but soft, soft cotton.

The most common variation in early Louisiana weaving is a horizontal wool striping that is distinctively Cajun. Some authorities believe that the striping in original Canadian Acadian fabrics may have denoted family or village/clan identities, much like Scottish tartans. But that practice, if common in pre-Expulsion Canada, does not seem to have survived either in New Brunswick or in Louisiana. In Canada, the use of all-homespun materials also disappears early—nineteenth-century Canadian wool-blanket weavers eventually began to use store-bought white cotton threads to set up their loom warp—the parallel threads that hold the thicker wool in place. By 1875, homespun wool warps in Acadian Canada disappeared altogether. Handweaving of textiles continued extensively in Louisiana until after the First World War, though there are also old newspaper advertisements for mass-produced imitation Acadian blankets vying for the market earned by the handmade originals.

While Louisiana Cajun weaving can thus be said to have survived longer as a tradition than Canadian Acadian weaving, not as many samples of the former are extant as of the latter. In Louisiana, antique blankets and other bedding materials have tended to last longer than any of the other early Cajun textiles, because worn clothing was commonly recycled into braided rugs. Gladys is lucky to have saved several pillowcases her grandmother had stitched together from recycled bed sheets of unknown and now indeterminable age—a Cajun time warp and woof as it were. One patchwork quilt found for a bicentennial Louisiana furnishings show in Lafayette a few years back had seventeen different types of early Cajun cloth sewn into it—most of it, presumably, clothing scraps—including ten patches with five quite complicated warp-sequence variations. Vaughan Glasgow, chief curator at the Louisiana State Museum in New Orleans, found a quilt with 164 different textile pieces, the centerpiece of an extensive Acadian weaving show being prepared to tour Louisiana, France, and Canada in the late seventies. These early *cotonade* clothing fabrics were dyed in various shades of blue, and would have been used to make skirts and blouses, jackets and trousers. The indigo-dyed scraps left behind resemble thinning, faded blue jeans now, and indeed, out on the Cajun prairie where the United States cattle industry began, Cajun cowboy clothes may well have been a precursor of our modern Levi's.

Despite their diversity, Cajun textiles fall into four basic types of weave. These four also appear in French Canadian fabrics, but the Northern weavers went on to develop more complex looms, resulting in designs that went beyond these four basic, earlier forms.

The simplest Louisiana weaving pattern uses a solid color warp (usually white cotton) with alternating woof bands of colored yarns or threads—white with brown and/or indigo blue. The color bands may be equal in width or grouped in numerically related repeats. For a slightly more elaborate design, variations in warp size produce a textured striping—most commonly found in coverlets. Add variations of both warp and woof size, plus variations in color, and the simple Acadian materials acquire an astonishing complexity, including checked patterns. A fourth and final refinement of these various themes is called *boutonne:* the most complex patterns form intersecting checks, and woof threads are raised and "tufted" to make the intersection stand out. The most elegant Cajun bedspreads were all made that way, and were finished with borders of handmade, hand-tied lace— the original macrame. (Cajun fishnet making is macrame at its utilitarian roots.)

It takes about five pounds of cotton, all hand-carded and spun, to make one blanket. Acadian looms were customarily set up to make ten blankets at a stretch. The blankets were usually 73 inches by 80 inches or thereabout—almost square. On smaller looms, half pieces would be made and sewn together, again to make an almost perfect square. For either method, warp threads are prepared in wound-up bundles on a large oak or cypress frame known as a warping board, or *ourdissoir.* Gladys hangs hers on a wall outside in the carport. The board is lined with corncob pegs, though Gladys has replaced most of hers with wooden pegs, and the yarns are looped around and around them. Loops of equal length are then transferred by hand and knotted to the loom, with between 400 and 600 such loops needed to form a warp wide enough for a blanket. In the old days, lengths were measured by the *aune,* a measure which nowadays means nothing. But it so happens that thirty-six aunes made exactly the ten blankets needed.

The laborious operations involved in setting up a warp explain in part the practice of making several blankets at one time. But another reason has to do with the social roots of Cajun weaving: *l'Amour de Maman.* "Mother's Love" was traditionally expressed by the preparation of bedding material collections for each child—dowries for men as well as for women. These textiles would be accumulated for presentation at the child's wedding, as part of the supply of necessities for establishing a new household. Maman's goods would customarily last for the person's adult life, and the woman of the new household would in turn set about preparing sets for the next generation. A typical package per child might include twelve blankets, twelve spreads, six sheets, twelve towels, one feather mattress covering, one bolster, and two pillows—plus three mattresses stuffed with Spanish moss. These prodigious trousseaux often required a special set of storage shelves, where they gradually amassed, to the admiration of visitors.

The most important of these approving visitors were the other women of the extended family—a family sometimes grown into a village. They would gather at one another's loom rooms to work on projects together, singing special weaving songs that are now only half-remembered fragments. It takes the hands of four people to string up a loom from an ourdissoir. Carding parties were sponsored year round, but the weaving itself usually took place only in the late fall and winter months, after the crops were gathered.

In those cotton-growing Cajun communities prosperous enough to have their own gin mills, mothers would sometimes wait until the end of the commercial ginning season and set off all at one time to gin their brown cotton at the village's idle mill. The gin owners would not charge for this service—but would insist that the women wait until after all the white cotton crop had been finished, so as to keep scrap brown tufts from clinging to the machinery and mixing in.

Nowadays, Gladys Clark, one of the last of the practicing Cajun weavers, still does all her own carding and cleaning—aided by her mother, whose advanced age and arthritis have limited her participation to simpler tasks. Gladys no longer makes blankets with brown cotton, however, and if her granddaughters want a set of twelve blankets for a wedding present, they will have to weave them for themselves. Gladys uses the small amounts of brown cotton that she has for trim on small piecework items—mainly napkins and place mats —that she makes on her loom in the utility room. Next to the loom sits her sewing machine, on which she makes clothes for herself and her grandchildren, using modern store-bought cloth and thread. While working there during the day, she can see out of the utility room door and across the kitchen table, through the dining room and the living room, to the TV set, so she won't miss her afternoon soap operas. At night, watching television in the front room with her husband, she knots the tassels at both ends of the finished pieces, tassels made from cut ends of the loom's warp.

Instead of ten blankets at a time, she now makes ten place mats at a time. And with scraps from a nearby fabric shop, she also makes her own throw rugs and doormats for the wide expanse of shiny linoleum floor. Gladys LeBlanc Clark belongs to the modern Cajun prairie, but she is also one of the few housewives in America who can claim she has a loom but no vacuum cleaner.

Most of the rugs, napkins, and place mats she makes are delivered to St. Martinville's Longfellow-Evangeline Memorial State Park. There a small Cajun craft shop was established in the 1940's in a reconstructed Cajun cabin—Louisiana's answer to the reconstructed church at the park in Grand Pré. The cabin and the shop were assembled at the Longfellow-Evangeline park at the insistence of a legendary Cajun woman named Louise "Lulu" Olivier. The strong-willed Lulu, a spinner of fine dreams in her own right, was the woman who gave Gladys her first brown cotton seeds and insisted that she learn to weave goods that could be sold at the park shop. "Gladys, if your mother died," Gladys now recalls the gentle scoldings she received as a child at the hands of Lulu, "there would be no one to carry on."

Lulu Olivier is the most important person in the history of Louisiana Acadian handicrafts, because she just barely kept some of them alive through her recruitment and encouragement of people like Gladys. There had been previous Cajun craft revival movements as early as the 1880's, but Lulu's was the last and most important of the

big ones. Lulu Olivier was able, single-handedly, to form a network
that by 1959 produced 8,431 pieces annually, sold through thirty-nine
outlets. She managed the enterprise as its sole executive, promoter,
and delivery person. She was able to do it for two decades because
of a personality so compelling that she seems to be alive even now,
hiding among the boxes and boxes of documents in the LSU library
that house the archives of the now defunct Acadian Handicraft Association. That the archives exist at all, and that they are stored at LSU,
is due to Lulu's work through the LSU Extension Service. That agency
unleashed her to develop what she styled her "French Project," a
training, employment, and self-help program for rural Cajun women
far more ambitious and liberated than any joint women's undertaking
ever seen in Louisiana's French Triangle before.

Lulu Olivier's handicraft odyssey began in 1940 with an investment
of $37.80. It would have begun much earlier, except that it took Lulu
a good year to wheedle the money out of the Extension Service coffers
at LSU—and even then, she didn't spend all of the $50 grant she had
asked for and finally received. Back during those days, $37.80 was a
sufficient amount to enable her to purchase "one Louisiana cotton
blanket, one homespun blanket, one homespun bedspread, one spinning wheel, one handhewn chair with a cornshuck seat," and, her
meticulous records conclude, the necessary accessories of a "warp
beam box and thread carrier." With these materials, she put together
a small but soon widely famed "Acadian Exhibit" that traveled everywhere she could think to send it. Lulu's traveling handicraft show
made its debut on April 10, 1940—and an astonishing crowd of three
thousand people showed up in the rice, sugar, and dairy community
of Abbeville to see it. From Abbeville, she headed out to libraries in
Houma and Welsh in the Cajun country, and then north to Alexandria, Shreveport, Minden, Winnfield, and Natchitoches in the
predominantly Anglo areas of north Louisiana. In each town, she
would work out an arrangement with one or more interested shops,
and by 1942 she could boast of two groups of busy workers, including
seven full-time weavers.

The war years slowed her down, but not much. Through Abdallas, the Lafayette-based Lebanese-Cajun department-store chain with outlets in the major prairie cities and shopping centers, she was able to wangle enough war-rationed tires to complete her endless automobile trips over the countryside. Through lawyer James Domengeaux, then a Louisiana congressman, who caught Lulu's cultural-preservation fever and later started the Council for the Development of French in Louisiana (CODOFIL), Lulu obtained a letter of introduction that she used until it was brown and tattered. Most effectively, on her travels she showed the first film ever made about the Cajuns—French filmmaker André de la Varre's 16-millimeter silent classic, *Acadians on the Teche.* She collaborated with de la Varre on its conception and execution, and he promised her an extra print for use on her travels. When de la Varre found himself caught between technical difficulties at his New York laboratory and Lulu's relentless pestering for her duplicate copy, he sent her his own work print to use until the extra one could be made. Thus armed, Lulu was a formidable audio-visual presence in the days before that skill became more widely utilized.

Perhaps one of her most formidable skills was her acute sense of humor. She disapproved of de la Varre's use of the then-pejorative word "Cajun" in the subtitles, but Acadian descendants ashamed of their heritage and preferring to be thought of as "Creoles" were equally offensive to her. In a letter to her war-era friend, sometimes companion, and periodic collaborator, Alex Melancon, Lulu tells the following story: "I was visiting an Olivier cousin when the Cajun topic came up. She was taking up a firm Creole stand based on her Creole Olivier ancestors, our common ancestors being of Creole union, when suddenly the idea hit me that nobility was synonymous with 'No matter what circumstances I may be in, I am too proud to work.' Up on the scene popped great-grandmother Eloise Savoie, born in the Attakapas country in 1798, the spirit of courage, honesty, simplicity, economy, energy and perseverance! 'I am proud,'" said Lulu, quoting herself, "'that I have one Acadian ancestor who has balanced in me my false pride and my inherited leanings towards laziness.'"

Lulu had little time for laziness, though, for between trips, exhibits, and movie showings, she collaborated with Melancon on a series of articles that later appeared in the New Orleans *Times-Picayune*. The articles recounted some of the folkloric tidbits she kept encountering in her daily visits with the women of the French Triangle, including folk medicine tisanes, or teas, and one collection of reputed cures using tobacco. Soldier friend Melancon, who in off-hours on base turned her notes into finished articles, lured her into the project with promises to indulge Lulu in her favorite collecting passion, demitasse coffee spoons. In a curious sidelight to more recent American history, the Olivier–Melancon letters make frequent reference to the distrust the U.S. War Department had for its Cajun soldiers: the Cajuns, even as late as World War II, still spoke of themselves in conversation as *"les Français,"* while all English-speaking outsiders were *"les Américains,"* and the War Department was uneasy about where their political loyalties might ultimately lie.

However, Lulu Olivier's loyalties to her own people were never questioned. In 1955, when the state organized an Acadian bicentennial celebration, it was dedicated to Lulu. On her $165 monthly salary, she had given Louisiana a breathing space in which to regroup its forces and rescue its Acadian heritage—a heritage which even then was in precipitous decline at the hands of government road builders and urban radio and television broadcasters, with their relentless, Anglo-American, homogenizing cultural influences. The Cajuns liked their bicentennial so much that a whole new generation of festivals and organizations sprang up in its aftermath, and what is now called the French Renaissance in Louisiana was on. By 1961, at the annual October dairy festival in Abbeville, the Acadian revival had advanced to the point where, for the first time in a local country festival, Cajun crafts, music, dances, and storytelling were combined into a comprehensive cultural program that permeated the entire celebration. A year and a half later, Lulu Olivier would die at fifty-six and take the momentum behind her "French Project" with her to the cemetery at Grand Coteau. There were many unfinished tasks—LSU agriculture researchers would never agree to Lulu's demands for developing improved varieties of coton jaune, and the university eventually disbanded her project, because she had never taken the time to train a successor. And yet the successors of the next generation were all around her: some of them, like Gladys LeBlanc Clark, are seeing to it that their granddaughters will carry on as well. In retrospect, Lulu seems to have had a direct personal influence on everyone over forty in Louisiana who has made or is making a serious contribution to the Acadian revival. She inspired Catherine Brookshire Blanchet in the late 1940's and early 1950's to collect the children's folk songs that would have died out completely otherwise. She dragged Gladys and her mother *and* father to a national crafts exhibition in Madison Square Garden one year, and later to the Smithsonian; through such trips, she sparked a minor national interest in Cajun textiles that still tracks its way through the folkloric literature on that subject. And she also gave the necessary encouragement to Elvira Kidder to make her the last surviving Cajun practitioner of what was at one time Louisiana's most unusual and practical home craft, palmetto weaving.

Coton jaune is of an uncertain Louisiana pedigree—but not so the common palmetto, known to the Cajuns as *latanier* and to botanists as *Sabal minor.* Palmetto is, as its name implies, a dwarf palm, and though its heart is considered edible, its principal use is not as food. Palmetto is found all across the south coast, but nowhere has it seen as many uses as Louisiana's Cajuns have found for it. Cajun fishermen, for example, used it as packing material, with Spanish moss, for insulating fresh, cool shellfish in pre-refrigeration days. When the conch, an oyster-boring pest Cajun fishermen don't relish, began its invasion of Louisiana waters, the fishermen learned to attach palmetto fronds to half-submerged stakes to lure conch larvae out of the water to a sunburned death.

But the principal Cajun use for palmetto was weaving. Elvira Kidder learned her craft from her mother, and started out as a child making hats for her father, brothers, uncles, and cousins to use when they worked in the field. "All our *straw* hats had to be imported in those days," she recalls of her pre-World War II childhood, so it was cheaper and easier to weave your own "straw" hats from palmetto. From learning to hand-stitch the woven strips together to make her

A palmetto house, late 1890s. Typical trapper's shack GEORGE FRANÇOIS MUGNIER, COL-
LECTIONS OF THE LOUISIANA STATE MUSEUM

hats, she eventually turned to sewing "on the first sewing machine in our area," and soon came to the attention of Lulu Olivier.

Elvira's sturdy white woven baskets and hats are not made from the palmetto's familiar green, extended fan. She hires workmen to go into the swamps and fetch the sprouting palmetto spikes, which are most numerous during the October-to-December prime sprouting season. She leaves them out to dry for at least three months, and sometimes as long as nine, under a shed roof just off the utility room of her country farmhouse. Then she splits the spikes into more narrow straws. Her specialty is hats of the finest millinery quality—one sample of which she has kept with her for the last thirty-five years. Palmetto is some tough straw, *cher.*

Though Elvira is the last Cajun practitioner of this craft, some of the Indians who first taught it to the Cajuns still do their own palmetto work. In the French-speaking Houma Indian community of Dulac, in Terrebonne Parish, Marie Dean dries palmetto leaves on her clothesline for about a week, and makes fans and vases for dried flowers, as well as baskets and hats. Elvira Kidder once made slippers and handbags, too, and for weaving applications where palmetto alone will not do, corn shucks are also useful. Louisiana's Coushatta Indians, who fled to Louisiana from Georgia about the same time the Cajuns landed from Canada, supplement this weaving repertoire with swamp canes and pine-tree needles. Animal-effigy baskets made with pine needles will stay green if picked green, or stay brown if picked brown. They can also be dyed red with red oak bark and black with black walnuts.

Of all the French Triangle's wild forest weaving materials, the sturdiest and perhaps noblest weaving product is the split-oak basket. And the foremost practitioner of that craft turns out to be a blue-eyed black man from the picturesque St. Landry Parish village of Washington. Once upon a time, Washington was the head of navigation, the farthermost distance you could travel up a hill in a steamboat, for the Atchafalaya Basin's intricate bayou waterway system. Washington is now a tourist arts and crafts center, with Thonius Robinson and his assorted relatives' basket shops cornering the market for split oak. Thonius, who learned his craft from his father, opened his Washington shop in 1940, and has sinced passed his know-how on to a younger brother and a cousin, who run their own shops, too. The split-oak basket is said to have been introduced to the Cajuns by the Indians, and is also known in Appalachia, though the construction is not as complicated as in Louisiana. Thonius prefers to work his baskets with white oak, but will also use post oak and red oak, because, as he explains, only the bark and outside appearance differ. His main task is to find the wood growing and raw and "green"—because it handles better that way. Using a hand-held power saw, he scouts the woods around Washington in the morning and can produce three large baskets from his findings by later that afternoon. The oak is "ripped" along its natural lines and shaved to produce uniform weaving strips. The secret of a split-oak basket is to weave it while the wood is "wet" and to let it dry in its finished state—whereupon it becomes so hard and strong you can stand on it. Such durability made split-oak baskets an indispensable element of the Cajun farmstead scene.

This intimate Cajun knowledge of the working properties of their weaving materials—cotton, palmetto, oak, whatever they found growing around them—permits an economy of means and style, a frugality of form that is "modern" in the best understanding of that term. These skills are brought to bear most brilliantly in the construction of the classic Cajun chairs, which mix together all the various materials of Cajun weaving. Made from a multitude of green woods that are carefully cut and linked so they will cure and harden at the joints without glue or nails, the Cajun chair is every bit as long-lived as the split-oak basket.

The so-called Ville Platte chair, named for a prairie town at the peak of Louisiana's French Triangle, is similar in design to other American frontier chairs. But it differs in a number of subtle and remarkable ways from the near-look-alike Appalachian "settin' chair" that is its nearest cousin. Both share an affinity for the same basic construction techniques and general appearance, plus the use of hickory—when available—to form back slats and other horizontal structural pieces. The Cajun chair commonly uses oak or ash for posts, while the classic mountain-chair posts are usually made of maple. In both types of chairs, the front posts are spaced slightly wider apart than the back posts—but, overall, the Cajun chair is slightly smaller. Valex Richard, a disciple of Lulu Olivier, conducted a survey of Cajun handicrafts in the late 1940's and discovered that the seat of the typical Ville Platte chair is only fifteen inches off the ground. Usually, neither the Cajun nor the mountain chairs are painted, but are left to age from the effects of weather and hearth smoke.

The posts of the Cajun chair always stand upright, but the posts of the mountain chair are bent slightly at the top. Light decorative lathing is common on the tops of the Cajun chair backs. But the pointed tops and elaborate ladder-backs of its Anglo-American mountain cousin are completely unknown down the bayou or on the Cajun prairie. The seats of mountain chairs are commonly formed of hickory splints, or sometimes woven cornhusks—and it is here that the Cajun chair departs most dramatically from its Appalachian counterpart. In the cattle-rich areas of Louisiana, sun-cured rawhide is the only mate-rial that will do; it gives the Cajun chair a gentle softness and delicacy missing in other American frontier chairs. Researcher Richard reports that thrifty Cajun chairmakers could sometimes get as many as seven-teen seats from one piece of cowhide.

Hosea Thibodeaux, a craftsman of Ville Platte chairs from Bayou Chicot, still tans his own hides and turns his chair posts on a home-made lathe. Thibodeaux stretches and laces the cowhide seats into place, unaware that his Canadian ancestors long made their chairs in exactly the same way—with one tantalizing difference.

I saw that difference for the first time in Meteghan, Nova Scotia, on the so-called French Shore, where an old Cajun house from the immediate post-Expulsion period has been privately restored as a museum, La Vieille Maison. My first Canadian Acadian chair was sitting inside by the fireplace, its shape and construction eerily famil-iar, a *déjà vu* reminiscence.

But the seat! The seat was completely different, and yet the same —evocatively Cajun. Cowhide, yes, but cut into narrow strips, the ends of which were knotted around the rungs that formed the edges of the seat. The seat had been interlaced with these rawhide strips— held close-knit, strong, and supportive, like everything else the Cajuns seek to weave together.

8

How to Cook Cajun

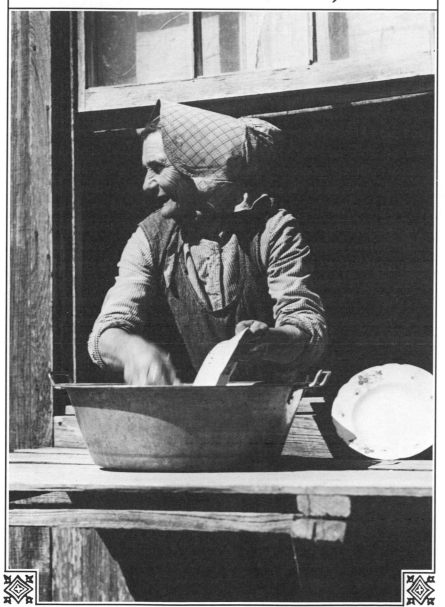

Old woman washing dishes, near Bayou Corne, 1943. The exterior window shelf, known as a tablette, *is a standard feature on old Cajun houses*
ELEMORE MORGAN, SR.

When Ruth Fontenot sets out to cook a gumbo, all the pots and pans and spices in her kitchen sit up and take notice. None is certain which one or ones will be used this time around, for both the recipe and the size of the serving will vary from day to day, depending on Ruth's mood and assessment of the tastes of her dinner guests.

A few things, certainly, will always be the same. Ruth will always use her black, cast-iron cooking pots, seasoned with oil by repeated cooking to attain the natural version of a Teflon finish. And her gumbo will always have lots of onions and peppers and garlic—*Mon Dieu,* it has *no* taste whatsoever without *beaucoup* of all the above. And of course, Ruth's gumbo will always start out with the same base mixture, a thick, rich, mysterious golden-brown sauce called a roux. As any south Louisiana cook old enough to lift a spoon will tell you, "First, you make a roux."

The roux is basically flour browned in butter, oil, or animal fat, to make a gravy base for the soup or other Cajun dishes—and there are as many ways to prepare one as there are cooks in Louisiana. But the basic idea, each time you make it, is to cook the flour slowly to a nutty brown without letting it turn so hot that it burns black and gets thrown away into the bayou. Ruth makes hers with lard, and says her Grandmother Dupré always used to tell her to cook the roux until it was the color "of an Indian's behind." Any roux cooked for less than an hour is merely a raw, greasy, unappetizing paste—but once that roux is a well-earned brown, and ready, the culinary possibilities open up like the Red Sea did for Moses, and all the strange little jars of home-grown spices above Ruth Fontenot's stove begin their anticipatory palpitations.

The gumbo Ruth makes could end up containing almost any imaginable form of meat, except beef. Seafood and chicken gumbos are the most common, but gumbos can also be made with duck, goose, guinea hen (a Louisiana favorite), or other wild game—sometimes with sausage or oysters mixed in. There is even a vegetarian gumbo, *gumbo z'herbes,* or "green gumbo," which was formerly made as a meatless dish for Lent. It's also delicious with bits of ham or sausage or shrimp. And of course, the very best gumbo in all the world has shrimp, oysters, and crab meat in it, with a little finfish or sausage thrown in to boot. Whatever you caught in the bayou that day, whatever was extra in your trawl or your neighbor's trawl, whatever is still left over in the refrigerator (like Thanksgiving turkey) or came back from the weekend hunt—any and all of that will make up into a gumbo day or night.

"Gumbo" is said to be derived from the African word "guin-gômbo," meaning okra—the peculiar seedpod vegetable that is added to most gumbos for taste and to thicken the broth around the various pieces of stewed and crumbling flesh and vegetables in the pot. "Gumbo" is also a name appended to a kind of Southern swamp tree and, more appropriately, to a dark, sticky soil formed by glaciers. But for cooks who know how to make one, gumbo can only mean a complete meal cooked up in one pot.

Chowders are common in the Maritime areas of Canada inhabited by Louisiana's Acadian cousins, but the meal-in-a-pot theme is the only similarity between the two cuisines. The Canadian *fricou* features potatoes, meat, and dumplings—seasoned, if at all, with a bunch of summer savory inserted top-down into the boiling stew, the savory's stalks poking insolently out between the pot and its lid. While nutritious and filling, such Canadian Acadian food strikes the Louisiana palate as having little or no taste.

Louisiana's Cajun gumbo has an unforgettable taste, not only because of its African but also because of its Spanish contributions. Hot peppers, and hot sauces like Tabasco made from them, have become indispensable ingredients in all Cajun cooking. The Indians pitched in a few ingredients, too: gumbos without okra can be flavored and thickened with *filé* powder, made from ground-up sassafras. Some linguistic detectives even suggest that "gumbo" is a variation of the Choctaw word "kombo," for sassafras. The pedigree of a good gumbo is as mysterious and complex as its taste.

Gumbo is usually served in a big bowl—or, in fancier Creole surroundings, a soup plate—ladled out over rice, the principal starch

in the south Louisiana diet. For their starch, Canadian Acadians cultivate and cook with potatoes, both because of post-Expulsion interaction with Irish immigrants and because of the climate. For the Cajuns'
Canadian cousins, rice is a dietary oddity, even though the grain was
known and used at Fortress Louisbourg and is included on period
menus at a Parks Canada restaurant there. The most complicated of
the Canadian Acadian potato dishes is something called a *poutine râ-
pure,* or "rapie pie." Grated whole potatoes are wrapped in cheese-
cloth and squeezed to remove the liquid and starch; the resulting
potato pulp left behind, mixed with animal fat, produces a kind of
crust for making chicken- or beef-filled pot pies.

Louisiana has found a use for this ancient and prolific Oriental
grain in almost every dish at almost every meal—from *calas,* or rice
cakes, for breakfast to rice pudding for dessert. Aside from their
gumbos, the Cajuns use rice most extensively in a dish called *jambalaya*
—a Cajun version of paella, without the peas and pimentos. A roux,
meat or crawfish, sautéed onions and other vegetables, plus tomatoes,
find themselves mixed together in a pot of water and rice. By the time
the rice is cooked, the jambalaya laced through it is ready, too. Whatever is left over in the kitchen goes into the jambalaya pot, especially
if there's not enough of it to make a gumbo.

Home-grown tomatoes are also an important ingredient in a complex of Cajun dishes like *court bouillon* and *sauce piquante.* Court bouillon is somewhat like the classic French bouillabaisse (*bouiller* = to
boil; *baisse* = to stop), a mixed fish soup with a heavily spiced tomato
broth. Bouillabaisse, however, usually includes wine, orange or
lemon peel, saffron, and other items a Cajun cook might find foreign
and fussy. And a Cajun court bouillon is thicker, slower to slide off
your spoon.

The basic court-bouillon sauce becomes a sauce piquante when it
is peppered up a bit and served over some meat other than finfish. The
meat from turtles, frogs' legs, chicken, quail, squirrel, pigeon, or
rabbit makes an excellent sauce piquante—as does squid. In tacky
tourist restaurants, you will find shrimp stewed in a watered-down
version of sauce piquante, served over rice and advertised as "shrimp
creole."

While all these dishes may sound exotic, they are easy to prepare from conventional ingredients; truly exotic expectations should be left for the dishes made with crawfish. Cajun folklore has it that the crawfish is descended from lobsters that followed the exiles from Maritime Canada to Louisiana. Leona "Tooti" Martin Girouard of St. Martinville is credited with starting one version of the tale, which has it that as the lobsters traveled farther, they became tireder and smaller. They were so friendly with the Acadians that they wanted to do everything the people did—which is why crawfish build mud chimneys for their houses. In low-lying areas, like the shallow ponds around cypress trees, whole "villages" of these mudbug chimneys will sprout in mushroomlike fairy rings. Each chimney tells you that, somewhere down underneath, there is a crawfish asleep.

Crawfish are most easily caught in the winter months, when the water is low, but their cycle begins in the summer. In late summer, the female crawfish lays her eggs, carrying them for a brief period on her abdomen. Because she then looks like a blackberry, the Cajuns say she is "in berry." In September, the peak of the egg-laying season, the older generation of males migrates aimlessly and frantically en masse, but biologists still can't tell us exactly how or why they do this. Depending on growing conditions, eggs hatched in the fall can produce the next generation of edible crawfish by January, when the crawfish season officially opens. They continue to be caught through June, but because they reach sexual maturity in April, later batches are harder-shelled and less desirable. "A warm, wet spring, combined with a large infusion of Mississippi floodwaters," notes Malcolm Comeaux, a leading authority on the Atchafalaya Basin, where most of the crawfish are harvested, "means a bumper crop of crawfish." In recent years, because of erratic flood conditions within the basin, complicated by the fact that the U.S. Army Corps of Engineers operates floodgates designed to "open" or "close" the basin like a big spigot, crawfish "farming" has begun in other areas. Louisiana's rice plantations have successfully experimented with hatching crawfish as an early spring "crop," and some Louisiana restaurants maintain their own farms to guarantee a steady year-round supply of the delicacy.

Crawfish tastes somewhat like lobster, although people in Louisiana will tell you it tastes better than lobster.

Indians fished them out of the bayous using sticks baited with roasted venison meat, and early Louisiana settlers used frogs' legs—gourmet diets for the little critters. Nowadays, crawfishermen use square pieces of netting about fourteen inches on a side. The net is lowered to the bottom of the pond or bayou, held with two V-shaped wire struts that have been inverted and joined to opposite corners, their intersections at the top forming a hollow pyramid. A piece of bait meat is tied to the center of the net, at the base of the pyramid, and the fisherman waits for crawfish to crawl across the net for a little nibble. When ready to pull them out, he pokes a hooked stick into the water and grabs the point of the pyramid. As the net is hoisted up, the weight of the crawfish causes the center to collapse, trapping them inside. You can also catch crawfish in more modern traps, made of chicken wire rolled into cylinders, with a cone-shaped entrance that lets them in and confuses them about how to get out again. In the year 1967, some unknown Louisiana bureaucrat sat down and counted 70,769 such traps in use in the Atchafalaya Basin alone. Tooti Girouard adds this tale: "When the coonasses who work on the offshore oil rigs went to Texas to work, they told the Texans that they were sexy because they ate crawfish fat. Well, when the Texans heard that, they started eating crawfish for the fat, and eventually they learned to eat the tail as well. And now we have a million-dollar crawfish business!"

The yellow crawfish fat is the secret of such deliriously delicious dishes as crawfish bisque and crawfish *étoufée*. The étoufée ("smothered") starts out with a roux, plus the usual sautéed onions, celery, bell pepper, and garlic. The fat is cooked with all the above, plus tomatoes, and the tails are thrown in at the last minute. For the bisque, you create a stuffing of bread crumbs, parsley, green onion, garlic, butter, and milk—and bake it inside the cleaned-out casing or "head" of the crawfish body. Étoufée is served over rice; for bisque, you drop the baked heads into the roux, add a little more water, and simmer for another half hour before serving.

If you're entirely too timid even to try to cook Cajun from scratch, several companies now package rice and seasoning mixes (with the roux included, in powdered form) that you just throw in a pot with some water and meat—and the results are sometimes creditable. On the other hand, canned gumbos are to be strenuously avoided. Cajun cookbooks are almost as prolific as Cajun cooks, if you really want to do it. And Ruth Fontenot one day promises to write her own cookbook, to be called—she winks—*First You Make a Roué.*

The recipes that follow have been synthesized from a variety of sources, including my own experimental attempts to develop recipes that could be prepared in electric frying pans or crock pots in places like Denver or Pittsburgh where fish (and well-seasoned iron pots) are not as abundant or inexpensive as they are in Louisiana. Electric frying pans have the advantage of temperature controls to brown your roux without burning it, and the whole meal can be cooked in the same dish. When using a cast-iron pot or regular skillet, make the roux over low heat; either add the other ingredients and simmer, or transfer to a larger pot.

Crock pots are ideal for making a gumbo, and I was surprised to see that neither manufacturers nor crockery-cooking writers have made that discovery for themselves. One author with more than 250 recipes boldly offers "Creole Steak Strips," whatever that is, and her own versions of Creole chicken and bouillabaisse—all in the same culinary ball park, I suppose. But not a single gumbo recipe!

The crockery pot presents a few problems, however. Onions and celery put in crunchy remain that way, so for the authentic Cajun texture, they should be sautéed first. Meanwhile, the crockery pot's slow-simmering capability blends everything together with fail-safe reliability and without scorched pots. If you leave the lid on, not allowing vitamin-rich tomato vapors and other ingredients to evaporate, the result can be even more nutritious than the traditional iron-pot gumbo. Dishes made with fish require at least five hours' cooking on "low"; dishes made with chicken or other meats require at least six hours.

Because I personally detest recipes with gibberish like "⅔ cup onions," quantities are measured in whole pieces, like numbers of stalks of celery. As Ruth Fontenot says, "I don't measure, I *put.*" Suggested servings are for four; if you need more, just proportion it out, and if you ever have any leftovers, don't worry. They're guaranteed to taste even better the next day.

Chicken is universally available in the United States, and all the following dishes can be cooked with it. If you can't get fresh okra, try the canned or frozen variety. Instead of pulpy or juiceless fresh tomatoes, it's okay to use canned ones. And for a thinner, quick gumbo, some cooks claim V-8 juice makes a devilishly tangy substitute. White ocean perch, sometimes frozen and packaged as Japanese turbot, is available in most supermarkets to add inexpensive "fill" to seafood dishes. With a little judicious shopping and foraging around in your refrigerator for useful leftovers, you'll soon learn that Cajun cooking is the best and most versatile gourmet bargain in America. Like everything else Cajun, just try it a few times and you'll get it right.

The Roux

If your dish includes chicken or wild game, brown the meat first in oil and use the drippings to make your roux. Lard, when available, or oleomargarine made with lard, will also do—as will any vegetable oil. One stick of butter or margarine, or half a cup of oil and/or drippings—is sufficient for the following recipes, which will yield four servings. Some insist you should use slightly more flour than oil; others slightly less—in either case, mix thoroughly before you turn up the heat. If using an electric frying pan, set the dial at approximately 300° F. and cook, stirring constantly with a wooden spoon so it doesn't stick. In a regular frying pan or cast-iron pot, keep the fire on low. The roux should bubble with a fine white foam and within fifteen minutes begin turning a caramel brown. It should cook for at least forty-five minutes. Garlic to taste and such things as celery salt may be added. Large batches can be prepared in advance and stored in your freezer, which saves both time and trauma. The roux is the only difficult part.

When using frozen roux, add a few drops of extra oil to the frying pan to help melt it, and then proceed.

Chicken and Okra Gumbo

Roux, as specified above (if frozen,
4–6 heaping tbs., plus another
   2 tbs. oil)
1 medium onion, chopped
2 stalks celery, chopped
1 clove garlic (or to taste)
½ bell pepper, chopped
About 2 qts. water
1 stewing chicken, quartered
   (2–3 lbs.)
1 lb. okra (1 14½-oz. can will do, or
   2 8-oz. cans, or 1 frozen package)

1 tsp. thyme
1 tsp. Tabasco or cayenne pepper
1 bay leaf

Optional ingredients:
2 large fresh tomatoes (or 1
   1-lb. can)
4 oz. sausage (andouille, Polish
   sausage, etc.)
1 tbs. Worcestershire sauce
1 8-oz. can oysters (add 10 minutes
   before serving)

Prepare roux. Sauté onion, celery, garlic, and pepper. Combine with roux and add 1 cup water, chicken, okra, spices, and optional ingredients as desired. Bring to a boil. Simmer for at least 1 hour, adding water as needed. Check seasonings and serve over boiled rice.

Seafood Gumbo

Roux, as specified in chicken
   gumbo recipe
1 medium onion, chopped
2 stalks celery, chopped
1 clove garlic (or to taste)
½ bell pepper, chopped
About 2 qts. water
1 lb. boiled, peeled shrimp
   (20–24 to a pound)

¾ pt. oysters and liquid
1 lb. white finfish
1 lb. okra (8–16 oz. canned or
   frozen)
1 tsp. thyme
1 tsp. cayenne or Tabasco sauce
3 bay leaves

Optional ingredients: 1 small can crabmeat, or up to 8 oz. cleaned from up to 10 boiled blue crabs. Save claws from this operation and toss them into the pot, cracking them later with a nutcracker to get their meat.

2 large fresh tomatoes (1 1-lb. can
will do)
4 oz. sausage (andouille, Polish
   sausage, etc.)
1 tsp. allspice

½ tsp. mace
8 cloves
Dash lemon juice
3–4 green onions
Fresh parsley for garni

Prepare roux as in chicken gumbo. Sauté onion, celery, garlic, and pepper. Combine with roux and add 1 cup water, fish, and other ingredients. Bring to a boil. Simmer for at least 1 hour, adding water as needed. Check seasonings and serve over boiled rice.

Gumbo z'Herbes (Green Gumbo)

32 oz. puréed greens (purée in blender), chosen from any of the following: lettuce, spinach, collard greens, mustard greens, turnip greens, cabbage, watercress, parsley, carrot tops, radish tops, kale, Brussels sprouts, endive, broccoli, beet tops, Chinese cabbage, chicory, scallions, dandelions, sorrel, fennel, bell pepper

2 bay leaves
2 cloves
1 tsp. thyme
½ tsp. cayenne
½ tsp. marjoram
¼ tsp. allspice

Pinch sage, dill, tarragon, and/or chives
3–4 links smoked sausage, or ½ cup ham, cubed, plus 2 tbs. oil, or 1 lb. shrimp (20–24 per lb.)
About 1 qt. water
4–6 tbs. roux (optional)

For vegetarian recipe, omit meat. If using ham or sausage, brown first in oil and then add all other ingredients. For shrimp, add 10 minutes before serving. Simmer for 1 hour.

Court Bouillon

Roux, as specified above (if frozen, 4–6 heaping tbs., plus another 2 tbs. oil)
1 onion, chopped
2 stalks celery, chopped
1 clove garlic, chopped (or to taste)
1 bell pepper, chopped
1 cup stock or water
1 1-lb. can tomatoes
1 tsp. thyme
1 bay leaf
1 tsp. Tabasco or cayenne pepper
2–3 lbs. fish (if fresh, filet and place

remainder of fish pieces in 2 cups water to boil into 1 cup stock)
4 scallions, chopped

Optional ingredients:
1 cup red or white wine
Juice of ½ lemon
¼ tsp. marjoram
¼ tsp. allspice
¼ tsp. oregano
¼ tsp. basil
1 tbs. parsley
2 tbs. Worcestershire sauce

Prepare roux. Sauté onion, celery, garlic, and pepper. Combine with roux and add stock or water, tomatoes, spices, and other ingredients, except fish and scallions, and simmer for 1 hour. Add fish and scallions, simmer 10 minutes more.

Sauce Piquante

Cut pieces from 1 whole chicken, or 16 frogs' legs, or 12 squirrels
Exact same ingredients and proportions as for court bouillon, except ½ cup oil instead of 2 tablespoons
Brown meat in oil and remove. Sauté celery, onion, garlic, and pepper. Combine with roux and add water, tomatoes, spices, and other ingredients, plus meat, and cook for 1 hour, stirring occasionally. Add more water if sauce thickens prematurely. Ten minutes before serving, add scallions and taste for hotness (the "piquante"). Add Tabasco to taste.

Jambalaya

1 frying chicken (2–3 lbs., 8 pieces cut)
4 tbs. flour
4 tbs. oil
1 medium onion, chopped
2 cloves garlic
½ bell pepper, chopped
4 oz. sausage or cubed ham
1 1-lb. can tomatoes
1 tsp. Tabasco or cayenne pepper
2 cups rice
2 cups water

Optional ingredients:
4 tbs. roux
Duck or turkey leftovers instead of chicken
Chicken stock or beer instead of water
1 stalk celery, chopped
Dash oregano, rosemary, and/or thyme
2 scallions, chopped (garni)

Coat chicken with flour and brown in oil. Remove and use drippings to sauté onion, garlic, and peppers. Combine all ingredients and bake on stove top in covered pot for 25 minutes or until rice is tender. Foolproof dish in a covered electric frying pan.

9

French Accordion
Folk Music

Nathan Abshire at the 1977 Cajun Music Festival in Lafayette
DAVID RICHMOND

The highway to Mamou breaks away from the Interstate at Crowley and heads north through the open Cajun prairie. The road is lined with continuous rice farms and cattle ranches—and the horizon is so flat that the occasional clumps of trees around coulees or farmhouses stand distinctly against the sky. The car's radio scoops up half a dozen different community stations from this seemingly endless great meadow, one station for each Cajun settlement of any size, and several from centers like Lafayette.

It is the village of Mamou, however, that on Saturday mornings commands the prairie airwaves with a sound such as your radio has never transmitted before. The sound of KEUN–AM rolls effortlessly across the unobstructed landscape from a bistro known as Fred's Lounge, broadcasting direct from the one-stoplight, one-intersection main street of beautiful downtown Mamou, population 3,275.

Off the highway to the right and back, Mamou's white rice elevator stands watch over a village noticeably well clumped with trees. A side road from the highway leads through the fields and directly into the center of town, where a jammed parking lot can be found next door to Fred's. The sound of the radio expands when you open the car door, for the broadcast comes not just from the antenna on the bar's roof but also through the air conditioners inserted in the cinder-block walls, and is further amplified by the openings and closings of Fred's front door. The cacophony spreads across a sun-soaked, mid-morning, weekend market day, forming a steady patter of music and French advertisements as a backdrop to the farmers and pickup trucks milling about their weekend business.

Many will drop in for a few minutes or an hour or so at Fred's, where the music and beer and a little light dancing begin flowing at 8 A.M. and continue heavier and thicker all the way through the morning until 11 A.M. About two dozen musicians form the backbone of the program's "regulars," playing with one another in different combinations on alternate weeks. There are also new faces from time to time at the microphone, which is haphazardly perched among the steadily growing collection of beer bottles on a requisitioned lounge table in one corner of the flamingo-pink room. Program host Revon Reed sits at a green Deco booth nearby, downing whiskey from his own special mug and reading the ads and introductions into the mike. The crowd is mostly locals, plus gaga-eyed foreign French-language teachers from the Lafayette-based CODOFIL agency who've never seen *any*thing like this back home, plus curious young musicians, journalists, and assorted other hangers-on. Their cumulative presence at this incongruously staged cocktail-party-of-the-air—before noon—sometimes leads to spirited dancing and jostling of the musicians while they try to play.

Standing out among the gathered musicians is a tall, wiry man, an elderly gentleman, seventy-four to be exact, whose accordion playing stands out as clearly as he does. His fingers are lithe and sure, his bright eyes behind the glasses riveted to the rhythm and at the same time drifting far, far away. His name is Ambrose Thibodeaux, and he is undoubtedly the most accomplished living performer of French Acadian accordion music, the power and intensity of which is probably one reason he is still alive to play it.

Though Ambrose may be the greatest, everyone present takes his democratic turn at a different instrument, and the one who just finished playing the triangle takes up the accordion while Ambrose sits one out. Triangles and guitars provide bass and rhythm accompaniment, while fiddles and accordions are lead instruments. As the band ranges from tune to tune, it shifts to varying sizes and performing roles and personal specialties as the morning wears on. The bow of the fiddle is pushed and pulled across its strings in a manner not at all like that used by symphony violinists, for the push and pull here is in time with and in imitation of the playing of the accordion—and every movement is well lubricated with beer.

One of the fiddle players, at least part of the time, is Merlin Fontenot, Ambrose Thibodeaux's son-in-law and a well-respected Cajun musician in his own right. One of the guitar players, again for at least part of the time, is Preston Manuel. Both helped back up Ambrose Thibodeaux in his first long-playing album, a recording issued in the late 1960's. That album, which relaunched Ambrose's professional career at the age of sixty-four, after four decades of rest, tells a revealing story or two about the nature and current state of Cajun folk music.

Ambrose first picked up the accordion at fifteen, he says, and played it until he married, sold the accordion, and settled down on the farm at the age of twenty-one. After years of farming corn, cotton, and sweet potatoes—plus enough sugarcane to make his own supply of syrup—Ambrose Thibodeaux neared the customary age of retirement, and his daughter Leola urged him to take up accordion playing again, as a hobby. Leola, who also plays triangle on the first LP,* finally persuaded her father to make a private 45-rpm recording in Lafayette that could be given out to family and close friends. They made the necessary arrangements with Carol Rachou, a Lafayette promoter who runs the La Louisiane recording company out of a converted garage on a quiet street not far from the University of Southwestern Louisiana campus. Rachou sat patiently at the controls for their first take, Ambrose recalls, but came bursting out of the control booth at the conclusion, demanding to know: "Can you play me twelve more like that?"

Well, they could, the four musicians replied. Why? "Because I want an album," snapped Rachou, hurrying back to the control booth. "But we came here prepared to make just one small record," chorused the four. "You'll *get* your 45," Rachou promised, closing the door behind him. "Just keep playing."

So they did. Twelve more songs, only eight of which they had practiced, and then only for a short period the day before. The other four were completely unrehearsed and played as well as they could remember them. Rachou allowed no retakes. Preston Manuel and Leola supplied unexceptional but adequate vocals where needed. Of the thirteen pieces they recorded, they picked the best dozen and left the studio that afternoon for a scheduled concert date at the Lakeview Club in nearby Eunice, not entirely convinced that Rachou was serious

---

*"Authentic French Accordion Music," available from La Louisiane, 711 Stevenson Street, Lafayette, Louisiana 70501.

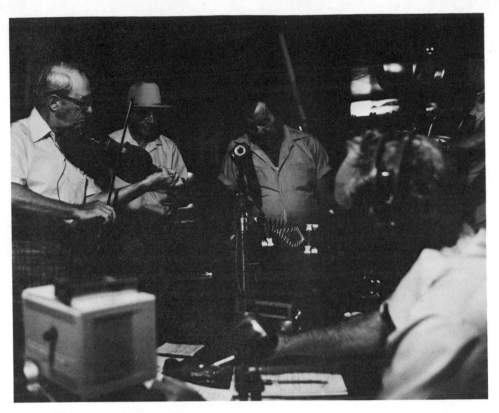

Saturday morning at Fred's Lounge in Mamou. Ambrose Thibodeaux and Nathan Abshire (center) *play into the microphone for KEUN radio host Revon Reed* (foreground)
TURNER BROWNE

about all that album business. The rest is, as they say, musical history.

So what was it that Rachou heard? If Ambrose Thibodeaux had laid down his accordion at age twenty-one, that would have been the year 1924—before Huey Long's roads and English-language schools, accompanied by English-language radio stations, had penetrated the French Triangle. The sound of that era is a sound gradually diluted in later Cajun music; it lay dormant for four decades in the person of Ambrose Thibodeaux, who busied himself in the meantime tending to his farm and family of four daughters, and who later drove a school bus down those paved roads to the schoolhouses. But Ambrose never forgot how to play the music he had heard as a child, and he never acquired much of an interest in the later Cajun music with its country-and-Western meddling from electric guitars and Nashville.

He also never forgot the kind of accordion he used to play as a kid. It was a Monarch in the key of D—a German make with a higher sound than the key-of-C accordions now most common in the Cajun dance halls. Leola's accordion gift for her father's retirement was a German-made Hohner in the key of C, and Ambrose says he didn't at all like the sounds it made. One lucky day, after delivering a busload of children to the Richard school, he was sitting in a grocery store owned by one of his cousins, having a Coke with him, the other bus driver, and their sometime companion, the Evangeline Maid bread deliveryman. The deliveryman owned a Monarch D that had belonged to his wife's father, but couldn't sing high enough to play it —and the wife was threatening to leave him if he didn't stop trying. The Evangeline Maid man needed a C, and though he wasn't interested in Ambrose's Hohner C, he was willing to sell the D. So Ambrose Thibodeaux bought it, writing out a check his cousin cashed right there in the store, and the rest was some more of that good old musical history.

Though the Ambrose Thibodeaux "style" is demonstrably more antique than the current style, the use of the accordion dates back only to 1822, when it was developed in Germany; later it spread to Belgium and France, where, as in Louisiana, it is still used in rural popular music. The Acadian music in Canada before and after the Expulsion had been led by violins, and continued to be in Louisiana until the German immigrants of the Midwest began remigrating south to the Cajun prairies in the railroad/rice boom years of the 1880's. The Balfa Brothers and fiddler Rufus Thibodeaux are the last major exponents of that violin-dominated music still surviving in Louisiana, for the accordion is now the undisputed champ. Folk-music researcher Catherine Blanchet reported in 1970 that the guitar had arrived on the scene only thirty-five or forty years before, a few decades after the accordion. By that time, the accordion had become so thoroughly entrenched that even the guitar could not dislodge it. Such is the time-bound musical pool in which Ambrose Thibodeaux was baptized as a young man. Out of that same pool came players like the legendary Iry LeJeune, who was killed at an early age like a Cajun James Dean but whose tunes are still in the Louisiana accordion players' repertoire. And players like Nathan Abshire, a guard at the Basile city dump by day and a plaquemine-faced music-box pumper by night—the Mean Man of the accordion, who stars as the hapless anti-hero of a haunting Public Broadcasting Service videotape documentary "The Good Times Are Killing Me." There are also musicians like Eunice's Mark Savoie, who make their *own* accordions, and do a booming business selling them to other performers.

Mark Savoie's principal peers in the Acadian instrument cottage industry are Sidney Brown of Lake Charles, in Savoie's general price range, and John E. Hébert of Lafayette, who tries to undersell his friends. Hébert complains that the Hohner brand has gradually reduced the number of "folds" in the bellows of the instrument from sixteen to fifteen to fourteen. He builds his bellows with eighteen folds in order to give the player more flexibility. The older ones who "never learned any better," he jokes, and won't allow themselves to play any worse, feel cramped by the wizened Hohner model and can't play their music on it effectively. Hébert's model permits that distinctly Cajun, expressive stage presence.

Hébert also manufactures his version with only nine keys instead of the standard ten. Only the most accomplished accordion virtuosos need ten keys, he maintains, and besides, most Cajun players seem to have hands too small for ten keys. Even so, a full two octaves are attainable on his instruments, which he can build to order in the keys of B, C, or D. "Violins and guitars don't like B or D," he suggests as an explanation for the general drift to C over the years. No more Monarch D accordions can be made, anyway, because the Americans bombed the factory during World War II, Thibodeaux laments. But one of the other major reasons there's no turning back now can be found in a small attachment Hébert adds to all his new accordions that none of the old ones ever had use for before: an electric microphone.

Mamou-born Jimmy Newman was the first Cajun to go electric and head for Nashville, where he made it big with a synthetic sound as exotic to the Anglos as it was, at that time, exotic to the folks back home. Newman became the major force behind the prevailing meld of traditional Cajun music with the country-and-Western instrumental and formal idiom. He signaled that successful synthesis with "Lâche pas la patate" ("Don't drop the potato," a multimeaning Cajun idiom for "Don't give up"). The record was a smash success in French Canada and Louisiana, as well as La Louisiane's first and only gold single.

Newman, in turn, helped pave the way for Doug Kershaw, who electrified his Cajun fiddle at the same time other young American musicians were electrifying their guitars, and went on to electrify the acid-rock generation with its first nationally recognized glimpse of Cajun music in the classic "Lou'siana Man." Kershaw, born in Lake Arthur, spoke no English as a child and learned to play the fiddle as an adjunct to shining shoes—his principal source of pocket money after "Papa Jack" committed suicide when young Kershaw was only seven. He plays twenty-eight other instruments and now lives in Nashville, but declared in his autobiography: "Everything I learned since I left there [Louisiana] was just trimmings." At the age of twenty, he joined the Louisiana Hayride, went to the Grand Ole Opry, and made what he considers his first real break, with the help of Johnny Cash. The *New York Post* once described him as a "mad water snake," while *Rolling Stone* observed that his wild playing was marked by "a distinct, fibrous rhythm that should get tiresome, but doesn't." Kershaw simply says, "You don't change your talent—you just change your style."

In doing so, Kershaw liberated the younger Cajun musicians born after World War II to explore a variety of instrumental and melodic combinations still rooted in the old forms. The most brilliant of these was Louisiana's short-lived group Coteau, founded by Jimmy Newman's son Gary. Young Newman, impressed with the "progressive" Austin sound in country-and-Western music, returned to the Lafayette area from Nashville, and through Rachou and other contacts met the core group of what became Coteau (Cajun for a ridged, geological outcropping). Their "progressive Cajun" sound, a sensation at the 1975 New Orleans Jazz Festival, started each tune in the traditional Cajun idiom before drifting into a mélange of rock/country-and-Western/bluegrass variations, blended and transformed with a conscious jazz sensibility. As soon as the playing started, however, dissension also started, and drummer Danny Kimball left the group to go back to shoeing horses. Fiddler Mike Doucet and lead guitarist Bruce

McDonald soon had reached a near-complete falling out, and the group split—with Doucet's faction returning to playing the Cajun classics under the name Beau Soleil. Beau Soleil is a regular fixture in the dance halls of the USL campus' entertainment strip. McDonald's faction, a precision progressive rock combo called Protein—also popular in the Lafayette area—allied itself with Zachary Richard. Richard is another young Cajun musician, virtually unknown in his own country, who has made it big in French Canada. Luckily, La Louisiane's tape library includes Coteau's only surviving studio tape, and one 45-rpm record was produced before the breakup—so the "progressive Cajun" sound is not lost. Exploring the same territory are the Lafayette-based Red Beans and Rice Revue, and interestingly enough, the young musicians of New Brunswick are simultaneously developing in their own "progressive" direction. Moncton-based 1755 can play the entire Louisiana accordion repertoire, plus the bluegrass-laced banjo music that has gradually infiltrated Canadian Acadian music.

Yet another strain of Cajun-influenced music is called Zydeco—a corruption of "les haricots sont pas sal," or "beans aren't salty." Zydeco is black Cajun music, popularized principally by Clifton Chenier. The Zydeco players went to Texas for some country, but retained their soul, and came back to the bayou electric and hot.

Varied as these permutations are, they all share the common ancestry that Ambrose Thibodeaux's accordion still sings, in one of America's most diverse and unusual folk-music traditions.

We know almost nothing of the very earliest Acadian music, but we do know that in early Louisiana (and certain areas of New Brunswick today) there was a form of Acadian music played entirely without sophisticated instruments. Usually the performer would sit, singing, clapping, and tapping his feet, and using a few sticks or kitchen implements to amplify the beat. In LSU professor Harry Oster's intriguing 1958 record and text set prepared for the Louisiana Folklore Society, recorded in Mamou, one of the songs is accompanied by spoons.

Professor George F. Reinecke of the University of New Orleans has identified one version of the sixteenth- and seventeenth-century folk classic "La Fille du Roi" as the earliest-known Louisiana French folk song—a piece which is narrative and didactic in content, like a Gregorian chant. Sung a cappella, it consists of numerous versions of what happens to a young woman when she is propositioned by various soldiers and sailors; personal honor is stressed, regardless of how the concluding details are handled.[1] Reinecke is convinced that the violin was the only European instrument to accompany the Acadians and their ancient European folk songs to the New World, and that these songs were composed principally for home presentation and "handing down" in the company of children and friends. One genre of these a cappella songs, notes Catherine Blanchet, is *les cantiques des morts*— sung during the days when there were not enough churches for conducting a formal funeral Mass. These quasi-pagan practices have disappeared entirely, except in Blanchet's own folklore song-and-dance troupe, as has the tradition of *les danses rondes*—a matchmaking spring exercise that once upon a time was the only form of public entertainment allowed young people during Lent.

Dancing, in one form or another, has always accompanied Acadian music, and is an integral part of all later Cajun music. In fact, critics and defenders alike will agree that it is not only the best music for dancing but positively useless and lifeless without it. Out of the milieu of violins and spoons eventually evolved the use of the *'tit fer,* or triangle, as a clear, light, bell-like rhythm section. Drums were too overbearing and intrusive for acoustic performances, and useful only in the more recent electric, country-and-Western-influenced bands. The use of two or more instruments dictates the eventual assemblage of a band, and the resulting increase in noise level serves to animate dance gatherings of a substantially larger size than the immediate household. We have it on authority from the aggrieved Bishop of Quebec that by no later than 1742 the Acadians had developed a flourishing interest in community mixed dancing as evening entertainment. As is the practice in Ambrose Thibodeaux's family today, any large Cajun family was certainly capable of mustering up a respectable band. A separate social class of musician-entertainers never developed, for everyone could play at least one instrument, even if it was only the 'tit fer. Most "professional" Cajun musicians have other means of livelihood, like Ambrose Thibodeaux's farm. Nonetheless, given the extended nature of the Acadian family then and now, several branches living in the same neighborhood or village might cull their clan and mount their own group of the family's all-stars for community-wide dance gatherings. Black Cajun accordion wizard Bois-Sec Ardoin and his enormous Ardoin Family Band exemplify this custom. ("Bois-sec," an expression still common in Poitou and other rural areas of France today, is a Cajun idiom for "drink up.")

These home-based entertainments were easy if you had a large house or yard. One common practice was to move all the furniture out of one front room for dancing, and to place a pot of gumbo and some beer in the other front room for refreshments. Eventually, the wall between the two came down and the Cajun fais-dodo developed, bringing with it an architectural package for the evolving Cajun music. Fais-dodo is Cajun baby talk for "go to sleep," as in "put all the small kids in a back bedroom to sleep," so that their parents and older brothers and sisters and aunts and uncles can play music and dance together all night in the front rooms. The first fais-dodo halls were built as family gathering spaces—perhaps on a convenient corner of grandfather's farm—when the cleared-out front rooms would no longer accommodate the crowd. Like a modern-day child's playhouse writ large, the family fais-dodo hall, based on the four-room Acadian cottage, was something of a caricature. It had one long, unobstructed room across the front, where in the original houses there had been two, plus two rooms in back—one with beds for the infants, *le parc aux petits,* as they called it, and another, where non-dancing menfolk could retire to play cards. Wooden benches were placed around the wall in the front room, and those too old to dance sat and watched, clapped, or tapped along, anyway. "It might be taken for a barn or warehouse" by the uninformed passer-by, notes Cajun prairie authority Lauren Post of the old fais-dodo hall. "Outside, a distinctive feature, of course, was an abundance of hitching racks where the horses were tied."

Larger and more complicated forms of this structure eventually evolved as the villages grew, like Oneziphore Guidry's famed fais-

Onzeiphore Guidry's fais-dodo hall, Rayne, 1935   LAUREN POST, LOUISIANA STATE UNI-
VERSITY PRESS

dodo hall, which survives only as a photograph. Later, these larger
halls would evolve into the enormous commercial nightclubs that still
dot the Cajun countryside today. But their origins were non-commer-
cial. They were sometimes built and maintained by one member of an
extended family as an expression of his personal prestige or generos-
ity. Fifteen cents might be charged to dance, in the old days, but you
were admitted free if you planned to sit in without dancing. As at the
more private house parties, custom dictated that the young women
were not permitted to leave the main area unchaperoned—if you left
alone, as the saying had it, you were not to be admitted back! The
men, on the other hand, were free to gather outside to drink hard
liquor, play pranks on one another, gamble beyond the indoor card
games, or engage in other social activities peripheral to the dancing.
Refreshments sold inside, combined with the fifteen-cents admission,
would cover the upkeep and provide an honorarium for the band.

In the smaller Cajun communities, American Legion halls or
church recreation centers still provide this same sort of community-
based, non-profit housing for the ritual weekly dances—but in all the
larger towns, and especially in the Lafayette metropolitan area, large
and commercially lucrative nightclub operations thrive. There,
largely part-time, "amateur" bands use fiddles, triangles, and accor-

dions, supplemented by one or more guitars and drums and the electronic amplification needed to fill the hall. In places like New Iberia's Blue Moon, the old barnlike wooden structure remains, but there is a stage at one end and refreshments sold at a full-service bar. Long tables with chairs around the room's central dance floor have replaced the traditional benches. At La Poussière ("Dust") in Breaux Bridge, the interior pattern is familiar, but arrayed within a more modern cinder-block barn. If you took a dozen suburban two-car garages and set them side by side, four long by three wide, you'd end up with an area equal to the large but low-ceilinged space that is La Poussière—ballroom-size in floor area, but still residential in scale and feeling, to the curtains on the windows and the checked cloths on the tables. All age levels participate, though an increasing number of the younger people are college-age tourists out to sample what is left of the old fais-dodo feeling. The younger ones no longer do the two-step danced by their elders, but do a sort of jitterbug of their own invention, using the two-step rhythm—a hybrid dance step in the disco and Dick Clark age that even the elders are beginning to adopt.

There is no surviving practice of group dancing in Louisiana like the Packetville festival's community quadrille, or even the Anglo-American square dance. Couples dance as separate units, even though the bounce of the Cajun two-step can give the dance floor the appearance of an outsized quadrille that has broken formation. The bounce of the two-step is a result of its shuffle, for the two-step glides across the ground instead of stomping it. Heel-kicking improvisations are not discouraged, nor are they deemed all that necessary. The two-step rocks contentedly across the dance floor, relaxes without exhaustion —so the dance can go on all night, while the infants sleep until the age when they can begin to join in.

At La Poussière, I have watched the two-step lose ground, and sometimes the band even sings in English. The erosion is more pronounced at Boo-Boo's—a slick, city-type, disco-equipped roadhouse between Breaux Bridge and Lafayette—and perhaps most pronounced at Allen Fontenot's Cajun Bandstand nightclub in Kenner, a New Orleans suburb. Fontenot's bar, with a Quonset hut paint-and-foil wonderland dance floor out back, is the closest nitery to the New

Orleans International Airport, your first drinking stop off the plane, *cher.* Fontenot, who stocks a complete Cajun souvenir and record shop in his sprawling complex, also leads the house band, and resignedly confides that the crowds these days mostly prefer country-and-Western. He'll throw in a Cajun number every now and then, and sometimes the visitor to his hall will find small groups of determined Cajuns stranded in the city and homesick enough to huddle together here, keeping the requests for the old music coming. As late as the 1955 Acadian Bicentennial music festival in St. Martinville, recordings were not even allowed, nor were electric instruments, nor were scores. But the family base and oral tradition of the music had already been seriously compromised even then, and in the intervening years the Cajun musician has found himself inexorably pulled off in other, sometimes alien, directions by the demands of the modern commercial American music industry and the record-buying tastes it has cultivated.

How and where it's played are easily determined aspects of Cajun music. What it says, since it says it in the Cajuns' own brand of French, and what it all means, are much more complex knots to untangle. Worse, no one even started recording, collecting, transcribing, and sorting through the Cajuns' once endless musical treasure trove until relatively recently. Corinne Saucier, later to become a faculty member and folklorist at Northwestern State College in Natchitoches—a French-influenced enclave and the state's first European settlement, on the Red River just northwest of the Cajun triangle—wrote the first scholarly thesis on the subject. But that was not until 1923. Saucier was working on a final draft of a later, lengthier manuscript when she died, but neither her publisher nor her estate has had it prepared for publication. Saucier collected original recordings and made a number of important transcriptions from them, as did the Lomax brothers, John and Alan, who stored their working papers and other findings with the Library of Congress.

The value of this early work was soon eclipsed, however, by two other events that largely determined what musical knowledge survived and how it was evaluated. The first book to be published on the subject is still the definitive work, Irene Thérèse Whitfield Holmes's 1939 *Louisiana French Folk Songs,* published by the LSU Press—which happens to be the custodian of the as yet unpublished Saucier manuscript. The other major turning point was the production of the first commercial record of Cajun music, on July 6, 1925, "Allons à Lafayette" ("Let's Go to Lafayette"), by Joe Falcon of Rayne. What has been recorded and what has been lost since then are the results of a haphazard pile of accidents. Falcon's Rayne neighbor, Leroy "Happy Fats" LeBlanc, the originator of the famed "Allons Dansez Colinda" (Colinda is a woman's name; but, more significantly, the name of a slave dance banned in Louisiana in 1843 for its licentiousness), organized a band called the Rayne-Bo Ramblers, which apparently holds the all-time Cajun recording title, with eighty 45-rpm records and two long-playing albums. Other LP collections have been assembled by Arhoolie in California, which brought Clifton Chenier to national prominence; by Swallow (owned by Fred Soileau) in Ville Platte; and by Boo-Ray in Lafayette—basically a country-and-Western label, though they also distributed the Coteau single. But even with all these and the Oster set, plus scattered private tapes of assorted vintages in Louisiana research libraries, we have nothing compared with what is known and recorded of Canadian French folk music.

For her 1970 master's thesis at USL, Catherine Brookshire Blanchet, another protégé of Lulu Olivier, pored through thirteen thousand texts and another seven thousand tapes and phonograph records at Quebec's Université Laval. This helped her to sort sixty children's folksongs collected from Vermilion Parish south of Lafayette between 1942 and 1954. Ambrose Thibodeaux, in his first album, included only one tune that was already an "old" one when he first started playing, "La Two-Step Richie," though much of his own original material from that era (and the material he has reassembled from memory since) incorporates fragments of the otherwise lost genre.

Such a comparatively meager assortment of printed and recorded fragments—gathered together, you could easily carry them in one armload—is not the most desirable data base from which to suggest or prove any definitive theory about Cajun music. Nonetheless, a few clear patterns and themes emerge. Irene Holmes opens the discussion: "They [the songs] seem endless in length, because they are played over and over again until they run on and on and on like the flat country of the southern part of the state that developed them. They fit the pushing and pulling of the accordion, having been made, so to speak, of, by and for the accordion." Such a structure gives the music an infinite flexibility of form, she says, and indeed, every Cajun extended-family village has its own version of how a commonly shared tune is to be "correctly" played. The music has impure tones, complicated by the portamento style of singing (the "glide" effect, as produced by a trombone), which is why the music sometimes seems so wailing and melancholy on first, or even second, hearing. An irregular location of pulse, she says, plus an irregular number of lines per stanza affords plenty of room for improvised grunts and other ad-libbed "fillers" to flesh out a stanza that might otherwise meander away from its instrumental backdrop. So you get a *"mais"* thrown in here, or an "oh" there, and an extra *"chère"* or *"la belle"* along the way—so that the same song inevitably develops a variety of versions.

All of this irregularity just barely submits to standardization, but the use of simple harmonic structures and quarter-time intervals can be deemed typical. Blanchet found that only three of her sixty children's songs were chromatic, or non-harmonic, and concluded that the music's folk character tends to "eliminate difficult intervals or unfamiliar melodic formulae." The regularity of quarter-time intervals is promoted both in the waltz forms that invaded the Cajun country from the same German sources that brought in the accordion and in the more lively-paced "two-step" rhythms later developed in the Cajun dance halls.

Music of this sort is entirely too loose to be an effective vehicle for religious purposes, hero worship, or nationalism—which require a martial orderliness of presentation Cajun music steadfastly denies. Cajun music is almost entirely secular and joyous. Sometimes it is unabashedly bawdy in its celebration of the sensual pleasures of life —but, Blanchet insists, "there is no worry about appropriateness for children." There is also a tinge of melancholy in some Cajun songs —abetted by the wailing sound of the instruments?—in which the singer laments "what life and fate have done to him," observes Holmes. "There is no attempt to conceal his misfortune, because nothing is his fault, anyway. He enjoys his suffering enough to want to tell the world about it." The most common affliction is the loved one who marries another. In many of these songs, the state of Texas makes an almost-ritualized guest appearance as the faraway place of self-imposed exile, escape, and attempts at recuperation from a broken heart. Human foibles, misfortunes, and ironic dilemmas are also often recycled into tales about animals (as surrogate people) in foolish predicaments: "Saute Crapaud," for example, where the frog does not jump fast enough and loses his tail. Other common characters are the *maringouin* (mosquito) and the alligator.

Whether joyous or melancholy, observes Revon Reed, the host at Fred's Lounge on Saturday mornings, the music always ends up coming back "down to earth," and never worries itself with abstract issues. "If a Cajun soul has a voice," he insists, "that voice is Cajun music."

In a concrete, rough-edged manner, Cajun music consistently promotes one set of values and world views in preference to other possibilities. Cajun music tells us it is better to live a full life, even with its pitfalls, than simply to exist, and that a full life lies close at hand, sometimes even within oneself. Cajun music tells us it is better to sing loudly and laugh coarsely than to curse fate or grumble about the human condition. And Cajun music relentlessly tells us, over and over again, that it is better to love and to trust than to fight and to fear.

Ambrose Thibodeaux leafs slowly through the scrapbook his daughter Leola made for him, a scrapbook for the memories not framed on the walls. You watch him and wonder if Cajun music is already a museum piece, another carcass for the nostalgia industry. Popular groups such as The Band ("Acadian Driftwood") and Taj Mahal ("Cajun Waltz") have paid tribute to the Cajuns and their music, but authentic Cajun folk music will require further attention to avoid extinction.

Ambrose Thibodeaux is doing his part. He can't read a note of music, but his head is a veritable jukebox of otherwise forgotten tunes. Tape recordings allow those tunes to be gathered and stored, so they can be imitated later without the direct laying-on of hands that marked their transmission when Thibodeaux was young.

The tape recorder that makes modern audio technology possible was already in widespread use when Ambrose Thibodeaux made his comeback—and he learned how to put it to an unusual use; he may be the first folk musician to have done so. Ambrose can compose music on a tape recorder, even though he can't read a note, because he can play pieces over and over again, erasing and rerecording until he gets it the way he wants it. The result is a score you can hear, instead of a score you can read—and the potential of Ambrose's technique is limitless. "After you know what the music is, you can assemble it in blocks," he says, and rearrange the blocks to make different tunes from the same vocabulary. A taped library of the constituent vocabulary of Cajun music—or jazz, or any other folk music, for that matter—could be the basis of an instructional course, perhaps even the cornerstone of a Louisiana Conservatory of Folk Music that could live on forever, at least technologically.

Ambrose Thibodeaux, in person, is a virtual one-man music school. Young accordion players come visiting all the time, to try to learn his style. He will play the tune or fragment he wants to teach, then hand the accordion to the student and criticize the student's try until the student finally gets it. "You have to be able to hear your mistakes in order to know how to get it right," he says. Ambrose figures he can teach his style to almost anyone, for interest is as important as talent. One of his favorite students was a young man who in polite conversation just happened to mention who his mother was. It turned out the man was the son of one of Ambrose's cousins, unbeknownst to either of them before this chance encounter. "I don't know you," Ambrose recalls telling the boy, "but I know who you are."

10

"Laissez les bons temps rouler"

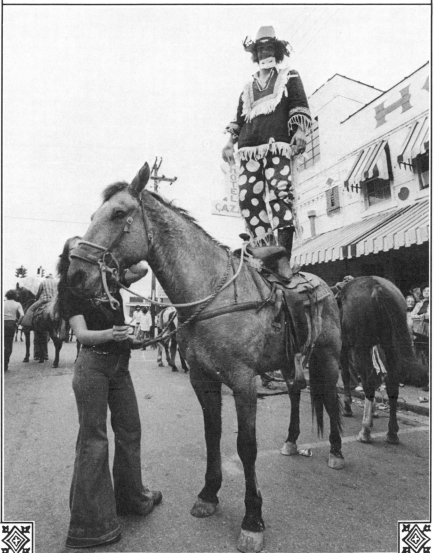

Mardi Gras rider, Mamou
DAVID RICHMOND

The highway to Mamou breaks away from the Interstate at Crowley and heads north through the Cajun prairie. The road is lined with continuous rice farms and cattle ranches—and the horizon is so flat that the occasional clumps of trees around coulees or farmhouses stand distinctly against the sky. The car's radio does not scoop up the sounds of Fred's Lounge this morning, however—for this is not Saturday, but Tuesday, Shrove Tuesday, Fat Tuesday, Mardi Gras.

Suddenly a band of horse-mounted, masked men materializes around the last bend and scatters, surprised, off the highway to the right and back, where the white rice elevator stands watch over a village well clumped with trees. Once again, it is Mamou. A side road from the highway leads through the fields and directly into the center of town, where Sixth Street is blocked off and crowded with Mardi Gras revelers.

Blink again. The masked riders are back in the farmyard now. There is horse sweat on the patchwork costumes, most of them baggy and one-piece, resembling clown suits crossed with jump suits. The hats are covered with scraps of the same fabrics, patches of cheap satin and old draperies with a little glitter. They peak like the hats of wizards and Kluxers and dunces; the Cajuns call them *capishons* (*capuchon*). The costumes are soaked not only with horse sweat but with the beer foaming from the cans in the hands of all the riders except their *capitaine*. He wears a cowboy hat but no mask, and they all fall silent behind him, behind their masks, looking you straight in the eye as he sings out, *"Voulez-vous recevoir les Mardi Gras?"*

The Mardi Gras maskers in his wake are received at farmhouses all over the Cajun prairie on the Tuesday morning of the "run"—for Mardi Gras is the last day of the previous year's calendar in the pre-Christian era's way of marking time. The stores of winter have sufficed so far, but must last until the coming of the first spring crops. The birth of the following year's growing cycle is reason enough to celebrate, but that celebration is of a very specific and essential sort

—one last splurge to honor the bounty of the past, followed by a period of reduced consumption in the warming weather until the ground gives forth sustenance again. When Catholicism spread over Western Europe, the Church turned this pagan celebration-and-pause sequence into Lent. In its original form, prudence was the point—not the guilt-ridden penitence that shifts around the calendar with each year's recalculation of Easter. Throughout their history, the Cajuns have never needed a forty-day rest to recuperate from their Mardi Gras. Moreover, Louisiana's early spring, which arrives at Mardi Gras instead of waiting for March's vernal equinox, is hardly a time conducive to penance.

The seasonal transition in Cajun country has evolved into a community ritual, a song, a chant. Everyone participates, for if you do not ride with the maskers, they will bring the party to your door. And if you are willing to receive the Mardi Gras, as both the maskers and the celebration are known, they will come into your farmyard to *faire le macaque* (make monkeyshines) and sing the remaining verses of their traditional Mardi Gras song. As the assembled family stand on the farmhouse galerie to watch, the Mardi Gras will dance, yell, and spill their beer over one another, all the while trying to disguise their voices behind the masks, and changing horses periodically to further their ruse.

The audience is endlessly amused, but fooled for only a short time, and as the anonymity wears off, the capitaine will step forward to lead his next call, demanding some small payment for the entertainment given by his Mardi Gras, *"Donnez-nous autres une 'tite poule grasse pour qu'on se fait un gumbo gras"*—"Give us a fat little chicken so we can make a big gumbo."

Instant replay: In video gray there is a "mystery chicken," a character from "The Good Times Are Killing Me," a Public Broadcasting Service documentary about the prairie Mardi Gras of 1975 in Mamou, Eunice, and Basile. The chicken squawks into the hand-held camera as both are carried from the farmhouse to a side field, where the chicken is thrown against the sun, and the Mardi Gras swarm through the screen, scattering costume remnants and chicken feathers through the last season's stubble. The successful captor holds the mystery chicken by the neck, and swings it, feathers and squawking everywhere, until it goes limp, then throws it into a pile of other strangled chickens in the pickup truck.

"Les Mardi Gras vous remercient bien pour votre bonne volonté!" the captain thanks his hosts, bringing the scene to an end. And he reminds them, as he happy-trails it with his drunken band to the next farmhouse down the road: *"On vous invite tous pour le gumbo gros et le bal à soir, mais là-bas."* Gumbo and dancing, over there, back in the tree-filled village under the rice spires.

The captain wears no mask. There is no chance, then, of wild bands of thieves marauding the Mardi Gras countryside in costume, despoiling what is left of the community's food supply. In fact, the group visit serves as a sort of community inspection of each farmhouse in the area, to make certain that no one will be left destitute until the spring—thereby eliminating the need for anything more disruptive than mock mischief.

3 P.M. Mardi Gras day on the main street of Mamou: the shouts are not what you hear first, but the horseshoes on the tarmac—the castanets of the hunchback in the rice cathedral, perhaps? Or steel cicadas in residence in the fields? Or just exhausted horses followed by whoops and car horns, *Mais oui!* Now they round the corner by the Hotel Cazan and ride into the middle of the crowd. The street has been blocked off to all traffic except that on foot, on horseback, or on the big flatbed trailer parked in the middle of the block. On the platform, Jack Leger, one of the Saturday broadcast regulars at Fred's Lounge just down the street, and his band speed up their tempo to welcome the riders with a smart, sassy salute. Some of the riders fall off their horses onto the platform; others fall off to the ground or are in some other way helped off their horses and into the nearest bar. Old women and LSU students, neighbors and cousins, all dance and whoop it up in the street, stopping only briefly to toast the riders before ducking inside a bar to grab another beer. Of the establishments that line both sides of Sixth Street, the main drag of downtown Mamou, the nine big enough to build signs projecting out over the sidewalk include five bars—Fred's Lounge, plus four others, that hose down the street with beer on Mardi Gras day.

But the Mardi Gras main event is to be found on Main Street, not Sixth Street. Around the corner from the Hotel Cazan, tucked away down the block, is Main Street's Evangeline post of the American Legion—where the riders have dropped off their chickens, and where the Mamou women are busily preparing the community-size "gumbo gros." Members of the Mamou Homemakers Club assemble at the kitchen of the Legion Hall Shrove Tuesday at 7 A.M., each member bringing along her homemade batch of roux. To supplement the dozen or so chickens and an occasional duck the riders will bring in later that afternoon, the cooks contribute three dozen "bought" hens, and start several pots a-cooking on the kitchen's big black stoves. Batches are taken outside at regular intervals and dumped into open iron kettles over a dugout pit's wood fire. Because of subtle differences in rouxs and pots and dumplings, no two bowls will taste exactly alike. You can test it for yourself, as many bowls as you want, ladled up at no charge. Though the gumbo is lagniappe, the limited number of bowls helps keep the crowd in the Legion Hall's side yard manageable. Finish your bowl and they'll wash it out in a soapy pan on a table by the kitchen door and pass it to the next hungry one to come along. Beer is sold all day long, and the eating continues until about 6:30 P.M., when everything pauses in anticipation of the big fais-dodo inside the hall from seven o'clock on.

Though variations of this celebration have existed for centuries, and were a regular part of the Cajun prairie until 1910, Les Mardi Gras des Grand Mamou are a comparatively recent invention of Mamou lawyer Paul Tate. In 1953 he became "captain for life" of the revived riding band, but he resigned a few years ago and picked Jasper Manuel as his successor. When the revival began, most of the participants were around the age of thirty-five, he recalls, but the range has since dropped to the early twenties. Women have periodically attempted to join the run—they have their own separate run in Church Point—and a few have even attempted to cross-dress and pass, Tate says, but the Mamou run remains male-only. "We don't claim to be democratic," he adds, rather relishing his role as a community patriarch. There's no committee to handle the arrangements, he says; "everyone just does it." Some of it is done out of the Sixth Street law

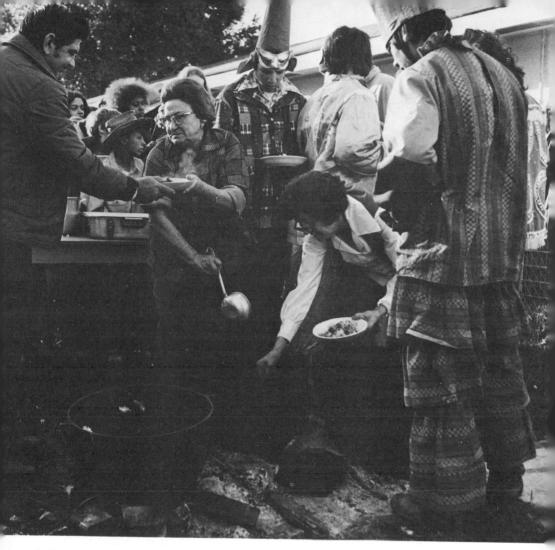

Gathering around the communal gumbo, Mardi Gras in Mamou   TURNER BROWNE

offices of Tate, Tate and Tate, a tan brick building with blue trim and a pink door, standing at the opposite end of the block from the Hotel Cazan and just across the street from Fred's Lounge, which is owned by Paul's cousin Fred Tate. Fred Tate, in turn, is Mamou-born singer Jimmy Newman's nephew, and on and on it goes—the typical tale of a Cajun family affair. Paul Tate freely admits that the revival of the Mardi Gras was an extended-family Cajun reunion. "It replaces funeral homes," he says dryly, downing another swig of beer. "You only have to come home one day a year this way. Even on a private visit, you won't have time to visit everyone from house to house—so seeing everyone in the street or over the gumbo pot keeps you from offending any relatives because you didn't 'pass by' to visit them at home." To visit a Cajun home, you must stay all day or you are considered rude—so the street, the gumbo, and the evening dance provide an easy, face-saving entertainment for all. Tate says 150 people come back annually from Lake Charles alone, and they keep streaming back from all the other area towns and villages as well. If you're from Mamou, you might end up mixing with five hundred or more known blood relatives by the time the day is over. "These people all know each other," he says, eyeing me with a scornful suspicion of the Mardi Gras I left back in New Orleans. "This is not a crowd of strangers."

The communal gumbo, with its Mardi Gras and fais-dodo attachments, is only one of the Cajuns' wide variety of self-entertainments. Any time of the day or year, the Cajuns can find a reason for getting together to put things into a common pot—later scooping out a whole greater than the sum of its parts. One such prairie practice during summers past was the *boucherie,* a communal slaughtering operation for cattle or hogs in the days before refrigeration, when fresh meat had to be eaten immediately to prevent spoilage. Cajun men, again usually interrelated, would arrange it with one man among them who was skilled as a butcher. Each participant except the butcher would bring one animal per week for a series of weeks equal to the number of families, sometimes as many as two dozen, choosing lots to see who was responsible for which week. The men would bring in their live-stock on the day before, usually Friday for a Saturday-morning carving up. The carving up would take place in a small shed, still commonly seen throughout the prairie. Inside the shed was a simple chopping block and a scale; outside, a raised crossbar for hoisting up the animal, and a pen where it spent its last night. The butcher divided the finished product into equal piles for the participants, plus one pile for himself for his trouble. The butcher brought no animal of his own—though today, in the informal variations that survive mainly among the black Cajuns, that practice may differ.

Regular cuts of meat were weighed and passed out, but brains, entrails, and other leftovers were put aside for the socializing part of the boucherie ritual. Intestines were stuffed with a mixture of chopped liver, brain, and other goodies, with onion, peppers, and garlic, and cooked in butter or oil in a big iron pot. Stomachs stuffed with this mixture are called *paunce bourré,* which is one of the Cajuns' most exotic dishes. Boudin sausages made in this manner usually include the slaughtered animal's blood, so that not even that is wasted. A bloodless white sausage, *boudin blanc,* is made with rice added to the stuffing. Boudin stands and even modern butchery/boudin-takeout stores have sprung up all over the French Triangle, for there is nothing quite like wasting away the afternoon on hot, spicy boudin and cold, cold beer; no self-respecting Cajun public activity is complete without them both.

For Louisiana Cajun wedding feasts, you'll find the beer and boudin outside, under the bride's parents' oak or chinaberry trees. The action moves inside only for the evening dancing. In days past, the actual ceremony was rarely attended by the mothers—who considered the event "too sad"—but by the evening's end, the whole community would be there to celebrate. Cajun courtship tended to be short and marriage early, and yet the girl was always free to say no—sometimes in the form of a paper-doll cutout of a young man sent to her suitor in an envelope, as a sign of rejection. Her father could speed up the process of getting her out of the house by painting the topmost part of his bousillage mud-and-stick chimney with whitewash, as a sign that a marriageable daughter was available within.

Of all their put-it-in-the-pot rituals, Cajun weddings were—in the old days, at least—the most extravagant. Judge Felix Voorhies, a Cajun from St. Martinville with a Dutch surname, whose grandmother told him stories, as a child, of her own childhood, relates in his 1907 volume, *Acadian Reminiscences:* "As soon as the marriage of a young couple was determined, the men of the village, after having built a cozy little home for them, cleared and planted the land parcelled out to them; and while they so generously extended their aid and assistance, the women were not laggards in their kindness to the bride. To her they made presents of what they deemed most necessary for the comfort and utility of her household, and all this was done and given with honest and willing hearts." After the wedding ceremony and feast, the village would march the newlyweds to their new home, and the party would continue into the night.

Though building and furnishing the newlyweds' house does not seem to have survived the transition from Canada to Louisiana, at least one element of the ritual is still carried on: flocking the bride. The community's women, who tended to the family's chickens and other fowl, would bring one young chick from each of their flocks to start up a new brood for the new bride. Of all the forms of sisterhood around the loom or the cooking pot, this traffic in future hens may have been one of the most important: for it was customary that wives could sell their surplus eggs for pocket money their husbands were never to control. The men were allowed to go out once a year in their masks to seize one chicken per farm—the only concession their wives would allow—which may, in part, explain why the men so adamantly refused to let the women join them on the ride!

The whole community was also expected to be involved in another kind of wedding celebration, called a *charivari,* reserved for those who marry late in life, or for a widow or widower starting out a second time around. The wedding ceremony itself would usually be private, sometimes even secret, and always quite beside the point as far as the rest of the community was concerned. It would be afterwards, when the newlyweds returned home, that the neighbors would arrive with pots and pans to raise a racket in celebration. The LSU Rural Life Museum includes in its collection some special charivari noisemakers, so elaborate was this ritual. However it was made, the charivari racket would continue until the newlyweds finally agreed to invite the neighbors in for dancing and gumbo—once again, an insistence that even the most private joys and decisions should always be celebrated with public and communal reinforcement.

The pots that are the most fascinating to watch the Cajuns fill are the ones they use when they gamble—those times of risk for unearned gain, times when life is rich enough that it doesn't matter if you lose.

Acadian boucherie de compagne, *1935*   LAUREN POST, LOUISIANA STATE UNIVERSITY
PRESS

In the Cajun-devised card game of *bourré,* the pot plays a role unlike
that in any other popular, contemporary card games. The word is
derived from *bourrer,* "to stuff"—as in such things as *paunce bourré.* In
the card game, it means to "stuff" the gambling pot: that's what the
loser must do.

A cross between poker and pidgin bridge, bourré is a fixture in
every Cajun bar's back room. In Mamou, the Hotel Cazan has a
bourré parlor fronting on the street; Fred Tate has one just off the
dance floor of his lounge, with two round tables and the old rawhide-
seat Cajun chairs. The lampshades over each table are taped and
patched, and suspended from the ceiling with old ropes that anchor
them back to the wall—where a small sign suggests a $5 pot with a
50-cent bottom limit.

The game is played with all fifty-two cards, but no jokers or wild
cards. Two to eight can play, but the mathematics are most interesting
when five, six, or seven play. After each player has anted up, the
dealer deals five cards down, one at a time to each player, and turns
up his own fifth card to determine the trump suit.

The object of the game is to win the largest possible number of
tricks from the five, playing one card per participant in succession. If

you don't think you have a chance to win at least one, you can bow out before the play begins. If you play and win no tricks—and here comes the punch line—you get bourréd and must fill the pot with the ante for all the players' next game. That game will be played at your expense with the same number of chips as were in the pot for the game you just lost. Whoever takes the most tricks wins the pot, and as long as you keep winning it periodically, you can afford to play.

Bourré has acquired a fearsome reputation outside Louisiana, because if you keep losing, you can end up losing big. In a game of five players, one player need win only two tricks to win the pot, while three others remain safe with one trick apiece and the fifth one bourrés. If you don't have a good hand, it's better to chicken out early, or else you might find yourself thrown in, squawking, to feed the pot.[1]

The moment of truth comes after the dealer has turned over the game's trump suit and has offered the players an opportunity to exchange any or all their cards—like draw poker. You can stay in and bet further on your hand, or you can drop out, beginning to the dealer's left, where play also starts. Since everyone is playing against everyone else, and since all would like to see someone else in the group bourré the next round's pot, the play is nothing short of cutthroat.

The Cajun gambling fever is a year-round part of the way life is celebrated in Louisiana. It is part of the cycle that follows the sun, the Cajun festivals, and the fais-dodos throughout the year, accompanied by dancing and boudin and beer. The fever peaks in the Cajun horse-racing season, for every small town has its quarterhorse track; it eases in the late fall and winter, during the long nights before the dawn of Mardi Gras, when the instinct for survival is certain to gnaw most intensely.

Winter in south Louisiana is unpredictable. New Orleans lies at the same latitude as Shanghai and Cairo—the worldwide sunbelt—so that clear, warming, sunny days are the winter's general rule. Cold weather comes most frequently with sundown, or with the occasional front moving in from the north and west, spilling cold thundershowers everywhere when it hits the warmer, moist Gulf air. By Thanksgiving, these weather monsters can kill banana trees or burst exterior water pipes when the temperature plummets thirty or forty degrees in just a few hours. Winter in the south of Louisiana is nothing like the winter of Acadia, however, for it won't kill you directly; and if snows ever reach as far down as the 30th parallel, they usually do so only as a New Year's salute to the Sugar Bowl. Something of the threat implied in that northerly wind, however, survives with the Cajuns, who begin one of their most secretive social rituals right after the American Thanksgiving, on weekend evenings when you can huddle together until three or four in the morning in warm defiance of the glacial shivers awaiting you outside.

The wind is cold and quiet and stills momentarily as you pull abreast of a nondescript cinder-block wall, part of a small, windowless shed built behind a roadside nightclub at Cankton—a town that is really just a few houses and a roadside sign north of Lafayette just over the St. Landry Parish line. It is not only quiet but dark, for there are no windows in the shed, and only by feeling your way along the wall do you suddenly find a wooden plank door hinged to it. Even if you have your gloves on, it feels rough and weathered with cracks, through one or two of which a thin light burns as bright as it burns cold, almost blue. The door opens to an entryway narrowed like Tut's tomb, but lined with concrete blocks in lieu of carved rock. There is a plywood covering over the low-ceilinged passageway, and beyond it—slightly higher—there is the low white ceiling of the widening room inside the shed. That ceiling is shiny from its four rows of surface fluorescent lighting tubes, arranged parallel but looking from below as if they were radiating out above you. The end of the passageway is blocked with people, and the bleacher seats built into the walls are also filled with people in a way that obstructs your view of what else is going on in the crowded little room—though you can soon see as many as a hundred heads. No one heard the door squeak open, for all hundred are talking at once, and even the man standing an arm's length in front must be poked to secure his attention. He turns and steps aside, jostling the man in front of him, who does likewise, and through a crack in the people, the central object of the room's atten-

Crawfish race, Breaux Bridge crawfish festival TURNER BROWNE

tion can be seen in a flash of feathers and squawks. Two roosters tear the shit out of each other; sprays of blood and ripped plumage hang in the dust cloud inside the dirt ring or are splashed out through the chicken-wire enclosure that demarcates it. Pay a buck to the big fat man in the pocketed apron who has pushed his way over to staple a torn business card to your lapel and you can come in to sit, if you can find a seat, and watch.

You can also bet on the outcome of each cockfight; and so Jay's Lounge and Cockpit in Cankton is one of the most wide-open and heavily patronized roadhouses in the French Triangle, where on the nearby dance floor musicians like Clifton Chenier do regular gigs and the beer flows freely until dawn, even on Sunday. In Louisiana, cockfighting is a local option, left to the discretion of the sheriff—at the express wish of the current Cajun governor, Edwin Edwards, and with the acquiescence (1972) of the Louisiana Supreme Court. It is not particularly lucrative for anyone, for the betting pools for a whole room full of people seldom exceed $100 per fight. That means you can double anything you bet, and lose it just as easily, just like bourré. The betting is mostly among family and cockfighters and friends, anyway—a deterrent to Anglo fears of "organized crime." Governor

Edwards says he sees no reason to prohibit cockfights, though he also says he "wouldn't walk across the street to see one," in part because his own sporting ways tend more toward Las Vegas gambling tables.

When the governor says, *"Laissez les bons temps rouler,* Let the good times roll," he means dice. He sums up the prevailing French Triangle attitude: "I've won more than I've lost, and I'm a tight son of a bitch —I could stop tomorrow." And with just slightly lowered tail feathers: "I'll never retire on what I've won"—he laughs—"or go bankrupt on what I've lost."

Winning or losing at cockfighting is like winning or losing at bourré or life—it's largely a matter of luck. But that doesn't stop Cajun cockers from trying to breed what they hope will be prize gamecocks. From 1940 through 1965, the terror of the Louisiana cock rings were the Duhon brothers of Lafayette—Ben, who worked for USL, and Osa, a school-bus driver. They cross-bred local roosters— mostly with smooth bodies, few feathers, and nasty tempers—with Asil varieties from Texas and an imported strain of Spanish roosters from a mysterious Mr. Thrasher in Kentucky. The Duhons were not effectively challenged until 1959, when a three-man syndicate in Crowley took Asils from California and India to blend with the Texas and Kentucky birds. Jay Saucier of Cankton, who has been breeding fighting roosters for the last quarter century, came into prominence after both those groups had declined, opening his own dance hall and pit nine years ago. The hundred or so birds in his collection—a low figure, he assures us, since seventy or so of them are young biddies —live in a wire-and-wood city of separated roosts in the field behind his nightclub. He trains them inside an eight-foot pen, chasing each one around and around with a red bandanna on a stick. To make them even more muscle-bound, Saucier has his own special training secrets, such as an inclined platform covered with carpet remnants that he makes the chickens climb "to build up the strength in their legs." At the end of their training sessions, they are rubbed down with alcohol, just like boxers.

The nights they fight, they are weighed on a scale, on a small shelf at one corner of the ring, with a bet collector watching to make certain that any two opponents will be within two ounces of each other's

Cockfight at Jay's Lounge, Cankton   TURNER BROWNE

weight. "That's equivalent to five pounds in a man," says Jay, as he wraps his next bird. Shaving its natural spurs with a pocketknife, while the rooster tries to bite off a shirt button, he can fit a larger and longer spur over the resulting stub. The fighting spurs are natural, grown from a different set of birds that are bred to grow long ones. Removed, they are "cured" by drying and filled with progressively smaller spurs and a little glue to make a more solid, and more vicious, but still entirely natural, fighting spike. He attaches it with surgical tape.

There is a collection of Mexican roosters in Cankton for this evening's match, accompanied by a shy party of men in one corner who drink their tequila straight from the bottle and joyously pass it around to all takers in the crowd. An occasional rooster will be set down between matches to exercise in the pit, where it nervously runs in circles for fear of being stepped on by the bettors who climb into the pit to check out the combatants personally and to trade pleasantries with the owners.

At last it is time for the match to begin, and the ring is cleared of everyone but the referee and two trainers, who cradle their birds in crossed arms as if they were about to coo a lullaby. The roosters in the wooden, pitch-roofed carrying cages scattered around the room sense the excitement as the room's din diminishes, diminishes enough so you can hear them crow. The trainers step toward one another sideways, their chickens' necks reaching out into the open space between them, snapping and recoiling like serpents.

Opening thrusts and parries, once the roosters are riled up enough to be released, go mainly for the tail feathers. But the fiery Mexican birds jump higher than their Louisiana cousins, landing with wings flapping and spikes flailing. Jay's bird, its sleek black feathers trimmed with a downy gold the color of rice shocks, goes beak-first for the head. Both birds have their combs deliberately clipped back away from the eyes, because fighting cocks will always lunge for the comb —and if they were to hit the eye instead, the match might end prematurely from blindness, instead of from fighting skill. When Jay's bird finally succeeds in grabbing the Mexican's comb, he throws him into the dust for a few sharp kicks. It looks like judo with feathers constantly in the way, as both birds fly at each other, jab, and fall back, and each raises his head through the other's feathers in a dizzying progression of hammerlocks and pirouettes.

If one rooster fails to fight before the referee has counted to ten, the birds are separated while he counts to twenty. Each trainer grabs his bird in the meantime, washing off the blood. Jay leans over and opens his mouth over the black and gold bird's glistening neck and blows gently to cool and calm it down; he utters a few words of encouragement. His all-time favorite rooster—named Blind Man because he eventually lost both eyes—went for a record twelve fights before finally meeting his match. Although some of Jay's chickens last as long as three years, their prime is between twelve and eighteen months. Jay doesn't have names for all of them. He has no name for the black warrior he throws back into the center of the pit at the referee's signal.

They're at it again, after a brief territorial run around the pit. One collision almost throws them over the protective chicken-wire barrier and into the audience. The spurs gouge holes in the breast or neck or head, and by now both birds' heads are bleeding. One weak moment and the black one stands still, while the Mexican bird rolls over, away from the kick. If the referee finishes his count without either bird attacking, the match is called a draw. But the black bird turns, regains its breath, and lunges again, sending the Mexican through the air and on its back, flopping around. The Mexican trainer concedes the match —and both birds, injured fairly seriously by rooster standards, are retrieved for that odd, cradled hold again, and a few loving wipes with warm water. Those that lose won't make it into a gumbo like the spring birds of Mardi Gras. Those that last will be back on their own two feet eventually, strutting those feathers, determined to live yet another day. "They're tough enough to fight," jokes Saucier, stroking and comforting his still-shaking rooster, "but too tough to eat."

Cajun Portrait Gallery

Evangeline

Evangeline Bellefontaine, "God's little angel," the "bearer of good news," is the reigning superstar of Acadian folklore and mythology. Glenn Conrad, director of the Center for Louisiana Studies at the University of Southwestern Louisiana, has counted 270 editions of Henry Wadsworth Longfellow's 1847 narrative, plus another 250 books and scholarly articles produced for the centennial of her sad sojourn. There have also been 130 translations, three plays, six orchestral productions, and an opera done in her honor. In the person of Dolores Del Rio, the tragic heroine made her debut on the silver screen in the 1929 classic *Evangeline*. Miss Del Rio subsequently posed for a statue that was donated to the town of St. Martinville, where stands the fabled Evangeline oak, under which she is said to have espied her long-lost Gabriel. According to a tale popularized by St. Martinville judge Felix Voorhies, his grandmother adopted an orphan named Emmeline Labiche when both were exiles in Maryland en route to Louisiana. Emmeline allegedly went mad after discovering, under her oak, that fiancé Louis Arceneaux had given her up for lost and married another woman. The rough outline of this tale was supposedly passed on to Longfellow by Nathaniel Hawthorne via a minister friend. Using William Darby's 1816 book on Louisiana geography —Longfellow had not visited either Louisiana or Acadia—the poet completed his own version of the story in a mere four months. Its reception has not been unanimously favorable, however. In 1848, a critic by the name of G. W. Peck opined that the work was "not really fine, but tawdry." Today the verses are considered by most critics as old-fashioned, rather than classic. Judge Voorhies's cousin Franklin Mouton is positively incensed by the legend of the poem's source: "His grandmother was a Mouton born in Lafayette, and not a refugee foster mother from Acadia."

A symbol of the Acadian diaspora, Evangeline—whoever she was—has nevertheless become a widespread commercial success; she has lent her name to the world's only Acadian daily newspaper, and to everything else from bread companies to highways. There are twenty-five commercial Evangeline entries in the Lafayette telephone directory alone, including a beauty salon, a paint company, a seafood market, and a chiropractic clinic.

"Gabriel's Heir"

Thomas J. Arceneaux, Dean Emeritus of the College of Agriculture at the University of Southwestern Louisiana, is a descendant of the family of Louis Arceneaux. According to local legend, Louis was the model for Gabriel Lajeunesse in Longfellow's *Evangeline.* Also according to legend, pirate Jean Laffite buried some of his long-lost treasure at the Arceneaux family's plantation in Carencro, now a suburb of Lafayette.

In his own right, Dean Arceneaux is the designer of the Louisiana Acadian flag. It was commissioned by France-Amérique de la Louisiane Acadienne in 1965, and is now seen across Louisiana's French Triangle in forms ranging from auto license plates to corporate logos to official city seals.

"To symbolize the French origin of the Acadians," explains Arceneaux, "a portion of the arms of their mother country—three fleurs-de-lis, silver on a blue field—is used as part of the flag. To symbolize Spain, the nation which controlled Louisiana at the time of the Acadian migration to Louisiana and under which they prospered after years of exile, the old arms of Castile—a gold tower on a red field—appear in one section of the flag. The gold star on a white field represents Our Lady of the Assumption (Maris Stella), patroness of the Acadians. The star also symbolizes the active participation of the Acadians in the American Revolution, as soldiers under Gálvez."

Dean Arceneaux, a member of the faculty at USL for thirty-one years, until he retired in 1973, trained almost singlehandedly an entire generation of Cajun rice and cattle farmers and county agents. He supervised extensive research into chemical control of south Louisiana's luxuriant weeds, and also designed technical assistance projects for underdeveloped French-speaking countries in the Third World. In 1955, he chaired the steering committee for Louisiana's Acadian Bicentennial celebration.

Yankee Cajun

There are those who call him Louisiana Lightnin', and others who prefer the Ragin' Cajun, or just 'Gator. By any name, the Ron Guidry they're talking about has become the best-known Cajun in the country. For his performance in the New York Yankees 1978 championship season, he was unanimously voted the Cy Young Award for the best pitcher in baseball.

Consider his 1978 accomplishments: a 25–3 season record, the highest winning percentage (.893) in baseball history; nine shutouts, tying a 1916 record set by a Boston pitcher named Babe Ruth; a new American League record for strikeouts in a single game (18). There are those who feel Guidry's early season efforts (he was 13–0 at a time when the Yankees, without him, would have been 31–33) kept his team's hopes alive long enough for them to edge out Boston in the pennant race. Even with his history of arm trouble, Guidry beat Boston three times in the last twenty-four days of the season, giving up not a single loss, and won a crucial game in the World Series, too.

Son of a Southern Pacific railroad conductor from Lafayette, the lithe and quiet-spoken Guidry was an early all-star sports standout. Former grade-school classmates recall that when he stepped up to pitch, the game was as good as over. Though offered scholarships to Notre Dame and other major sports schools, he decided to stay at home-town USL and study architecture. In 1971 he was signed by the Yankees and left school, spending several years shuffling back and forth to farm clubs before his first big break at the end of 1977—when he won eight of his last nine games.

When not playing baseball, he says, he'd rather be back in Louisiana hunting with childhood friends. Like many Louisiana refugees in the Big Apple, Guidry imports certain essential food supplies from home. "I'm not about to go six months without real coffee," he asserts, not able to stand the weak substitute served in New York. He brought fellow Yankee pitcher Jim 'Catfish' Hunter home for gumbo once, but "never again. I didn't get anything to eat."

Cajun Schoolteachers

Ed and Catherine Blanchet were dissatisfied with the Cajun cultural awareness their seven children were getting from Louisiana's public schools, so they decided to build one of their own. Located on their farm at Meaux, between Lafayette and Abbeville, their school opened its doors in 1971, offering instruction in all twelve grades.

The schoolhouse has four rooms around a central hallway that also doubles as a library between visits of the parish bookmobile. One room is used for elementary grades taught by an assistant from Lafayette, while Catherine teaches music in another room, and Ed teaches other courses in a third. Everyone joins in the art and weaving activities in the fourth room. Both Blanchets were trained as teachers: Ed in math and education at USL and LSU; Catherine in music at Sophie Newcomb College and later at USL, where she completed her master's degree with a thesis on children's songs from the surrounding Vermilion Parish countryside. Both conversational Cajun French and standard written French are taught, the former using James Faulk's Cajun grammar book, which emphasizes Vermilion dialect. And all students participate in a performing group that presents Cajun folk songs and dances at various Louisiana festivals and museums.

"Traiteur"

Gloria Breaux Ducrest of Broussard is a "treater," or practitioner of Cajun folk medicine. Trained as a nurse at Catholic Hôtel Dieu Hospital in New Orleans, and married to the village pharmacist, she discovered her "gift" only in 1959. A devout Catholic, she keeps an image of Our Lady of Perpetual Help near the kitchen sink of her modern ranch house and firmly rejects any suggestion that her healing powers conflict with established Church doctrine.

In accordance with the usual pattern among Cajun treaters, she is left-handed and is the niece of an earlier treater in the family. Gloria's first patient was the doctor who had hired her as his nursing assistant, and she now receives regular referrals from other medical personnel, and occasionally even clergy. Though she has treated a variety of ailments, she says her specialty is warts.

Unlike some other Cajun treaters, she uses no special rites or accessories. Belief in the process is essential, she says, for those seeking treatment for themselves, but at the request of third parties, she will also treat patients who may be unaware of her intervention. Healing does not need to be done in person; it can be done by telephone. She accepts no fees, explaining that she is only the vehicle for this healing power, not its source.

Born in Rayne on Louisiana's Cajun prairie, she is Aunt Gloria to Crowley's Seventh District Cajun Congressman John Breaux, the son of her brother. Has she ever treated the Congressman? No. She laughs. But she once treated his daughter Beth for—of course—a case of warts.

Cajun Confederate Hero

Standing in a small triangular park in front of Lafayette's City Hall is a 1922 statue erected in memory of General Alfred Mouton by the United Daughters of the Confederacy. The park stands at what is now the political center of Lafayette, with the French-Spanish Trade Mart (housing the offices of the Council for the Development of French in Louisiana, CODOFIL) on one side and the American Bank tower (housing the offices of the Quebec legation) on the other.

The statue's inscription reads "Raised a company of Confederate volunteers 1861, which became part of 18th Louisiana Regiment of which he became colonel. He led his regiment at Battle of Pittsburgh Landing 1862. He was severely wounded at Battle of Shiloh, April, 1863, and promoted to rank of Brigadier General. Died Battle of Mansfield, April 8, 1864," when he was only thirty-five years old.

Alfred, son of Louisiana's first Cajun governor, Alexander Mouton, was a leading figure in the Battle of Labadieville on Bayou Lafourche, and is credited with capturing a contingent of Yankee forces at Brashear City (now Morgan City). It is perhaps a measure of both the Cajuns' antebellum prosperity and their legendary resistance to political intervention that Louisiana's main Civil War action—after the fall of New Orleans—was concentrated in Cajun areas. After recapturing Brashear City, Yankee forces fought their way up Bayou Teche one bend at a time, fending off constant guerrilla attacks while the main Confederate army evaporated every time the invaders tried to charge. In this manner, Confederate forces drew their bedraggled Yankee prey as far north as Mansfield, where Mouton and his men finally prevailed. Unfortunately, the victorious leader was shot from his horse by a Yankee sniper after ordering his own men to cease fire.

"Mouton Blanc et Mouton Noir"

J. Franklin Mouton III is a thirty-three-year-old graduate of Pratt Institute who gave up a New York design career—cosmetic packaging, Lord & Taylor windows, among other things—to return to Louisiana to find his roots. After seven years of research, he has managed to track down almost every descendant of Salvador and Jean Diogène Mouton. According to Louisiana legend, they were the first Acadian settlers to arrive in the state.

Among the cousins Franklin found was Oscar Dewey Mouton, sixty-eight, a retired jazz musician and house painter who now raises black Angus cattle on a modest gentleman farmer's thirty-one-acre spread just outside Lafayette—the Cajun capital city founded by their common ancestors. They are pictured sitting on the grave of Oscar's paternal grandfather and grandmother—a black Haitian beauty named Mathilde Schoal. In 1888, she married Charles Alexander Mouton in Lafayette's Roman Catholic Cathedral of St. John the Evangelist, which towers over the graveyard. Charles Alexander was the brother of Civil War hero Alfred Mouton, the son of Governor Alexander Mouton, and the grandson of Lafayette's founder, Jean Mouton —who donated the land for the cathedral.

Franklin and Oscar are also distantly related through Oscar's maternal great-grandfather, Solasty Roy, once one of the wealthiest planters on Bayou Teche. Solasty had several white and black wives, and one of them was the mother of P. S. Roy—Oscar's grandfather, and the only black man in the South ever to own his own cotton gin.

Oscar Mouton plays alto saxophone, and during 1932–35 toured Louisiana with the band of Willie "Bunk" Johnson, a trumpeter who is said to have had a major influence on Louis Armstrong.

Bayou Refugee

New Iberia-born Jim de la Houssaye was a Ph.D. biologist teaching college in Arizona when he finally decided to abandon the rigors of academia and go back home. He moved a trailer house into an isolated section of Bayou Teche between Franklin and Jeanerette, and now supports his wife and child by fishing. He fishes mainly for catfish, using primitive equipment: a trotline (multiple hooks on one line) and an occasional hoop net he makes himself. "If you can get into macrame, you can get into this," he jokes.

In July 1975, he and three other men—who would sometimes break the loneliness of nighttime fishing with coffee and a little chat—decided to form Louisiana Freshwater Fisheries, Inc. The proposed cooperative would serve fresh-water fishermen in and around the massive Atchafalaya Basin, the Everglades of Louisiana. Collection points would be set up in Catahoula, Bayou Sorrel, Pierre Part, and Franklin, and a main dock and processing plant would be established next to a crawfish plant in the Indian village of Charenton. De la Houssaye's half-million-dollar project is still awaiting word on a grant requested from the federal government. He estimates that the 175 fishermen eligible to participate could harvest an annual crop worth $1.3 million—though under current conditions they may receive as little as 27 cents per pound for their catfish.

Organizing the co-op has proved to be slow going. "They're a mostly self-sufficient group," he says of his fellow fishermen; many of them are illiterate and still living in isolated communities that can be reached only by boat.

But, despite the hardships, de la Houssaye finds his new life "immediate and satisfying." With twentieth-century communications and conveniences stripped away, the result, he says, is a life where he is dependent "only on the weather and my own energies."

Clifton Chenier

Storm clouds gather over the hazed-in skyscraper towers in the distance, and the breeze flaps the huge blue canopy over the outdoor stage. It is the 1978 New Orleans Jazz Festival—and it's time for the last act on the last day. Doing the honors is Clifton Chenier and his Red Hot Louisiana Band; the storm clouds are held mysteriously at bay while the crowd gathers round to cheer one of its favorite favorites.

The stage crew wears Clifton Chenier T-shirts. Most of the band wear emerald-green suits. The saxophone player, looking like a banker in a three-piece gray suit, leads the group through its first set. Only then does Clifton Chenier emerge—his shiny mocha Palm Beach suit just a shade lighter than he is. The fingers dancing across his Hohner accordion ivories are covered with rings of the same gold that flashes generously in his smile.

And Clifton Chenier is full of smiles as his band launches into a dizzying repertoire that ranges from rhythm and blues to jazz and rock. The accordion and saxophone are a surprisingly strong combination throughout. Chenier's brother Cleveland plays a rub board strapped across his chest. Clifton's accordion straps are tied behind him with an old necktie, and he wears a headband to hold down his sweat-soaked curly hair.

"Blues boogie's all right," he shouts when he has succeeded in driving the sea of hats, sunglasses, and bare shoulders into a screaming, beer-swilled frenzy. "But I'm a Frenchman." With that, his playing takes on a new flavor. He clips his accordion runs in much the same way the Cajuns and black Creoles around his native Opelousas clip their French. Occasionally, he'll linger over a Cajun riff and transform it into a jazz pirouette before coming back to the basic tune.

Now a national cult figure, Clifton Chenier and his Zydeco group are still strongly rooted in the tradition of what Louisiana's country people call a "chanky-chank" band. As his hour's performance draws to a close, he pauses to announce, "Here's one for the Cajuns—for all you people from the bayou." When the roar subsides, Clifton Chenier is singing in French, polishing off the set with "Jolie Blonde."

The Kings

The tilted crown is a recurring visual image in the French Triangle, signifying success by merchants and other assorted characters. Lafayette businessman Albert LeBlanc strikes this pose on homemade billboards for all his enterprises, though his original claim to fame is as the King of Mobile Home sales. Another LeBlanc, a jeweler, styles himself the King of Diamonds. The proprietor of Lagneaux's Restaurant is the self-proclaimed King of Seafood. Zydeco musician Clifton Chenier can still be seen in old publicity pictures garbed as the King of Zydeco—but legend has it that his colleague Gatemouth Brown, who wears a Stetson cowboy hat, kept ribbing Chenier until he finally gave up wearing his crown in public.

FOR
LEASE

COMMERCIAL

ALBERT
Le BLANC

984-0461

Cajun Newspaper Publisher

Revon Reed has emerged as the dean of Cajun letters. Trained by the Christian Brothers and now retired from teaching, he wrote the first book describing Cajun Louisiana in a mixture of standard and Cajun French (*Lâche pas la patate,* published by a subsidiary of the Parti Quebeçois in Montreal in 1976). He also helped launch a small Louisiana magazine devoted to the intricacies of local culture, and has most recently decided to turn his home base of Mamou into a two-newspaper town.

Reed's *Mamou Prairie* is unlike anything else in English or French journalism. Resolutely local in advertisements and emphasis, it offers a mixture of stories in English and Cajun French. Though its circulation is small, the *Mamou Prairie* is rich in humor, particularly in its tales of Sosthene and his dog, Fideaux.

In telling the history of Mamou, which was founded in 1907, Reed can concoct a myriad of explanations for the town's unusual name. "Mamou" is variously explained as an Indian word from the Mobilian dialect, an African word for sweetheart, or a word derived from the Russian. In yet another version, an English-language newspaper is credited with describing the area as a "mammouth prairie," later spelled "mamouth" and pronounced by the Cajuns as "mamout'", or, ultimately, "Mamou."

Reed's favorite version begins with settlers bringing their cattle into the area. The calves would cry out "maa" for their dinner; and their mothers would respond with a "moo."

Cajun Governor

At the age of fifty-one, Louisiana's only modern Cajun governor, Edwin Edwards, is still matinee-idol handsome and always flamboyantly dressed. His mother was a Cajun, and of his childhood in Avoyelles Parish—the apex of Louisiana's French Triangle—he says, "I do not remember when I could *not* speak French." His father, of Welsh heritage mixed with Cajun blood, was a sharecropper with a third-grade education, used a mule to plant his cotton and sweet potatoes, and later grew prosperous enough to open a one-room general-merchandise store. In 1933, young Edwards started first grade in a one-room schoolhouse and vividly recalls the days when official state policy forbade the speaking of French on school grounds.

Having completed high school, college, and law school, at the age of twenty-one he moved to Crowley in 1949 as "one of only two attorneys who could write a French will." As late as the early 1960's, he recalls, older clients would flock to his office because he continued to conduct his practice in French. Elderly witnesses in simple land-title suits or divorce actions or auto-accident cases were often questioned in French; English interpreters were used for preparing the final court record.

From his first election to a seat on the Crowley City Council in 1954, he moved successfully to the State Senate and the U.S. Congress before returning to Louisiana for the hotly contested governor's race of 1971. With a skillfully conceived coalition of voters from the French Triangle and upstate urban areas, Edwards narrowly squeaked through—the first French-speaking Catholic candidate in almost half a century to break the political hammerlock of north Louisiana's Protestants.

Edwards hated life in Washington, and claims he has no plans to return there or to leave the state for any reason when he completes his second term. Prohibited from seeking a third consecutive term, he is toying with sitting it out for four years and running for governor again in 1983.

An irrepressible wit, he tells endless stories like the one about the elderly Cajun woman who confided to him after his first-term election, "I sure am glad we have a governor who don't have no accent." Edwards neither drinks nor smokes and doesn't dance—but he loves to gamble, hunt, and cook. When dealing with Protestants or Yankees, he speaks flawless English. But when dealing with the folks back home—or ladies of any variety—he shifts effortlessly into a *chère* here or a *c'est bon* there. "You'd be surprised"—he winks—"how it warms them up."

284

George Febres 72.

Appendices

Moonlight on the Teche, 1885. Illustration originally appeared in Harper's
HISTORIC NEW ORLEANS COLLECTION

The heart of the Cajun culture is its language. And the heart of modern Cajun cultural politics is a cutthroat debate over what form Louisiana's French language preservation/revival effort should take. The debaters fall into two general camps: the forces of orthodoxy gathered around the Council for the Development of French in Louisiana (CODOFIL), a government-funded agency, who insist on the use of standard French; and a loosely organized, sometimes utterly disorganized band of dissidents who stubbornly insist that the Cajuns should speak their own brand of French, *merci.*

Although standard French and Cajun French share a number of elements, the Cajun patois comes very close to what its purist critics roundly denounce as "Frenglish," or, more frequently, just "bad French." Not only are there numerous incursions of English words and sounds and usages—you'll also find miscellaneous scraps from Spanish, German, Portuguese, and Italian, as well as words and ideas taken intact from the cultures of neighboring blacks and Indians. And, to make matters worse, Cajun French is entirely oral, lacking both a body of written literature and grammatical standardization. Revon Reed's *Lâche pas la Patate* (1976) was the first book ever written in the language the Cajuns speak—and its CODOFIL reception was lukewarm, at best.

Outright hostility greeted the publication of the first Cajun grammar book, *Cajun French I,* in June 1977. This 375-page volume, written by former Crowley High School language instructor James Donald Faulk, was developed during a three year trial period in his country classroom and focuses primarily on the version of Cajun spoken in Vermilion Parish. It includes an 87-page glossary with over 3,000 entries—no small task to compile. Composed on a typewriter and illustrated with stick-figure cartoons, Faulk's book was printed privately in Michigan and sold at $18.95 a copy (plus 80 cents handling, from The Cajun Press, Route 4, Box 388-E-3, Abbeville, Louisiana 70510). Word of its publication spread so rapidly over Louisiana and the French-speaking world that the first edition of a thousand was soon sold out. Cajun-born Faulk did undergraduate work in French and Spanish at the University of Southwestern Louisiana and graduate work leading to a master's degree at the University of Missouri—then taught French in Louisiana high schools for two decades. From the outset, Faulk decided to use a phonetic system of his own devising, based almost entirely on English sounds, and wrote all the Cajun French words and phrases in that phonetic system only. To the horror of CODOFIL partisans, he refused to add a third column of standard French spellings.

The project originated with a complaint from one of Faulk's students: "I've been learning French so long, and I still can't speak to my grandma!" Most of his Cajun students are headed for local oil or farming jobs after graduation from high school, and, for them, learning standard French seems to make less sense than learning Cajun. Even those who go on to college but settle in the French Triangle need to know at least some Cajun French to do their work most effectively. Considering the problem of medical care for elderly rural residents who speak little, if any, English, Faulk included an entire chapter of specialized Louisiana terms for health and the body. "It's for our own good," he insists, and whether CODOFIL likes it or not, "Cajun French is part of our heritage."

Not all of Faulk's fellow Cajuns, however, share his pride or enthusiasm. Professor Barry Ancelet, director of USL's Cajun folklore center, opposes Faulk's system of phonetic Cajun as applied to the written word. He points out that "Southern children never see 'y'all' written on the blackboard, but they all learn to use it anyway and they all know what it means." Ancelet—who works closely with CODOFIL—wants his students to learn enough "good" French to be able to communicate with other members of the French community in the world beyond Louisiana, and on an equal basis.

Professor Richard Chandler, chairman of foreign languages at USL, takes a middle-of-the road position, proposing that Faulk's course be taught in Louisiana schools as an adjunct to standard French. And Cajuns who carp about Faulk's methodology could always have written the first grammar book themselves, he snaps.

The controversy is most intense at Louisiana State University's main campus in Baton Rouge—where CODOFIL's Lafayette-based political influence is less strong. In the fall of 1977, after Faulk's book was published, a determined group of Cajun undergraduates succeeded in forcing LSU to offer an elective Cajun French course. "Les Cajuns," as they call themselves —still denied official campus recognition and funding as a student group— draw unremitting fire from CODOFIL chairman James Domengeaux. Ulysse Ricard, a graduate student in linguistics who teaches the Cajun French course at LSU, replies: "Francien was not adopted as the official language of France until the King's edict of Villers-Cotterets in 1539," and there were fifteen different dialects from which to choose and standardize a common tongue. L'Académie Francaise—the committee appointed to work out the standardization details—was not organized until 1633, well after immigration to Acadia had begun. And the Academy's dictionary, which synthesized Burgundian pronunciation and northern grammar, was not issued until 1694. The Cajuns, then, had their language before there ever was a standard French —and those who look down on the rich Cajun patois are, in Ricard's view, "linguistically naïve."

Not only is Cajun French different from the Parisian-accented idiom that is now accepted as standard or "true" French, but both differ from "joual" —the French of Quebec (the word is archaic for *cheval,* horse). These three differ markedly from the Caribbean-influenced French spoken by Louisiana's largely rural black Creoles. And all four differ markedly from the once-flourishing Creole French of white New Orleans. In his pseudonymous *Les Francophones de Louisiane,* Jean-Jacques Peyronnet, France's former consul-general in New Orleans, notes that Louisiana's upper-class "Creoles speak French the way that Tolstoy spoke French"—more as a cultural affectation than as a living language. CODOFIL posters urge: *"Soyez à la mode: parlez français"*—but, protests Peyronnet, *which* French?

Les Cajuns have countered with two additional grammar books. Ricard's *Lagniappe: A Louisiana French Reader*—a compilation of Cajun and Creole folk tales written down in his own adaptation of standard French spellings for Louisiana French sounds—is being tested in the classroom. *Conversational French I,* put together by two Baton Rouge undergraduates, Randall P. Whatley and Harry Jannise, is being used in informal conversation classes and is available in soft cover for $7.95 in bookstores (or $7, plus $1.22 in tax and handling, from The Chicot Press, P.O. Box 21988, Baton Rouge 70893).

Despite such guerrilla efforts, CODOFIL remains immensely powerful. Domengeaux, a descendant of Governor Alexander Mouton and a U.S. Congressman from 1941 to 1949, remains a political powerhouse in his septuagenarian years. He is seen outside Louisiana as the Cajun ambassador to the international Francophone community—Le Grand Jimmy, Mister Cajun. Domengeaux started the agency in 1968 and imported the first thirty French teachers in 1970; by 1978, CODOFIL commanded an educational force that reaches 43,000 elementary- and secondary-school students. With state and federal funds—plus aid from Canada, France, and Belgium— CODOFIL sponsors a ceaseless stream of foreign visitors, conferences, scholarships, and exchange programs. Its success in international public relations has led to the establishment of similar organizations in the English-dominated Canadian province of Manitoba (CODOFIM) and in New England (CODO-FINE). CODOFIL publishes a bilingual newsletter that is available free of charge ("Louisiane Française," Boite Postale 3936, Lafayette, Louisiana 70502); a bilingual academic journal, *Revue de Louisiane;* and has secured a state charter for a *Television Louisiane* French-language channel. CODOFIL's free translation services for municipalities and private business have resulted in an explosion of bilingual street signs, billboards, and newspaper advertisements all over the French Triangle—as well as promotional gimmicks such as a series of McDonald's posters advertising free French fries if you order in French.

This CODOFIL-orchestrated French Renaissance has been accompanied by a series of eye-opening international economic and political developments. A French firm has begun assembling offshore oil-drilling rigs at the Gulf coast fishing village of Morgan City, and Cajun oil workers have been extensively recruited by France's state-owned oil company. CODOFIL and the French government graciously arranged for Louisiana public officials to visit the French superport on the Mediterranean when the Louisiana Offshore Oil Port (LOOP) superport was first proposed for Cajun fishing waters.

While there is no danger of a separatist movement in Cajun south Louisiana comparable to that in Quebec, there is no doubt that French capitalists view Cajun Louisiana as a safe place to do business—and the French government is not above overt use of its Louisiana ties in disputes with Washington. At the height of the debate over the use of the supersonic Concorde airplane at Kennedy and Dulles Airports on the East Coast, for example, French President Giscard d'Estaing flew one into both Lafayette and New Orleans.

The high-falutin' international antics of some of Domengeaux's CODO-FIL forces generate endless jokes from Les Cajuns. Robert LeBlanc, an LSU geology major from the coastal fishing village of Cameron and Les Cajuns' crusading chairman, is fond of describing CODOFIL partisans as *aristocrottes*. "I'm Cajun, I speak Cajun French, and it's not a birth defect," he says, and laughs. He dismisses CODOFIL's standard French as *tcheue poule* ("chicken ass") because of its—for a Cajun—exaggerated puckering.

The directness of CODOFIL's critics is matched by the basic, blunt, and brevity-prone nature of the language they seek to preserve. Cajun French is characterized by simplification and shortening of standard French grammar and pronunciation at almost every turn—perhaps the inevitable consequence of its oral tradition. The adjective *petit,* for example, almost always emerges as *'tit*—as in *'tit noir,* a demitasse-size serving of black coffee, or *'tit nom,* a nickname. Numerous diphthongs and consonant clusters also are abbreviated or deformed. And the familiar *tu* is used almost universally for "you"; the more formal *vous* is never used except with priests or outsiders or as a form of mild mockery. (The setting of Cajun French—always spoken within the family, or in a village that is often little more than an extended family—may help to explain this.) Moreover, many Cajun adjectives have only a masculine form, an interesting distinction from black Creole, or "gumbo" French, in which the feminine article *la* is used almost to the complete exclusion of the masculine *le.*

Complex or irregular forms of verbs have also virtually disappeared. All Cajun French verbs have been regularized, except for limited variations of "to be" and "to have." The first-person-singular form of the verb is used throughout all conjugations except third person plural (for example: *j'aime, tu aime, il* or *elle aime,* and *nous aime,* but *ils aimont*).

Tense forms have also been greatly simplified. Sentences using the present participle ("John is eating") follow a Cajun formula of subject plus a form of the verb "to be" plus the adverb *après* ("after") to modify the infinitive form of the main verb: *"Jean est après manger."* Future tense utilizes what Faulk calls a "helper verb" form of "to go," properly conjugated and inserted before the infinitive form of the main verb. Unlike standard French, where "John will eat" can be *Jean mangera* as well as *Jean va manger,* Cajuns use the helper-verb construction exclusively. Because Cajun French does not have the means of rendering the construction *"parlez-vous,"* this and other questions are posed by simply giving the affirmative statement a different inflection: *"Tu parle Cajun?"*

Cajun French is economical, essential, uncluttered, and rational—values that in some spheres are considered quite modern. And yet Cajun French is also an exotic antique. Cajun verbs include a number of usages—nautical forms, for instance, that survive to describe non-nautical events. "To knot one's shoelace" is *amarrer,* as in "to moor" a boat, rather than the standard French *nouer.* Or to "turn around," as in an automobile on a street, is *virer de bord,* as in "to come about" with a sailboat, rather than the standard French *tourner.*

It is the Cajuns' extensive borrowings from non-French sources, however, that provide their language with its diversity and spice. From the Spanish overlords of Louisiana at the time of the principal Acadian immigration come words like *lagniappe* ("a little something extra," from the word *ñapa*). Also the word *gouerre* (from *güero,* meaning, alternately, someone blond or someone stupid). From African-Americans, the Cajuns acquired *congo* for water moccasin, and *gris-gris* for voodoo charm. From the Indians came an assortment of terms: *bayou; ouaouaron* for bullfrog; *plaquemine* for persimmon; *chaoui* for raccoon *(raton laveur);* and *pichouette* for little girl *(jeune fille).* From English come all sorts of words for which there were no known seventeenth- or eighteenth-century French words: "concrete" instead of *beton;* "bootleg" instead of *vendre en contrebande;* "peace cop" instead of *agent de police.* Oftentimes, English words acquire full or partial gallicization of pronunciation or grammatical form ("Frenglish"), as if they were French words: *gambleur* for gambler; *gomme* for chewing gum; *l'office de doctor* for doctor's office; *la maison de show* for movie theater.

The controversy over Cajun French has contributed to a major resurgence of ethnic pride, far beyond the institutional limitations of schools and CODOFIL. Classified newspaper ads are cropping up all over Louisiana for classes in "native" French, and Faulk is preparing tapes and workbooks for eventual distribution to language labs and radio stations. Father Roland Vaughn of Grand Chenier has even prepared a translation of the Mass.

Some observers, armed with census statistics, have predicted that the native speaking of the language will disappear altogether by the end of this century. But the Cajuns, resilient as ever, have started circulating an underground slogan which challenges that and other outside assumptions. *On va les embêter,* sounds their new rallying cry: roughly translated, "We shall overcome."

*The first existing play written and
produced in North America*

**by MARC LESCARBOT
1606
Translated from the French by EDNA B. HOLMAN**

"Neptune's Theatre in New France, given on the waves of Port
Royal, the fourteenth of November, 1606, at the time of the
return of Sieur de Poutrincourt, from the country of the
Arouchiquois."

Cast

NEPTUNE.
SIX TRITONS.
FOUR SAVAGES.
A GAY ATTENDANT.
THREE OR FOUR FRENCH GENTLEMEN (*two of whom are* POUT-
RINCOURT *and* CHAMPLAIN) *who do not speak, but politely receive
the compliments of Tritons and Indians.*

Dramatic Directions

The scene is a seashore with a blue expanse of water. In the
background, a gateway or large doorway representing the entrance to the fort. Above the gateway, the French fleur-de-lys,
wreathed in green, and also the following three mottoes,
wreathed in green:
  DUO PROTEGIT UNUS.
  DABIT DEUS HIS QUOQUE FINEM.
  INVIA VIRTUTI NULLA EST VIA. (See author's note, at
end of play.)
  The play is well suited to outdoor production, at a beach, or
lakeside vacation resort or camp. Or it may be given on an indoor
stage with seaside scenery.
  NEPTUNE, an old man, wears blue robe and buskins, long
hoary hair and beard. The TRITONS are dressed similarly but not
made up as old men.
  The four Indians, dressed in regular American Indian rig,
carry, one a quarter of meat representing venison; one, small furs
representing beaver skins; one, some beaded scarfs or other Indian fancy work; the last, a spear.
  The French gentlemen should wear French court-costume of
the early seventeenth century, and the gay attendant a page's suit
of that period in France.
  NEPTUNE'S chariot may be represented by a rowboat or
canoe, festooned and decorated as for a water-fête. Or, if the

performance must be indoors, a decorated boat may be used in the style of a float in a parade.

Suggestions concerning the last part of the play will be found in footnotes.

Neptune's Theatre

(At the beginning of the play, NEPTUNE *enters, riding in his chariot, attired in blue robe and buskins, his hoary hair and beard long; his trident in his hand. The chariot is drawn on the waves by six* TRITONS, *up to the shallop in which* SIEUR DE POUTRINCOURT *and his men are making their landing from the barque. The men make fast the shallop.)*

NEPTUNE Pause, Captain,* pause here, and look upon a god who cares for you. If you do not recognize me:—Saturn was my father; I am brother to Jupiter and Pluto. In olden time the universe was divided among us three: Jupiter had heaven; Pluto, Hades; and I, more daring, had the sea; to me fell the duty of governing this portion. Neptune is my name, Neptune, the one of the gods who has most power under the heavens. If a man wishes for prosperity, let him pray to Neptune. For whoever lives a domesticated life at home deserves merely the title of cook. I make it possible for the *Flamingo* to travel, swift as the wind, in a short time even into China. I make it possible for a man riding on my waters, from another pole, to see foreign luminaries, and to traverse the confines of the Torrid Zone, where the billows of the liquid element are boiling hot. But for me the French king could not have received from the Persians the victorious gift of a proud elephant. And but for me, French soldiers would never have planted their arms in the countries of the Levant. But for me and my billows, the daring Portuguese would have stagnated, without fame, on their inland streams, and the beauties of Aurora would not have risen, which are so madly adored by the wondering world. In short, but for me the merchant and the pilot and the sailor would be cooped up at home as in a basket, hardly able to emerge from their province. A prince could not aid a brother prince, except that my deep waters lie between. And you, after all your fine exploits in the French War, but for me, you would not have had the pleasure of landing on this strand. 'Tis I who carried your vessels

---

*The Indian word "sagamore" is used—as in several places in the play.

on my back whenever you have wished to make me a visit. And again, it is I who lately have a hundred times preserved from Fate yourself, your men, and your ship. Even so, I desire always to assist your plans. And I desire that your efforts shall never be in vain because you have courage so strong as to come from afar to explore this shore, so as to found here a Kingdom of France, and establish here my statutes and my laws. By my sacred trident, by my sceptre, I swear that I will be mindful to favor your project, and never shall I have repose within myself, unless all around I see my waves laden with the weight of ten thousand ships, doing your bidding in the twinkling of an eye. Go then, in happiness, and follow your path wherever fate leads, for I see destiny preparing for France a prosperous Empire. In this new world, here afar, shall brilliantly flame the immortal renown of De Monts and of yourself, —under the mighty sway of Henry, your King.

(A trumpet sounds loudly, signal for FIRST TRITON *to speak.* SIEUR DE POUTRINCOURT *holds his sword in hand, unsheathed, not putting it back in the scabbard till the* TRITONS *have all spoken.)*

FIRST TRITON. You, great Captain, may call yourself fortunate, now that a god promises you friendly help in the important enterprise which, with a bold heart, you resolutely undertake, braving the violence of Aeolus, Aeolus, who is ever changeable and light, sometimes kindly, again, driven by envy, wishing to thrust you and yours into peril. Neptune is a great god, who will banish that envy like mist in the air. And we, his postboys, despite the efforts of Aeolus, shall publish abroad the fame of your valor, which already flies into all countries.

SECOND TRITON. If Jupiter is king in the sky, governing men here below, then Neptune, in these regions, holds similar sway. And we, his attendants, greatly wish to see the time and the day when you will receive the reward of your exertions, so that these shores may e'er-long reverberate with the glory of mighty Neptune and likewise that your memory may be eternal.

THIRD TRITON. O France! You have reason to praise the devotion of your children, whose courage is manifested more grandly in this era than it was in ancient times, being fervently desirous of sounding your praises even among strangest peoples, of engraving immortal praise of you even on this mortal world. Aid, then, and assist an undertaking so noble, Neptune offers himself as helper. Refuse not the good a god provides!

FOURTH TRITON. He who dares run no risk shows he has a coward's heart, but he who with stout heart and a glorious purpose scorns the raging waves easily convinces everyone that he is all girded and clothed with courage and valor, desiring only that silence may hold his name in forgetfulness. Even so, great Captain, your name shall resound upon the surges now and forevermore, now that, coming upon the sea, you have discovered this new world, and planted here the French name and the majesty of your Kings.

FIFTH TRITON. *(A Gascon, who speaks in dialect)* Ah! What think you? August Neptune, the old man, once on a time played the gallant, admiring himself like a beau, and thinking only of making love. He kissed a young girl at first politely and elegantly, but pressing his suit day by day, he said, "Don't be disdainful to graybeards! For in their affairs they are no laggards in love!"

SIXTH TRITON. Hail Henry! great king of the French! who now makes to live under his laws the nations of New France, under which we have hope of seeing Neptune e'er-long reverenced as much here as he was honored by his subjects on the Gallic shores, and in all places where the stout courage of their ancestors in bygone times carried them. Neptune also, will, on his part, befriend their descendants who sincerely labor to further their beautiful undertaking. All their plans he will bring over the waves prosperously.

(NEPTUNE *moves aside, to make room for a canoe in which are four Indians, each with a gift for* POUTRINCOURT. *The Indians land, and the first approaches* POUTRINCOURT, *carrying a quarter of meat.*)

THE FIRST INDIAN.*(Presenting a quarter of elk or venison)* On behalf of the savage peoples who live in these parts we render the homage due the sacred fleur-de-lys into your hands, for you represent the majesty of your prince. We foresee the time when you will have made this province to flourish in piety, in civilized customs, in everything which serves to the establishment of what is fine, which belongs to a royal government. Sagamore, if you have any love for our services, we offer them to you and to your followers. Our gifts are a little something from hunting, which we wholeheartedly offer you, assuring you that all we wish for is to live ever in your favor.

SECOND INDIAN. *(Carrying bow and arrow, and presenting some beaver skins)* See my hand, my bow, and my arrow, which gave the mortal wound to the animal, whose hide may serve as a cloak, great Sagamore, for your highness. Receive, then, from my littleness, this offering, which I present to your greatness, with my best love.

THIRD INDIAN. *(Presenting scarfs and armlets made by the hand of his mistress)* It is not only in France that Cupid rules, but in New France as among you, he with his flame lights his firebrand and roasts our poor souls. And my mistress, hearing that you were coming, bade me for love of her to come find you. Then receive cheerfully this present I give. I am filled with gentleness for the love of my mistress, who is now in grief, and will have no pleasure until I come quickly to her side, to caress her. [*These verses are full of ingenious rhymed conceits, allegresse, maitresse, détresse, vitresse, etc.*]

FOURTH INDIAN. *(Unsuccessful as a hunter, carrying a spear, and making excuses)* Captain, excuse me for coming in this style, for having no present for you. Fortune does not always favor the good hunter. That is why, after for a long time scouring the woods, invoking Fortune, I am having recourse to a master who is more reasonable, and am resolved to serve Neptune. Diana in the forests favors whomever she wishes, and I regret that I spent my youth ranging through valleys, woods, and plains, at a cost of a thousand exertions, and all for vain hopes. And now I mean to see if along this seacoast I cannot find something wherewith to furnish the table. And now, if somewhere in that shallop you chance to have a bit of caracona (bread) I beg you give it me and my party!

(SIEUR DE POUTRINCOURT *reverently kneels to* NEPTUNE *in gratitude for his kind promises; and, with courtly bows, acknowledges the Indians' good will and devotion and beckons them toward the fort* [*where there is always "caracona"—bread—for them*].)*

ALL. *(Singing)*

> Vray Neptune donne nous
> Contre tes flots assurance

---

*Much liberty is allowable in giving the last part of the play. The French lines to Neptune, for instance, may be twisted to fit, after a fashion, the traditional melody of
> "Sur le pont d'Avignon
> On y danse, tout en rond."

Or the English translation (see footnote below) may be recited by all and the recitation followed by instrumental music (a "sarabande" or "courante" on a small orchestra, or MacDowell's sea pieces for four hands). As the troupe is marching into the fort, if singing is desirable, a cheerful old melody of the habitants of French Canada may be used, such as "En roulant ma boule roulant," a song which came out to the colonies from France in the period of the early settlements and is still heard among the French Canadians.

Et fay que nous puissions tous
Un jour nous revoir en France.*

(After the singing, a trumpet sounds, and thunder sounds, resounding from all sides, "caused by echoes sent by the shores back and forth from one to another, lasting for more than a quarter of an hour." DE POUTRINCOURT approaches gate of fort.)

GAY ATTENDANT. *(Who meets* DE POUTRINCOURT *at gate of fort, having awaited him)* After long, Captain, desiring your return in this place, at last angry heaven has had pity on us, and shown us your face, blessed us with unbelievable favor.† We cookshop-keepers, pursers, man-cooks, scullions, pastry-cooks, squanderers, tavern-keepers, spendthrifts, have thrown down our pots and plates and kitchens. What matters so long as each has his full quart! I see them all changed as the world would be without water. (Sient terra sine aqua.) Here, boy, hurry! Cooks, are the ducks on the spit? Kill the chickens! Put them on to broil! Come in, messieurs, you are welcome. Drink, to drive out all chilly humors and fill your brains with sweet vapors.

(Trumpet sounds within the fort, and all, in an informal, light-hearted procession, go their way into the gateway of the fort.)

Note by the Author

I pray the reader to excuse if these verses are not so polished as fastidious men might wish. They were made in haste. Still I wished to insert them in my history, that they may serve the purpose of showing that we lived joyously (pour montre que nous vivions joyeusement). In addition, for the sake of better commemorating the return and our performance, we had placed over the gateway to our fort the arms of France, surrounded by wreaths of laurel (which grows abundantly along the edge of the woods) with the device of the King: "Duo protegit Unus," and below, those of Sieur de Monts with this inscription: "Dabit Deus his Quoque

*i.e., "Truly Neptune gives us confidence against the surging billows, and will enable us all to see France again some day."

†This speech runs into nonsense-verse, containing words without English equivalents and bristling with alert, crisp puns, play on words and combinations of letters needing to be heard, not seen in print; recalling somewhat the cadet's song in Cyrano de Bergerac, beginning: "Nous sommes les cadets de Gascoigne."

finem," and those of Sieur de Poutrincourt with this other inscription: "Invia virtuti nulla est via." All these also surrounded with garlands of laurel.

Curtain

Chronology

Europe and America before the Founding of Acadia

1500—France enters the sixteenth century with six times the population of England, twice that of Spain, and half again that of Italy. Predominantly Catholic, France has a ravenous appetite for fish and a restless, independent-minded seacoast population capable of sailing to the New World to obtain it.

1504—The first recorded confirmation of a French fishing vessel on the Grand Banks off Newfoundland.

1515—King Francis I pulls off a strategic marriage, incorporating the independent duchy of Brittany into metropolitan France, thus vastly enhancing his political power and beginning to create the France of today.

1516—Francis I wangles from the Pope the power to appoint French bishops, thereby establishing royal political control over the French church.

1517—In response to the political and cultural conflict provoked by expansionist Catholicism, Martin Luther initiates the Reformation.

1519—The Brittany fishing village of St.-Malo establishes a "wet" fishery drying area on rocks near her harbor. This commercial advance permits French fishing vessels to bring their catch back to France "wet" in the hold, rather than putting in on the American coast to dry it first—and enables the French fleet to expand its operations to both a "dry" (dried in America) and "wet" fishing season.

1521—Cortes takes Mexico.

1523—At least three vessels from the Protestant stronghold of La Rochelle are recorded on the Grand Banks.

1524—A peasants' revolt in the German province of Swabia produces twelve demands, ten of them secular, that graphically illustrate the political problems of the day. They demand abolition of serfdom and the system of "tithe" payments from their crops; removal of restrictions on hunting or fishing on nobles' land reserves; regulation of overlords' often excessive punishments; and the training of priests responsive to their own unique personal and community needs. These demands seek restoration of the social order that prevailed before Catholic feudalism, and suggest the motivation for early Acadian immigration: escape from Christian religious and political oppression.

Giovanni da Verrazano, aided by Protestant merchants from Rouen, sets out to explore the American coast from Florida northwards, hoping to find a quick route to China. An educated Florentine, he knew of Virgil's use of the word "Arcadia" to describe an earthly, secular paradise—an idea further glorified in a sixteenth-century novel by Jacopo Sannazaro. The first New World area to receive the designation "Arcadia" was actually Kitty Hawk, North Carolina, where Verrazano was impressed by the trees. In subsequent maps, the word goes through several spelling changes and moves steadily up the coast until it settles on the Nova Scotia peninsula, where the Micmac Indians used the word "Akade" for a similar concept of paradise.

1529—The fisheries catch of Normandy grows so large that some of the French cod is reexported to markets in England.

1533—French Protestant dissident John Calvin is convicted of heresy and must eventually flee the country.

1534—A momentous year: Paul III becomes Pope and attempts to rebuild the Church to counteract the Reformation.

Jacques Cartier sets out for the New World, attempting, too, to find a quick route to China. He discovers Prince Edward Island and the coast of New Brunswick, where he makes contact with the Micmac Indians.

1535—Cartier's second voyage, with an abortive attempt to found a colony.

1536—Calvin, now residing in Geneva, writes the treatise that will make Huguenot Protestantism a divisive French political and cultural problem for several decades.

1540—The Jesuits are founded by Ignatius Loyola in an attempt to counter the Reformation.

1541—Another abortive attempt to settle Canada, this time by Huguenot refugees, who by now constitute a substantial portion of the fishing and fur-trading classes of coastal France, where centralized Catholic control continues to be most remote.

Hernando de Soto discovers the mouth of the Mississippi River.

1545–63—The Council of Trent attempts to clean up the Roman Catholic Church, while the Reformation rages on.

1547—Henri II comes to power in France, caring little to pursue his country's American discoveries.

1548—Gastaldi's map is published, identifying the Acadian/Nova Scotia peninsula as "L'Arcadie."

1550—The St. Lawrence River Valley as far inland as Tadoussac is visited regularly by French fur traders, following on the heels of the cod fishermen. They barter the skins of beaver, otter, deer, seal, and marten for bread, peas, beans, prunes, tobacco, kettles, hatchets, iron arrow points, awls, cloaks, blankets, and baubles—initiating friendly relations that will greatly influence the subsequent development and history of North America.

1559—A record number of fishing vessels, forty-nine from La Rochelle, are engaged in fishing the Grand Banks.

1562—Two ships of Protestants leave Dieppe to establish Fort Charles in Florida—but they are massacred by the Spanish.

1578—Troilus de La Roche de Mesgouez sets out on his first attempt to establish a permanent New World base for the French fish and fur trade, but does not succeed.

1589—Protestant Henri IV becomes King of France.

1593—Henri IV renounces Protestantism in the hopes of reuniting his strife-torn country.

1598—La Roche finally succeeds in planting a colony/trading post at Sable Island, a desolate, crescent-shaped sandbar in the Atlantic Ocean's fishing banks 100 miles southeast of the Acadian peninsula. His ragtag group of soldiers and ex-prisoners is gradually whittled down to eleven survivors. Five years later, they are rescued and removed.

Henri IV issues the Edict of Nantes to permit "separate but equal" treatment and development of Catholics and Huguenots.

1600—Pierre de Chauvin de Tonnetuit, a Huguenot officer given exclusive rights to the St. Lawrence trade by Henri IV, sets off to found a permanent fishing/trading base at Tadoussac. In his expedition: Pierre du Gua, Sieur de Monts.

Acadia's Early Beginnings

1603—De Monts persuades Henri IV to grant him colonization and fur-trading rights between the 40th and 46th parallels, including all of what is now New England and Nova Scotia.

Elizabeth I of England dies and James I succeeds to the throne.

1604—In the spring, de Monts sets off with Samuel Champlain, the king's geographer, as captain, and sails around the southern tip of the Acadian peninsula, discovering the Annapolis Valley and charting the Bay of Fundy. On a minuscule island 300 by 125 yards that they named St. Croix (near the mouth of the river of the same name that currently divides the province of New Brunswick from the state of Maine), they establish a colony with seventy-nine men. The rocky island has no fresh-water supply, provisions are poorly figured, and Indian medicines and survival techniques learned from Cartier's voyages are apparently not utilized. So thirty-six members of the colony die of scurvy, including both the Catholic priest and the Huguenot minister in the party—who are buried in the same grave by the survivors, contemptuous of their petty rivalries.

1605—When supply ships return the following year, de Monts moves all the remaining colonists and supplies, plus two buildings, to the more protected area of the Annapolis Basin. Champlain draws up plans for a fortlike series of wooden buildings surrounding a courtyard (with a well to assure fresh water), and they name the settlement Port Royal, one of the first permanent European settlements in North America. De Monts and another important member of the party, Jean de Biencourt de Poutrincourt (who had earlier been granted most of the land around the new habitation), return to France to attend to business matters.

1606—Poutrincourt returns to the colony accompanied by Parisian attorney Marc Lescarbot, whose diary contains the first account of life in Acadia. A lime kiln is established, along with North America's first water-powered grist mill. America's first wheat crop is planted. Poutrincourt and Champlain set out to continue their explorations, leaving Lescarbot in charge. Upon their return, he writes and produces North America's first play, *The Theatre of Neptune,* staged in Indian canoes along the waterfront of the habitation. To pass away the boredom of winter, Champlain devises L'Ordre du Bon Temps, a social club that arranges feasts and other entertainments for dark evenings.

1607—Jamestown is founded.

De Monts loses his trading franchise from the crown. The habitation is left to the care of Chief Membertou, a Micmac Indian ally and trading partner, until Poutrincourt can return.

1608—Champlain founds Quebec.

1610—Poutrincourt returns to Port Royal and finds that Membertou has kept his promise to guard the habitation. Accompanying him is a party of forty men (and two women, whose subsequent lives are not recorded), including a Catholic priest, who converts Membertou and twenty-one members of his family. Acadia's first cattle also make this voyage. Son Charles de Biencourt returns to the French Huguenot port of La Rochelle with the first cargo of furs from the revitalized colony.

Henri IV is assassinated and his widow—Marie de Médicis—falls under the influence of the Jesuits as she sets out to create the Regency.

1611—Because of court intrigue, Poutrincourt's Huguenot partners are bought out by the Jesuits, who send two priests to the colony with Charles de Biencourt and his mother.

1612—The first of several internal power struggles in the colony: a rival trading post is set up across the Bay of Fundy at the St. John River.

1613—The Marquise de Guercheville, aided by increasingly ambitious Jesuit interests, sends thirty settlers, with goats and horses, to retrieve the priests at Port Royal from the company of Protestant infidels and establish a third, competing settlement—this one at St. Sauveur on Mt. Desert Island, Maine.

Late this same year, the Virginia pirate Samuel Argall, with the sanction of that English colony's governor, sets out to sack any French settlements found south of the 45th parallel. He destroys the colony at Mt. Desert Island and moves into the Port Royal harbor. While the men are out in the fields, Argall captures the habitation without a fight and burns it, removing livestock and provisions. The colonists flee into the hills, and those who survive live with the Indians in rude huts at a bare subsistence level for the next decade, continuing, on a haphazard basis, their fur trade with France.

1614—Poutrincourt returns from France to find his colony burned out, but leaves his son Charles and two important newcomers—Claude de Saint-Étienne de La Tour and his son Charles—to try to revive the fur trade.

1615—Poutrincourt and son Charles are killed in France in a religious riot, leaving the surviving son, Jean, as the Acadian seigneur.

1616—From trading posts at Port Royal, Cape Sable, Penobscot, and the St. John River, the colony ships 25,000 pelts back to France.

1619—Four Recollet missionaries—rivals of the Jesuits—leave France for Acadia, but flee five years later when the Scottish take over.

1620—The Pilgrims arrive at Plymouth Rock.

1621—Sir William Alexander, a Scotsman who gained power at the English court with the accession of James I, is granted a charter to found a "Nova Scotia" in what is still French Acadia. His first expedition, sent out the following year, gets only as far as Newfoundland.

1623—Jean de Biencourt (Poutrincourt's surviving son) dies, so Claude de La Tour claims possession of the colony and moves its headquarters to Cape Sable on the Atlantic Coast.

1624—Cardinal Richelieu comes to power; the Huguenots' days are numbered.

1625—The Jesuits establish a beachhead in Quebec. Charles I succeeds James I in England.

1626—The Dutch found New York.

1627—War breaks out between England and France. Cardinal Richelieu reorganizes the Company of New France and excludes Huguenots from any further economic ownership of the colony.

1628—Alexander finally succeeds in establishing a New World colony on the Gaspé peninsula of Quebec with seventy men and two women.

In the French religious wars, the last Huguenot holdout, La Rochelle, finally falls.

1629—The Scottish pirate brothers Lewis, David, and John Kirke (possibly born in the French port of Dieppe) force Champlain to give up Quebec. The Gaspé settlers are relocated in Port Royal, and the captured Claude de La Tour is taken prisoner to London. However, by the end of the year, opportunist La Tour shrewdly persuades Charles I and Alexander to confer Scottish baronetcies on himself and his son Charles, who had remained behind. Neither has a strong attraction to either Catholic or Protestant regimes, and they are able to vacillate back and forth in their political and religious loyalties for decades, while their colony remains essentially out of direct European control. The Treaty of Suza ends the war.

1631—Louis XIII, now King of France, wants his Canadian possessions back, and Charles I agrees when Louis hands over the dowry of Princess Henrietta Maria. Charles La Tour wangles an appointment as lieutenant governor of the colony from Louis XIII, his new overlord, and the colony effortlessly returns to French jurisdiction the following year with the Treaty of St. Germain-en-Laye. Most of the Scottish colonists depart either for New England or home, but the Acadian surnames Melancon and Pitre (originally Peters) survive from Scottish-French intermarriages during Alexander's brief possession of the colony.

1632—Cardinal Richelieu continues dabbling in New World politics, appointing his cousin Isaac de Razilly governor of Acadia. Razilly, in turn, appoints Charles de Menou d'Aulnay his lieutenant governor in a move that creates years of friction with the La Tours. Three hundred additional settlers arrive at Lahave on the Atlantic Coast on the eve of the Feast of the Assumption and eventually retake Port Royal. Unsuccessful Scottish colonizer Alexander is paid £10,000 for the loss of his colony and is granted other English lands in what is now the state of Maine.

Among those names known to be in the 1632 expedition: Doucet, Bourgeois, Petipas, Boudrot (Boudreaux), Terriault (Theriot, Terriau), Daigle, Sire, Poirier, Richard, LeBlanc, Thibadeau (Thibodeaux), Girouard, Granger, Comeau (Comeaux), Cormier, Robichaud, Hébert, Blanchard, Brault (Braude, Breaux), Morin, and Belliveau.

1633—Charles La Tour attacks the New England colony of Machias.

1635—Razilly dies, leaving d'Aulnay in charge of the colony. D'Aulnay repairs to Port Royal, where he establishes a new "Fort Royal" five miles upriver from the original habitation, where the Allain River joins the Annapolis. La Tour, however, asserts a conflicting claim to the colony based on his 1631 commission from Louis XIII, and he moves his headquarters from Cape Sable to the St. John River, where he builds a fort and engages d'Aulnay in a fifteen-year civil war. With the help of his father's prior English connections, La Tour secures periodic assistance from Boston in raiding d'Aulnay, while Europe generally ignores the developments.

Additional Acadian names known to be in the colony by this date: Aucoin, Gaudet, Martin, Dugas, Trahan, and Landry.

1639—La Tour attacks one of d'Aulnay's ships and attempts to storm Fort Royal.

1641—D'Aulnay persuades the French court to appoint him governor.

1642—D'Aulnay receives authorization to capture La Tour and arrest him.

1643—Louis XIII dies, and another regency is established for Louis XIV.

1647—While La Tour is away, d'Aulnay succeeds in capturing and destroying his fort at St. John. Mme La Tour dies at his hands.

1650—D'Aulnay's canoe capsizes on a sandbar, and he is drowned. La Tour secures a new patent to consolidate his control of the colony the following year. In a surprise strategic move, he marries the widowed Mme d'Aulnay the following year (at the age of sixty), and has five more children by her.

1651—An estimated forty families are living at Fort Royal.

1652—Emmanuel Le Borgne, one of d'Aulnay's creditors, captures Fort Royal. Ultimately, his son Alexandre will marry one of the daughters born of La Tour and Mme d'Aulany, thus consolidating by marriage several decades of conflicting claims to land and power. Alexandre Le Borgne is named seigneur of Grand Pré, which is not settled until 1682.

1654—Massachusetts forces are armed by Robert Sedgwick to take New York from the Dutch, but just before they embark, a ship arrives (June 20) with news of peace. So, instead of heading south, they head north to cause trouble for the French, capturing Penobscot, St. John, Fort Royal, and a completely surprised La Tour. Exhuming his one-time Scottish title, he successfully negotiates, by 1656, his return to the colony as English governor-designate under Cromwell. Eventually, he relinquishes control to Boston trader Sir Thomas Temple (an heir of Sir William Alexander), who fights off everyone (including more raiding parties from d'Aulnay's creditors) until his claims to power finally go unchallenged one year later. Meanwhile, the first rudimentary council of colonists is established, headed by Guillaume Trahan.

1657—After much maneuvering, Bishop François Laval is selected to head the first episcopal see in New France, and arrives in Quebec in 1659 with an edict banning Protestantism from the colony.

1660—Cromwell dies and is succeeded by Charles II.

1661—Louis XIV takes possession of the French throne.

1663—Bishop Laval establishes the first seminary to train Canadian priests.

1667—Over Governor Temple's protests, Acadia is ceded back to France by the Treaty of Breda. The colony's official population is estimated at four hundred by an English census prior to the transfer.

1670—Colbert comes to power in France, and Acadia finally assumes the status of a crown colony. A succession of professional governors arrive to attempt to reassert European control over what was by this time a virtually self-administered society.

Acadian Expansion under the French

1671—Governor Hector de Grandfontaine conducts a census that shows that Fort Royal has sixty-seven families, totaling 340 persons, with 650 cattle and 430 sheep. Scattered settlements are also reported at six other locations. Some fifty new settlers arrive from the vicinity of the former dissident citadel of La Rochelle. Additional Acadian names known to be in the colony by this date: Giroire, Joffriau, Raimbault, Babin, Bertrand, Brun, Cyr, Savoie, Dupuis (Dupuy), Bourq (Bourg), and Saulnier.

1672—Jacques Bourgeois, former surgeon to d'Aulnay, establishes his own and five other families in the Beaubassin area, thus beginning a process of outmigration and shift of population center from Fort Royal to the other dikable marshlands of the peninsula. Not all the marshlands around Fort Royal have been depleted, however, leading historians to speculate that these pioneers merely wanted to distance themselves from the government's reinforced garrison and its attempts to regulate such things as illegal trade with the New Englanders.

1676—The first school in Acadia is founded at Fort Royal by Abbé Louis Petite, a graduate of Laval's seminary in Quebec. Petite becomes the first priest to establish a full-time ministry in the colony.

1678—Within two years, additional Acadian names: Chaisson, Cottard, Hache, Lagace (Lagasse), Leger, Mercier, Aubin, Mignault, Mirande, Perthuis (Pertuit).

1679—Yet another census shows 515 people in the colony, a remarkable 25 percent increase over the last decade.

1681—La Salle, a former Jesuit from the Quebec seminary, sets off to sail down the Mississippi River from Quebec.

1682—In April he discovers the Mississippi's Gulf terminus, and he names the surrounding territory Louisiana in honor of his king.

In the Minas Basin, site of the village-to-be of Grand Pré, Pierre

Melancon leads a settling party that includes a Terriau, a LeBlanc, and a Landry.

Witchcraft trials are finally ended in Europe.

1683—Another French census pegs the colony's population at 800.

1685—Sisters of the Congregation found a school for girls at Fort Royal, and Abbé Louis Geoffroy arrives to set up more schools at the other settlements.

Louis XIV revokes the Edict of Nantes.

1686—Another census puts the size of the colony at 875.

Bishop Jean de la Croix St. Vallier, who had been the king's personal chaplain prior to arriving in Quebec, makes his first visit to Acadia. A church is established at Beaubassin.

1687—A church is established at Grand Pré.

1690—Sir William Phips leads an expedition that sacks Fort Royal; in a rehearsal for deportation, prisoners are taken to Boston. English hostility to the settlement increases its outmigration of young people. Benjamin Church organizes a raid of the Chignecto and Beaubassin areas, inflicting heavy (but temporary) damage.

1692—In February, Indians friendly to the French massacre the inhabitants of the New England town of York.

1698—Pierre Thibaudeau, a miller, persuades members of the Blanchard family to join him in establishing settlements along the Petitcodiac estuary in what is now New Brunswick. In a well-protected cove of the Bay of Fundy, these settlements eventually grow into what is now metropolitan Moncton—which, with its French-speaking university, is now the center of Canadian Acadian culture.

1699—Iberville and Bienville, exploring along the Gulf Coast, enter Louisiana's Lake Pontchartrain inland bay as far north as Baton Rouge. They bring the first Jesuits to Louisiana.

1701—Another census tallies 1,450, and for the first time the Minas Basin with 487 surpasses the Fort Royal colony with 456.

The European war over the Spanish succession begins.

1704—The French, under the governor of Quebec, seize and burn Deerfield, Connecticut. In retaliation, Benjamin Church returns to Acadia to repeat his previous pillaging, and he attacks the Minas Basin.

1707—The last French census before the English raids of 1710 reveals a total population of 1,800.

1708—French governor Daniel Subercase remarks in a letter: "The more I consider these people, the more I believe they are the happiest in the world."

1709—The continental war cuts off the colony from France. Some thirty-five English ships are taken by Acadian privateers.

1710—Francis Nicholson, lieutenant governor of the colonies of Maryland and Virginia (governor of Virginia in 1698), broods over the French presence and decides to send a raiding party to capture the Acadian colony. Nicholson, with the aid of New York businessman Samuel Vetch, arrives in Boston on July 15 with six naval vessels and sets out for Fort Royal on September 18. On September 24 he arrives in the Fort Royal harbor with 3,400 men, to oppose Governor Subercase, badly outnumbered, with only 300 men, in a deteriorating fort. Subercase holds out valiantly until October 16 and wins honorable terms of surrender. Vetch becomes governor, and the village is named Annapolis Royal in honor of England's Queen Anne.

Years of Transition: Acadia under the British Empire

1713—The Treaty of Utrecht establishes English control over most of the Nova Scotia peninsula, excluding Île Royale (Cape Breton Island) and Île St. Jean (Prince Edward Island). Control of New Brunswick remains disputed, with the French fort of Beauséjour established on the north side of the Missaguash River and the English Fort Lawrence on the south side, defining what would later become the boundary line between the two provinces. Periodic raids and the Indian war of the 1720's would disturb the tranquillity, but the Acadians resolutely remained "neutral" in accordance with treaty terms—refusing to assist either European contender for administrative control of their society. Population estimate at this date: 2,300–2,500.

1714—Queen Anne dies, bringing George I to the throne. Governor Vetch writes a report advocating expulsion as the solution to what he regards as a hopeless political problem. Major Paul Mascarene—a Huguenot officer in the English garrison, later to become lieutenant governor of the colony—is assigned the task of authorizing the election of four "deputies" from the major settlement areas to handle communications between the governors and the governed. By 1748, there will be forty-eight deputies, whose leadership abilities enable the widely scattered Acadians to survive the travail to come.

The first permanent European settlement in Louisiana: Natchitoches.

1715—The French fort of Louisbourg on Île Royale now has a population of 700, and increased fortification efforts begin. Louis XV ascends the French throne.

1717—Colonel Richard Philipps succeeds the scandal-ridden Nicholson-Vetch regime as governor, and appoints Huguenot Captain John Doucett as his lieutenant governor through 1726. Doucett remains in Annapolis Royal to run the colony when Philipps moves—first to the English-speaking fishing village at Canso in 1721, and then England in 1723.

In Paris, John Law's Company of the West is founded to colonize Louisiana with German immigrants.

1718—New Orleans is settled. Population as of June: 68. Rice is first brought into Louisiana.

1719—A soldier-adventurer named François Semar de Belle Isle is marooned after a shipwreck, and forced to live among the Attakapas Indians west of the Atchafalaya River in Louisiana. Belle Isle falsely accuses them of cannibalism, which effectively discourages settlement of their isolated lands until the Acadian immigrations of the latter part of the century require more expansion room.

1720—The so-called King's Bastion at Louisbourg is completed. Louisiana's population as of this year: 6,000.

1722—Four years of Indian wars begin in Acadia.

1724—The first *Code Noir* is adopted in Louisiana, requiring, among other things, that all slaves be baptized Catholics.

1725—In a manner typical of colonial administrative confusion, Major Lawrence Armstrong is appointed to a lieutenant governorship concurrent with Doucett, and continues in office until 1739.

1726—At the conclusion of the Indian wars, the Acadians of Annapolis Royal are summoned to the fort to be administered an oath of allegiance to the English crown. They demand that a clause be inserted exempting them from bearing arms, and letters from that period confirm that the demand was penciled in on the French copy—though it does not appear on any of the English-language versions that are still the only "official" documents to survive.

1727—George I dies and is succeeded by George II, who passionately hates Catholics. Residents of Annapolis Royal, upon hearing of his ascendancy, confer with Abbé Breslay and hold a protest meeting to demand that their religious independence continue to be protected under the terms of the Treaty of Utrecht, that French priests continue to be sent to them, and that they not be required to bear arms. Three deputies sent from the meeting to present these demands are imprisoned and Abbé Breslay is expelled. But in order to quell the subsequent uproar, which almost results in the town storming the fort, an English officer is sent out to capitulate to the residents' demands.

The first permanent contingent of Jesuit priests and Ursuline nuns is sent to Louisiana.

1729—Governor Philipps returns briefly to the colony, but departs again in 1731. While there, he determines to obtain oaths of allegiance from all the Acadian settlements, not just the one at Annapolis Royal. Abbé

Breslay is brought back as a gesture of appeasement. Philipps gets his oaths, but it is assumed from correspondence and later reports that he does so only by giving verbal assent to the Acadian demands not to bear arms.

1730—Some 900 people are counted at Annapolis Royal.

1731—Bienville is named governor of Louisiana (until 1743).

Before leaving Acadia, Governor Philipps issues strong orders against any Acadian trade with Louisbourg. Even though he offers half the value of seized goods to informers, he is unable to stop the smuggling which goes on along Indian paths over the Chignecto isthmus.

The first lighthouse in Canada is established at Louisbourg.

1732—Because the Acadian population continues to burgeon, Armstrong is authorized to confer title to "new" crown lands not previously settled.

1733—Agatha La Tour Campbell, a member of one of Acadia's "first families" who married a succession of English garrison officers after the 1710 takeover, receives a settlement of £5,000 to relinquish her claims to a defunct French "seigneurie" or feudal land grant. Acadia's seigneuries were never well respected or enforced, and hers was the last to go.

1737—Another census reveals 7,598 people in those sections of Acadia under English control. There are also 1,463 people at Louisbourg.

1738—The infamous Abbé Jean-Louis Le Loutre ("The Otter") arrives in the Fort Beauséjour area from France, determined to keep the Acadian settlers there Catholic and loyal to the French king. His ministry to the Indians produces many headaches for the English, who put a price on his head and detain him twice, unsuccessfully, in prison camps before the Expulsion. Le Loutre's aggressive activities are conceded by most historians to have been the principal cause of much of New England's paranoia about the "loyalties" of the Acadians in the event of another war. When the deportations begin, Le Loutre's bishop in Quebec writes him: "You have at last, my dear sir, got into the very trouble I foresaw, and which I predicted long ago."

1739—England goes to war with Spain.

1740—After Armstrong commits suicide, Major Paul Mascarene succeeds him as lieutenant governor (until 1749), ushering in the most benevolent period of English rule.

1741—Charles Lawrence, the villain of 1755, first arrives in the colony.

1744—Four more years of war between France and England begin.

1745—In a surprise attack, a group of New Englanders capture Louisbourg.

1747—The French return the favor with an unsuccessful assault on Grand Pré.

1748—The Treaty of Aix-la-Chapelle restores Louisbourg to French rule. The Acadians henceforth are known in various documents and reports of the day as the "French neutrals."

1749—Colonel Edward Cornwallis succeeds Philipps as governor and decides to establish Halifax as the new provincial capital and an Atlantic port/fort defense against Louisbourg. He brings 2,000 settlers with him. An English blockhouse is built to watch over Grand Pré. Lawrence joins the Cornwallis regime's executive council.

Le Loutre becomes the Beaubassin village priest and Fort Beauséjour is completed. The French governor of Newfoundland sends out explorers to mark claims to the Mississippi River Valley with lead plates.

1750—Louisbourg now has a population of 4,000; there are now 10,000 Acadians, half of them living in the Minas Basin region. Throughout the colony, they have diked 13,000 acres of land.

Cornwallis builds a road from Halifax to Pisiquid (now the town of Windsor) and builds Fort Edward in his own honor there, to reinforce his control. From Fort Edward, Lawrence attempts to take Fort Beauséjour and occupy Beaubassin, but is beaten back. That summer, the Indians burn the church at Beaubassin, probably on orders from Le Loutre, and the Acadians begin a confused migration to areas of New Brunswick behind the battlelines. Eventually, that fall, Fort Lawrence is built on the site of the burned-out church.

In Louisiana, Father Baudoin—the Jesuit superior—is named the first vicar-general in New Orleans for the Bishop of Quebec.

1751—Sugarcane is introduced into Louisiana from Santo Domingo by the Jesuits, who grow it on their New Orleans plantation.

1752—As the political situation in Canada worsens, more Acadian refugees head for Shediac and Beauséjour just over the de facto boundary line between English Nova Scotia and French New Brunswick, or else they set out for French-controlled Prince Edward Island. Most of those 2,663 headed for PEI will end up eventually in Louisiana. Another 2,586, joined by scattered refugees, will begin walking northward along the New Brunswick coast adjoining the Gulf of St. Lawrence, eking out an existence with the Indians and hiding from various English raiding parties until the fall of New France and the later granting of legal permission to reestablish their farms. Cornwallis, meanwhile, resigns as governor and is succeeded by the weak-willed Peregrine Hopson.

In the Louisiana Territory, there are now twenty-four French forts and settlements.

1753—The ambitious Lawrence is named president of the Council after

Hopson resigns, and ten months later succeeds to the lieutenant governorship.

Lunenburg, near Halifax, is settled with additional European immigrants, mainly Germans. They, the original Cornwallis settlers, and refugee-Tory "Loyalists" after the American Revolutionary War will make up the overwhelming majority of the population base of modern Nova Scotia.

1754—Five Mouton brothers and one nephew begin their immigration to Louisiana, the first Cajun settlers in the state. Louis, Pierre, Charles, and Jean, Jr., all die young or their lines terminate early, leaving only Salvador and Jean Diogène Mouton to carry on the family name—which disappears completely in Acadia.

Governor William Shirley of Massachusetts accuses the Acadian settlers of the Chignecto region of working with the French garrison at Beauséjour to storm the state of Maine. Actually, they just want to return to their Beaubassin-area farms, which the Abbé Le Loutre's Indians forced them to leave.

April 6—The first fully documented arrival of Cajun refugees in Louisiana: four families, totaling twenty people, who had arrived via New York.

July 3—George Washington abandons Fort Necessity.

September 17—Acting Governor Lawrence orders that there be no more grain shipments from Annapolis Royal or Grand Pré to the Beaubassin region.

October 29—The Lords of Trade in London caution Lawrence not to do anything rash.

Years of Chaos: The Expulsion and Beyond

1755—Canadian census figures show 10–11,000 Acadians still living in Nova Scotia, plus another 4–5,000 in PEI. A rough estimate of 18,000 is agreed upon by most historians.

May 22—Lawrence's secretly organized expedition of 2,000 men leaves Boston for Chignecto Bay.

June 3—Lawrence holds council at Halifax, and secretly plots the details of the Expulsion.

June 4—He sends out an order demanding that the Acadians turn in their arms, an order protested because of possible wild-animal attacks on their livestock. Troops from Halifax are sent to reinforce the Boston troops now at Fort Lawrence.

June 16—Fort Beauséjour capitulates to the English.

July 28—The Council issues Expulsion orders.

August 13—The Board of Trade sends additional cautionary instructions to Lawrence, instructions that do not arrive until the Expulsion is already well underway.

September 5, a Friday—413 men of Grand Pré are lured into church under false pretenses and held captive.

October 8–27—Ships at Grand Pré are loaded up. In all, some twenty-four vessels carrying 5,000 people are dispatched during the late fall and winter accompanied by three warships.

1756—Beginning of the Seven Years' War, our first true world war, on May 18. Scattered Acadian refugees dumped in Maryland, the Carolinas, and Georgia begin heading for Louisiana.

February 8—The *Pembroke,* the only English ship overpowered by its prisoners, arrives at the St. John River.

1757—The first chapel is established at St. James Parish, soon to become the principal settlement of the Acadian Coast along Louisiana's Mississippi River.

Lawrence is made a full colonel for his efforts.

1758—Louisbourg falls, after being besieged by 27,000 troops and three dozen ships. Remaining Acadian refugees found along the St. John River, and half the population of previously untouched Cape Sable, are rounded up for deportation.

1759—Some 200 additional refugees surrender at either St. John or Fort Cumberland (formerly Beauséjour), plus another 152 from Cape Sable, all of whom are imprisoned at Halifax. Quebec falls.

1760—Forces from Montreal make one last effort to rescue New France, but are surrounded and captured.

Another 300 refugees swept up from the St. John area are imprisoned at Halifax, while 2,000 new English settlers are brought in to take the Acadians' lands.

George II dies. George III takes the throne.

Caraquet, New Brunswick, is founded by Stephen Landry of Grand Pré.

1761—In Louisiana, the first Cajun name appears in the cattle industry's so-called brand book: Bernard.

1762—Louis Jules Mancini Mazarini, Duc de Nivernais, is sent to London to negotiate an end to the Seven Years' War on September 2.

October—Nivernais finds out about the Acadians being detained and writes Étienne François, Duc de Choiseul, the French foreign minister, for instructions. These are the survivors of 1,500 prisoners sent to Virginia, then expelled from there also.

November 3—The secret Treaty of Fontainebleau gives Louisiana to Spain. Minister Choiseul has private plans to develop French Guiana, and hopes that his ceding of Louisiana to the king's Spanish cousins will cause lasting problems for English colonial settlements in North America.

December 11—Nivernais finally begins treaty negotiations with Lord George Grenville, the English Prime Minister.

December 31—Nivernais secretly sends his secretary, La Rochette, to Liverpool, with a message of assurance for the Acadians imprisoned there.

1763—Founding of Poste des Attakapas (now St. Martinville) on Louisiana's Bayou Teche. Jesuits thrown out of the state. Some 2,542 Acadian refugees will end up scattered among ten French port cities by the end of the year.

January 18—La Rochette visits prisoners in Southampton. From 340 originally, their numbers have dwindled to 219.

January 20—Louis XV refuses to sign armistice with England unless Acadian prisoners are returned either to France or to Canada.

January 24—La Rochette finds 159 surviving prisoners at Falmouth.

January 31—La Rochette finds 184 survivors of 341 refugees imprisoned in Bristol. Total thus far: 866 of the original Virginia 1,500.

March 18—Nivernais letter to La Rochette: "Tell them [the Cajuns] of their coming liberation."

April 11—Choiseul writes from Paris authorizing final plans to bring the prisoners home to France.

April 18—La Rochette sent out to complete final arrangements.

May 16—218 Southampton survivors shipped to Morlaix.

May 26—160 from Bristol to Morlaix; 158 from Falmouth to St.-Malo. Population of total group has dropped from 866 to 833 during the three months of negotiation.

June 8—217 from Liverpool to St.-Malo.

July—383 surviving refugees in Pennsylvania hear of La Rochette's letter promising freedom. They protest Anglo-American conditions (using the word "slavery") and beg to be allowed to return to France.

August 23—Exiles in Georgia also write to La Rochette, charging that they have not been allowed confession or any other religious rights for eight years, and that many of their children have been indentured, kidnapped, or sold outright into slavery.

November 22—Choiseul sends a census to the new ambassador to London, Claude François Louis Regnier, Comte de Guerchy. There are still 4,397 survivors in the English Atlantic colonies, 1,043 in the Boston area alone.

December 2—Maryland refugees write that they have dwindled from 2,000 to 810, and also report stories of slavery and indentured servitude. Survivors will form the nucleus of the early Cajun settlement at St. Gabriel.

December 6—The English insist that they want no exiles sent to any tropical French colonies (like Choiseul's Guiana project).

1764—Lord Halifax flatly refuses to permit return of refugees to Quebec or Acadia. A census that year, however, shows that there are still 1,762 Acadians in Nova Scotia, 1,076 of them imprisoned in Halifax. 600 of them will set sail eventually for the French West Indies, and the survivors will migrate to Louisiana. In December, a boatload of 20 refugees turns up in New Orleans.

1765—February 27—200 Cajuns arrive in Louisiana via Santo Domingo.

April 8—Joseph "Beausoleil" Broussard, a resistance leader in Acadia, is appointed commandant of the garrison at Poste des Attakapas.

April 24—A unique contract between Bernard d'Auterive and the Cajuns "loans" them cattle with which to relaunch their cattle industry. The original number of animals, plus half the offspring, are to be returned after six years. Broussard is one of the signatories to this historic pact.

May 13—Forty-eight more families arrive in Louisiana, bringing the total since the first of the year to over 650 people.

October 20—Broussard dies and is buried near the Cajun town named for him.

October—Abbé Le Loutre surfaces again, this time leading a group of six families from Morlaix and St.-Malo to Belle-Île-en-Mer, an island off the west coast of France. But a drought sets in for six years, and all of the colonists return to their seaport refugee homes by 1772.

December 2—The entire refugee population of a small Canadian island is kidnapped by the English Colonel Haldimand to work his estate.

Louisiana under the Rule of Spain

1766—The first Spanish governor, Antonio de Ulloa, arrives in Louisiana on March 5. Some 216 more refugees arrive directly from Halifax.

1767—Expeditions of refugees are sent from France to settle the islands of St. Pierre and Miquelon off Newfoundland in May, October, and December, but return to France within a few months.

Another 210 refugees arrive in Louisiana from Minas via Santo Domingo and are dispatched by Governor Ulloa to the growing settlement of St. Gabriel de Manchac. The most common names on the passenger manifest: Hébert, Landry, Babin, LeBlanc, Richard, Fôret, Blanchard, and Brasseaux.

1768—The first revolt against a European power by an American colony takes place in New Orleans, led by Creole merchants upset with Spanish commercial policies. A force of Cajun militiamen enter the city to help establish an independent regime seeking reaffiliation with France.

1769—General Alexander O'Reilly, an Irish mercenary, gunboats his way into the New Orleans harbor and reclaims the colony for Spain, executing the ringleaders of the revolt.

Some 150 acres of the French estate of the Marquis de Saint-Victour near Limoges are set aside for an experimental refugee settlement for seven families, but the effort is abandoned in 1772.

A New Orleans census puts the population of the city at 3,190.

1770—The Cajun chapel at St. James is made a separate parish and records its first baptism, that of Alexandre LeBlanc.

1771—The first of several proposals is advanced at the French court to send the refugees to Corsica.

Land is granted to settlers in Clare, Nova Scotia, who walked there from Boston and refused to leave.

1772—Another French refugee settlement is established at Grand' Ligne, but no harvests can be produced in either 1774 or 1775.

Another census shows 1,249 Acadians still live in Cape Breton, Nova Scotia (mainly the Clare/Bay Ste. Marie area), and New Brunswick.

Ascension Parish, site of the second rural church for the Cajuns, is established in what is now Donaldsonville.

1774—Eglise Ste. Anne is founded on the new French Shore of Nova Scotia. The Act of Quebec is passed, giving the French increased civil rights, in an attempt by the English to keep them from joining the rebels in the American colonies.

1775—Some 1,500 refugees show up for a protest meeting at Grand' Ligne; 1,340 vote to return to the seacoast and end up mainly at Nantes. The 160 who remain behind form the nucleus for the largest remaining Acadian settlement in France.

1776—That other American revolution begins.

1777—The French government decides to send the refugees to Corsica. Meanwhile, word of the American Revolutionary War stirs new interest in Louisiana. Some eighty families send two delegates to Versailles to protest the Corsica plans and plead for relocation in Louisiana instead.

October 20—Two families, totaling 22 persons, leave France for the Cajun settlement at St. James.

1778—France intervenes in the American Revolutionary War on the side of the colonists. The Marquis de Lafayette, a principal force behind the French decision, declares that the plight of the Acadians helped convince him.

1779—George Washington is made a lieutenant general to Louis XVI.

New Iberia, Louisiana, is founded.

May 8—Spain authorizes Louisiana Governor Bernardo de Gálvez to harass English colonial holdings on the Gulf Coast to aid the American revolutionaries.

August—27—Gálvez leaves New Orleans with 600 Cajun volunteers.

September 7—They attack and capture the English Fort Bute on Bayou Manchac across from the Cajun town of St. Gabriel.

September 21—They attack and capture Baton Rouge.

1780—Mobile surrenders to Gálvez and the Cajuns, March 14.

1781—Pensacola surrenders to Gálvez and the Cajuns, May 9.

1783—End of the American Revolutionary War. Catholic Emancipation Act adopted in Nova Scotia. New Orleans druggist Peyroux de la Coudrenière (originally from the seacoast town of Nantes, with its large refugee colony) returns home to France after seven years in Louisiana. His mission: to bring back the Cajuns as Spanish colonists.

July 12—A group of refugees, including Nantes shoemaker Oliver Terrio, write to Don Pedro Pablo Abarca y Bolea, Conde de Aranda, the Spanish ambassador to France, requesting that Charles III of Spain remove them to Louisiana.

August 21—Peyroux sends his own memoir to José de Gálvez, minister of the Indies in Madrid and uncle of the victorious Bernardo, who is in Madrid for a round of honors when the letter arrives.

October 22—Charles III decides to accept Peyroux's proposal. However, Aranda does not find out until January.

1784—New Brunswick is separated from Nova Scotia.

January 21—The Spanish consul to St.-Malo informs the anxious Peyroux of Charles III's approval.

March 24—The Spanish chargé d'affaires contacts Charles Gravier, Comte de Vergennes, the French foreign minister, with the details of Charles III's proposal.

April 6—Thirty-five heads of refugee families write directly to the court, seeking acceptance of the Spanish offer.

April 27—Louis XVI accepts.

May 11—Vergennes so informs the Spanish embassy.

May 21—A Nantes judge mistakenly arrests Peyroux for suspected "foreign agitation."

July 18—Peyroux, finally freed, asks Terrio to publicize the plan.

September 13—1,508 refugees sign up for the Louisiana migration.

September 27—Manuel d'Asprès, a Spanish consular official, is sent to Nantes to arrange for boats.

October 9—D'Asprès receives bids of $30 per person for transportation.

October 28—D'Asprès meets with shipping companies for negotiations.

November 7—Final contract is sent to Aranda for approval.

November 19—Peyroux sends five clarification questions to Charles III.

1785—New Orleans population: 4,980. First visit to Louisiana by a Catholic bishop. Port Hudson (Thompson's Creek) becomes the third Catholic parish to be established for the Cajuns. Louisiana's first sugar mill is constructed.

March 5—Charles III responds to Peyroux's letter, and sends a copy of his personal instructions to Governor Gálvez.

April 4—D'Asprès finishes registering all the families that wish to emigrate.

May 10—First departure, Le Bon Papa, with 159 aboard. Arrives New Orleans July 29.

May 12—La Bergere departs with 273, including Oliver Terrio. Arrives August 15.

June 11—Le Beaumont leaves with 180, including Peyroux. Arrives September 22.

June 20—St. Remy leaves with 341. Arrives September 9.

August 12—La Amistad leaves with 270, arrives November 7; La Villa de Arcangel leaves same day with 309, arrives December 3.

August 25—Under Commissioner Anselmo Blanchard, the first expedition of these settlers leaves for Manchac.

October 15—Last expedition, La Carolina, leaves France with 80, arrives December 17. Tally as of this date: 440 families, totaling 1,624 persons (including 28 stowaways). Total cost to Charles III: $62,424.12.

1786—Nantes made French terminus for trade from Spanish Louisiana, July 2.

1790—By now, over 4,000 Cajun refugees have relocated in Louisiana.

1791—Slave rebellion in Santo Domingo brings Creole planters and slaves to join the Cajuns.

1792—Cotton gin is invented.

1793—Establishment of the diocese of Louisiana, second oldest in North America. A fourth Cajun church is set up at Valenzuela (now Assumption Church in Plattenville), and a fifth at St. Martin de Tours in St. Martinville. Sanctuary lamp and carved marble baptismal font are sent to St. Martinville as gifts of Louis XVI.

1794—First newspaper published in Louisiana, *Le Moniteur de la Louisiane,* in New Orleans.

1795—Coushatta Indians migrate to Louisiana from Alabama.

1796—First opera in United States staged in New Orleans.

Cajuns under the United States

1803—Louisiana returns to formal French rule for twenty days, but only as part of a maneuver whereby Napoleon sells it to Thomas Jefferson.

First Protestant sermon preached in Louisiana.

1805—Louisiana's first American constitution, written in French, restricts voting rights to those who own land and pay taxes, in an attempt to keep the state in Francophone hands.

1806—Donaldsonville is founded at the juncture of the Mississippi River and Bayou Lafourche.

1808—First public school is established in the state.

1809—6,000 additional refugees fleeing West Indies political turmoil arrive in Louisiana.

1810—The state's slave population is double its 1803 number.

1812—Louisiana enters the Union as the first state west of the Mississippi River. The governor is appointed by the House of Representatives until Alexander Mouton becomes the state's first elected governor decades later.

Catholicism in Louisiana limps along, with only twelve priests in the entire state. Voodoo and other unorthodox practices thrive.

1815—Andrew Jackson wins the Battle of New Orleans with a ragtag militia reinforced with large numbers of Cajun volunteers.

1818—The Church of St. Charles is established at Grand Coteau, the third to be built west of the Atchafalaya (the others: St. Martin de Tours in St. Martinville and St. Landry in Opelousas).

1820—The state's population has doubled in the last decade.

1821—Sacred Heart Academy begins operations in Grand Coteau. The Church of St. Jean the Evangelist is established in Lafayette by Jean Mouton.

1822—The first steam engine is adapted to use in sugar milling.

1823—Lafayette Parish secedes from St. Martin Parish.

Louisiana's first natural gas well is dug.

1825—The Marquis de Lafayette makes a hero's visit to New Orleans.

Louisiana adopts the Code Napoléon for its legal system.

1830—State capital moved from New Orleans to Donaldsonville, briefly.

1833—Shreve's "cut-off" at the confluence of the Red and Mississippi Rivers aids commerce in Alexandria and Shreveport, but floods out Cajun farmers in the Atchafalaya Basin.

1835—Louisiana Catholicism dwindles to six active churches and only two resident priests.

1840—Calcasieu Parish secedes from St. Landry Parish.

Vermilionville Academy is founded in Lafayette.

1843—Alexander Mouton becomes the first Cajun governor.

1844—Vermilion Parish secedes from Lafayette Parish.

1845—Louisiana's new constitution authorizes French and English public documents. Public schools are expanded during the Mouton regime, and the University of Louisiana (later to become Tulane) is founded.

1847—The first Acadian schools are established in New Brunswick.

Evangeline is published in Boston.

1849—Louisiana's state capital is moved to Baton Rouge.

1850—Half the state's territory is still unsurveyed.

1851—New Orleans booms, becoming the nation's fourth-largest city. Plans to build a railroad westward from the city are drawn up.

1853—Paul Octave Hébert becomes the state's second Cajun governor. Louisiana's worst yellow fever epidemic rages.

1855—Hébert's regime imposes a one mil tax to support public education. He also starts the state's library and organizes what will eventually become Louisiana State University.

1857—The railroad reaches from New Orleans to Morgan City and Berwick Bay.

1860—Louisiana's first commercial orange groves begin production.

1861—Former governor Alexander Mouton presides over the state's secessionist convention.

1862—After federal forces capture New Orleans, the Confederate government moves its capital to the Cajun prairie at Opelousas.

The nation's first salt mine is established at Avery Island near New Iberia.

1864—Confederate forces win the Battle of Mansfield, but lose General Alfred Mouton.

1865—The last Confederate military resistance collapses.

1867—The miracle of Grand Coteau leads to the establishment of the French Triangle's first major religious shrine.

    First shrimp-canning factory begins operations.

    Following the formation of the Canadian Confederation on July 1, in which they played no part, the Acadians of New Brunswick begin publication of the first Acadian newspaper on July 4.

1869—The nation's first sulphur mine begins work.

1870—Cameron Parish is established.

1872—The haul seine is adopted by Louisiana shrimpers.

1875—The first public schools for Cajuns are established.

1877—The first free public schools for blacks are established.

1881—The railroad builds west to Vermilionville, which is renamed Lafayette three years later.

1882—Acadia Parish is established.

1885—Southern Pacific Railroad is organized to operate the rail line from New Orleans to the West Coast.

1887—A record 6.8 million pounds of rice are harvested, twelve times the crop in pre-railroad 1880.

1889—Louisiana becomes the nation's top producer of rice.

1890—The first "central plant" for sugar refining is established in Franklin.

    College Ste.-Anne is established as the only bilingual college in Nova Scotia.

1892—Rice-monopoly politics lead to the formation of the Louisiana Cooperative Rice Milling Company on the Cajun prairie.

    Louisiana Folklore Society founded by Alcée Fortier.

1894—Rice irrigation pumps and canals begin operations near Crowley.

1895—First racially segregated Catholic Church parish is formed

1896—The nation's second rural free delivery service, the first in Louisiana, is established outside Thibodaux.

1897—First New Orleans-style Mardi Gras celebration in Lafayette.

1900—The population of southwest Louisiana is double the 1880 tally.

1901—The forerunner of the University of Southwestern Louisiana opens.

    Oil is discovered in Louisiana near Jennings.

1903—La Société l'Assomption is formed by Acadian activists in Waltham, Massachusetts.

1908—Louisiana Rice Growers Association is formed.

1909—Exxon's Baton Rouge refinery commences operations.

1910—Evangeline Parish is formed.

1912—"Blue Rose" rice is developed, ushering in the modern era in rice cultivation.

Allen and Beauregard Parishes are formed

1913—L'Assomption moves from Massachusetts to Moncton, New Brunswick.

1914—*Louisiana,* Alcée Fortier's encyclopedia, is published.

1918—The Diocese of Lafayette splits from the Archdiocese of New Orleans, starting out with forty parishes and fifty priests.

1922—Compulsory education is adopted; French-speaking on public-school grounds in Louisiana is prohibited.

1925—*L'Abeille,* the most important French newspaper in Louisiana, suspends publication in New Orleans.

1926—Lake Charles becomes the first Cajun deep-water port.

1928—Huey P. Long is elected governor.

1929—*The Mayor of Bayou Pom-Pom,* a minor literary classic with a Cajun theme, is published.

1930—South Louisiana surpasses north Louisiana in oil production.

The first blessing of the shrimp fleet along Bayou Grand Caillou.

1933—Published reports identify the Cajuns as the nation's "last unassimilated minority."

1935—The Louisiana Shrimp and Petroleum Festival is established in Morgan City.

Huey Long is assassinated.

1937—Acadia University (Baptist and English-speaking!) founded in Wolfville, Nova Scotia.

1938—Pope Pius XI declares Our Lady of the Assumption the patroness of Acadians worldwide.

Louisiana climbs to fourth place in national oil production.

1940—Governor Earl K. Long appointed first king of the Sugar Festival, largest in the French Triangle.

1945—Yambilee Festival (sweet potatoes) founded in Opelousas.

1947—The centennial of Longfellow's *Evangeline;* 270 editions have been published.

1951—France-Amérique de la Louisiane-Acadienne founded.

1952—Oil Center opens in Lafayette.

1953—President Eisenhower authorizes vast expansion of Louisiana offshore oil drilling.

1954—University of Southwestern Louisiana becomes the first state institution of higher learning to accept blacks.

1955—*Le Courrier de la Nouvelle Orleans,* the state's last French-language newspaper, suspends publication.

1959—Crawfish Festival started in Breaux Bridge.

1968—*Le Conseil pour le Devéloppement de Français en Louisiane* (CODOFIL) is established in May, and French returns to Louisiana schools.

1969—*Acadiana Profile* magazine begins publication.

Oyster Festival is started in Galliano.

1970—First foreign teachers of French arrive for CODOFIL program.

LSU Rural Life Museum opens.

Lagniappe on the Bayou festival starts, Chauvin.

1972—Cajun Edwin Edwards elected governor.

1973—First Cajun music festival held in Lafayette; Frog Festival started in Rayne; Gumbo Festival started in Bridge City.

1976—Over three thousand oil platforms are in operation in offshore Louisiana.

1977—Le Village Historique Acadien opens in Caraquet, New Brunswick.

Notes

Prologue: Cajunism

1. Linguists explain it this way: the New Orleans Creoles, with their tendency to shorten pronunciation, called the Acadians "Cadiens," leaving off the "a" and ending up with a word that sounds in English like "cod-yen." American settlers had trouble pronouncing the "dy" and corrupted the word further, to "Cajun" with a "j." Cajuns are also sometimes known colloquially as "coon-asses"—and there is an even more complicated linguistic history there. The consensus is that the word has little or nothing to do with raccoons, but derives instead from the no-longer-used *"conasse,"* a French cussword for a prostitute who has not had her regular health inspection. "Cajun" was at one time fightin' words in Louisiana, and "coon-ass" even more so —but French Triangle youngsters now often sport T-shirts or automobile bumper stickers with sentiments like "I'm proud to be a coon-ass."

2. There is another common misperception that the mixture of black blood and white blood in the United States was a one-way street—white blood mixed into black families. But there are two major episodes in American history in which the number of "mulattoes" recorded in federal census figures suffers an inexplicable decline—a decline suggestive of massive but hidden racial crossover.

The first of these incidents occurs in the decade 1840–50 in Louisiana, during the regime of Cajun Governor Alexander Mouton, when the state drops from 25,502 "free colored" to 17,462—slipping from the nation's fifth ranking in that census category to ninth. All other Southern states report net increases in their "free colored" population during that same period (except Mississippi, with a net loss of 436), and the national number of "free colored" goes from 377,932 to 424,920—figures in line with national-average birth rates and population growth for that period. Curiously enough, there is a small net gain of "free colored" in rural Louisiana, with New Orleans "losing" an astonishing 9,305 of its 1840 total of 19,266—almost half. It is worth noting that New Orleans had four-fifths of the state's "free colored" population in 1840 and that New Orleans was the most truly urban society to be found in the South of that era—so New Orleans had the "free colored" population with the best available trades and educations needed *pour passer blanc.*

While it is conceivable that some of New Orleans' Creoles of color were "lost" to other states or to yellow fever, we must also remember that Louisiana from 1840 to 1850 was the country's most prosperous, booming area. The "white" population of New Orleans zoomed from 59,519 to 91,431 (an increase of 65 percent) in that same decade. Louisiana's overall "white" population increased from 158,457 to 255,491 (an increase of 54 percent)—a much higher than average gain for a decade when the overall national white population increased from 14,195,805 to 19,553,-

068 (an increase of only 35 percent). Louisiana's boom years were characterized by a major in-migration of "outsiders" whose origins would have been largely impossible to ascertain. Therefore, we may never know exactly how many of the city's mulattoes moved across town or into the countryside during this period to set up housekeeping as "whites."

In pre-Civil War Louisiana such changes would not have been as difficult to manage as they would have been in other Southern states, or as they would become in Louisiana after the Civil War, when a more racist, Anglo-dominated government took control. Nonetheless, there is another curious period of mulatto "loss" in the decade 1860–70, during the confusion of the Civil War, and this time the loss does seem to be spread nationally. The total United States mulatto population in 1860 had grown to 588,363—but one decade later it had fallen back to 584,363. Mulattoes had constituted 11.2 percent of the nation's "colored" population in 1850, and had steadily increased to 20.9 percent by 1910—the result of an even and predictable statistical climb for all the intervening decades except the 1860's. Unknown thousands could have "passed" during this period, and one century later there could be millions of American "white" families with an unknown share of black blood.

3. Defenders of the more orthodox version of the faith will tell you proudly that the largest early Acadian immigrant-settler group managed to reach Nova Scotia's Atlantic coast in 1632 on the eve of the Feast of the Assumption. In 1638, the politically astute advisors around Louis XIII—at that time possessor of a tightly controlled state church—persuaded him to declare Our Lady of the Assumption to be the patroness of the French nation now scattering its population through various colonial domains. Three hundred years later, Pope Pius XI declared her to be the special patron saint of the Acadians. In the 1880's in the provinces of Maritime Canada (New Brunswick, Nova Scotia, Prince Edward Island), the Canadian Acadians held the first of their several Victorian-era "congresses" at Memramcook, near the original family settlements. At one of these congresses, a hymn was composed in Latin, "Stella Maris," that until after World War II continued to be sung at the beginning of every public gathering in Acadian areas of New Brunswick, like a "Star-spangled Banner" of the family or clan. Perhaps the most phenomenal development of Acadian nationalism during this period was the creation of a communal resource-sharing and development institution called La Société de l'Assomption. Organized in 1903 in Waltham, Massachusetts—another heavily Acadian area—but later moved to Moncton, New Brunswick, it now occupies that province's largest skyscraper complex. The sprawling Société has almost 100,000 members and annually hands out millions of dollars in payments through its insurance agency—reputedly the fastest-growing in Canada. Through Atlantic Gestion and other holding companies, the Société owns credit unions and finance companies; Bonnacord Realty; the Acadian Co-op chain of farm equipment and grocery stores; as well as an operation called Mother's Own Bakery. The Société is also in on Moncton's *L'Evangeline,* the world's only Acadian French daily newspaper, founded on July 4 of the year the province of New Brunswick was forced into the Canadian federation without its French-speaking inhabitants having any say in the matter. The Société's younger critics accuse it of having turned into a pillar of the Canadian Establishment, but it

has not yet completely lost touch with its communal, matriarchal roots. There is no comparable economic institution like the Société in Louisiana, and indeed, in few geographical or ethnic areas in North America can you find any self-administered institution of its size and scope.

4. There is a darker side to this communal cultural phenomenon, which French researchers Geneviève Massignon and François Rameau have addressed with diligence. Their evidence suggests that two-thirds of the Acadians who were alive in the middle of the eighteenth century—the ones who were deported—were descended from immigrants who were in the colony before 1671. Lack of sufficient "new blood" in the intervening eight decades sometimes led to excessive levels of consanguinity, which has produced a small but statistically significant incidence of genetic disease in some Cajun families.

One study of marriage records at Port Royal, the capital of the original Canadian Acadian colony, for example, concluded that 44 percent of all marriages consummated between 1729 and 1755 (the Expulsion) were between second cousins. In the single year 1740, a majority of marriages listed in the church register required dispensations from the Church.

The issue remains a problem in Louisiana in the twentieth century but was generally publicly ignored until a woman named Ada Jack Carver wrote *The Cajun,* winner of the 1926 Samuel French Prize in scriptwriting. In this Cajun remake of *Romeo and Juliet,* Julie has become engaged to Pierre. But there is a bad-news scene with Pierre and the priest, followed by disclosure that Papite—Julie's afflicted brother—is the reason she best not marry Pierre. The Carver production is somewhat melodramatic, with a cake knife poised in mid-air at one point, and an embarrassingly bastardized French accent.

In real life, Dr. Theodore F. Thurman of the LSU Medical Center's Heritable Disease Center reports this statistical irregularity: while the Acadian-dominated rural areas of the French Triangle account for only one-third of the state's population, they also account for between two-thirds and three-fourths of the state's cases of PKU (phenylketonuria), a genetic nerve disorder. Thurman has also found higher-than-average incidence of cystic fibrosis, muscular dystrophy, albinism, and eighteen other rare hereditary disorders, including two apparently new syndromes that have never been recorded in genetic literature before. The numbers directly involved in this problem are small, but that they are there at all in an ethnic population grouping the size of the Cajuns' is a source of interest to medical researchers—not just because of the problems, but because of the answers the Acadian family structure can provide us at a time when the world is realizing it must live as one big family in order to survive.

5. Geneviève Massignon's volume lists the ten most common Canadian Acadian surnames in the following rank, with parenthetical notation of the number of families bearing the name: 1. LeBlanc (2,749); 2. Arsenault (1,543); 3. Gallant (1,167); 4. Cormier (1,079); 5. Boudreau (1,054); 6. Richard (1,021); 7. Doucet (955); 8. Landry (910); 9. Poirier (760); 10. Robichaud (759). There is no comparable study of Louisiana's population, but an inspection of the metropolitan Lafayette telephone directory produces the following tally: 1. Broussard (730); 2. Hébert (468); 3.

Guidry (432); 4. LeBlanc (430); 5. Landry (383); 6. Trahan (353); 7. Mouton (316); 8. Breaux (299); 9. Boudreaux (263); 10. Domingue (249). Domingue is just one more than Richard at 248.

LeBlanc, Boudreau(x), Landry, and Richard are prominent in both lists—but there are interesting differences. There are few Gallants or Poiriers in Louisiana, and no Acadian Moutons in Maritime Canada. Hébert, the second-largest family on the Louisiana list, is 20 on Massignon's; Louisiana's ranking Broussard family has an even less common name there than in Canada.

Other large families, drawn from both sources and listed alphabetically, are: Benoit, Bernard, Bourque, Chaisson, Comeau(x), Cyr, Dugas, Duhon, Fontenot, Gaudet, Leger, Melanson, Roy, Savoie, Thibodeaux.

The addition of an "x" in Louisiana spellings is explained as follows: Acadian immigrants would pronounce their names to Spanish customs officers, who would write out their best phonetic transcription and ask the immigrant to affix an "X" of certification alongside.

1. Canadian Roots

1. Here is how Henry Wadsworth Longfellow puts Winslow's speech to verse in *Evangeline*:

"You are convened this day," he said, "by his Majesty's orders.
Clement and kind has he been, but how you have answered his kindness,
Let your own hearts reply! To my natural make and my temper
Painful the task is I do, which to you I know must be grievous.
Yet must I bow and obey, and deliver the will of our monarch;
Namely, that all your lands, and dwellings, and cattle of all kinds
Forfeited be to the crown; and that you yourselves from this province
Be transported to other lands. God grant you may dwell there
Ever as faithful subjects, a happy and peaceable people!
Prisoners now I declare you; for such is his Majesty's pleasure!"

9. French Accordion Folk Music

1. "Fille du Roi" literally translates as "king's daughter," but was also used to mean orphan or wayward girl. The phrase also refers to women sent to Canada (1665–71) to marry the colonists.

10. "Laissez les bons temps rouler"

1. Here is some basic bourré strategy:
Just as in bridge, if you hold a substantial number of trumps (four small ones, in this case) and it is your turn to lead, lead a middle one to try to flush any higher trumps out early.
If it is your lead and you hold the ace of trumps, and one or two other players

have drawn several cards apiece, lead your ace. Chances are that at least one of them didn't have any trumps until the draw. If you flush out another player's only trump early, you might be able to bourré him.

If it is your lead and you have only a fair hand, lead a throwaway—your lowest card in a suit other than trumps—hoping it will draw off high cards or trumps.

When drawing for new cards, discard non-trump aces *except* in games with two or three other players. Non-trump aces don't stand up well against trumps when five or more are playing.

As a corollary: *if* you possess a winning ace, lead the next trick with another card in that suit—hoping to flush out more of your opponents' trumps.

If your opponents are leading high trumps, exhausting your supply in an attempt to bourré you, keep your highest card until last and hope for the best.

If you drop out of any hand, don't worry about it: it's better to lose a little than be bourréd for a lot—the quintessential Cajun caveat.

Acadian Handicraft. Louisiana State Department of Commerce and Industry. Baton Rouge, 1955.

Akins, Thomas B., ed. *Acadia and Nova Scotia: Documents Relating to the Acadian French and the First British Colonization of the Province, 1714–1758.* Cottonport, La.: Polyanthos, 1972. Selected documents issued by the Anglo-Canadian government of Nova Scotia to justify the Expulsion.

Arceneaux, Thomas J. "Acadian Bicentennial Celebration, 1955–65." Southwestern Archives, University of Southwestern Louisiana (USL), Lafayette. Gift of personal papers by the celebration's chairman, formerly Dean of the College of Agriculture at USL.

——. "The Louisiana Acadian Flag," *Acadiana Profile,* Vol. 1, No. 1 (January–February 1969), pp. 1–2.

Arsenault, Bona. *History of the Acadians.* Quebec: Le Conseil de la Vie Française en Amérique, 1966. Brilliantly partisan historical sketch, unquestionably the most provocative Canadian volume on the subject. In both French and English.

Arthur, Stanley. *Jean Lafitte.* New Orleans: Harmanson, 1952. A revisionist historian's treasure trove, complete with reproductions of Lafitte's letters concerning his visit to Marx and Engels.

Babineaux, Lawson P. Jr. "A History of the Rice Industry in Southwest Louisiana." Master's thesis, USL, 1967.

Baird, Penny. "Some Southwest Louisiana Toys of the Late 19th and 20th Centuries," *Attakapas Gazette,* Vol. VII, No. 2 (June 1972), pp. 58–77.

Barrett, Barney B. and Ellen J. Ralph. *1976 Environmental Conditions Relative to Shrimp Production in Coastal Louisiana.* Louisiana Wildlife and Fisheries Commission, Technical Bulletin No. 21. New Orleans, 1976.

Baudier, Roger. *Catholicism in Louisiana.* New Orleans: A. W. Hyatt, 1939. Small type and wretched style make it difficult to read, but the volume nevertheless suggests the rich and seamy history of the Church in Louisiana.

Becnel, Thomas Aquinas. "A History of the Louisiana Shrimp Industry, 1867–1961." Master's thesis, LSU, 1962.

Blanchet, Catherine Brookshire. "Louisiana French Folk Songs Among Children in Vermilion Parish, 1942–54." Master's thesis, USL, 1970.

Boucher, Neil Joseph. "The Development of an Acadian Village: Surette's Island, 1859–70." Master's thesis, Acadian University, 1974.

Bourgeois, Lillian C. *Cabanocey: The History, Customs and Folklore of St. James Parish.* New Orleans: Pelican Publishing, 1957.

Bourque, J. Rudolphe. *Social and Architectural Aspects of the Acadians in New Brunswick.* Fredericton: Research and Development Branch, Historical Resources Administration, 1971.

Bradshaw, Jim. "The Economic Impact of Oil and Gas in Louisiana," *Acadiana Profile,* Vol. VI, No. 2 (Fall, 1977), pp. 21–70.

Brebner, John Bartlet. *New England's Outpost: Acadia before the Conquest of Canada.* Hamden, Conn.: Archon Books, 1965.

Brown, George S. *Yarmouth, Nova Scotia: A Sequel to Campbell's History.* Boston: Rand Avery Co., 1888.

Browne, Turner. *Louisiana Cajuns.* Baton Rouge: LSU Press, 1977. More photos by the young Cajun photographer, with an introduction by poet William Mills.

Burnham, Harold B. and Dorothy K. Burnham. *Keep Me Warm at Night: Early Handweaving in Eastern Canada.* Toronto: University of Toronto Press, 1972.

Calhoun, James, ed. *Louisiana Almanac, 1975–76.* Gretna: Pelican Publishing, 1975.

Campbell, Rev. J. R. *A History of the County of Yarmouth, Nova Scotia.* St. John, N.B.: J&A McMillan, 1876.

Campbell, Mrs. Stephen Roy and Dr. Isobel French. *Research Notes on Acadians, Cabahanoce-Verret, and Jacques Cantrelle, Sr.* Baton Rouge: Louisiana Genealogical and Historical Society, 1962.

Casanova, Jacques-Donat and Armour Landry. *America's French Heritage.* Quebec: La Documentation Française and the Quebec Official Publisher, 1976. Brief but tasty bicentennial survey of the various North American French cultural puddles, past and present. The English edition features a foreword by James Domengeaux.

Chachere, Tony. *Cajun Country Cookbook.* Opelousas: Cajun Country Cookbook, Inc., 1972.

Chambers, Mortimer, et al. *The Western Experience. Vol. II: The Early Modern Period.* New York: Alfred A. Knopf, 1974.

Chandler, Richard E. "End of an Odyssey: Acadians Arrive in St. Gabriel, La.," *Louisiana History,* Vol. XIV, No. 1 (Winter, 1973), pp. 69–87.

Child, Julia, with Louisette Bertholde and Simone Beck. *Mastering the Art of French Cooking.* New York: Alfred A. Knopf, 1961.

Clark, Andrew Hill. *Acadia: The Geography of Nova Scotia to 1760.* Madison: University of Wisconsin Press, 1968. Astonishing scholarship, thoroughly thought through and executed with style and grace. The best published work on early Acadia in English, and a definitive base for further research.

Clarke, George Frederick. *Expulsion of the Acadians.* Fredericton: Brunswick Press, 1955.

Coleman, Linda P. "The Acadians." Master's thesis, LSU, 1911.

Collections of the Nova Scotia Historical Society. Halifax, 1881.

Collin, Richard and Rima. *The New Orleans Cookbook.* New York: Alfred A. Knopf, 1977. The best Louisiana recipe book in print.

Collins, Rev. Charles W. *The Acadians of Madawaska, Maine.* Boston: T. A. Whalen and Co., 1902.

Comeaux, Malcolm L. *Geoscience and Man. Vol. II: Atchafalaya Swamp Life, Settlement and Folk Occupations.* Baton Rouge: LSU School of Geoscience, 1972. Informative text and photographs of some of Louisiana's exotica.

Conrad, Glenn R., ed. *The Cajuns: Essays on Their History and Culture.* Lafayette: USL Center for Louisiana Studies, 1978.

Craig, N. J. and J. W. Day, eds. *Cumulative Impact Studies of the Louisiana Coastal Zone: Eutrophication and Land Loss.* Baton Rouge: LSU Center for Wetland Resources, 1977. Authoritative compilation of scientific studies conducted over two decades, and a devastating analysis of oil-industry depradations in the coastal zone.

Davis, Edwin Adams. *The Rivers and Bayous of Louisiana.* Baton Rouge: Louisiana Educational Research Association, 1968.

Deveau, Alphonse. "The Status of Acadian Culture in the Maritime Provinces." Unpublished article, 1977. Prof. Deveau teaches at Collège Ste.-Anne in Church Point, N.S.

Dismukes, J. Philip. *The Center: A History of the Development of Lafayette, La.* Lafayette: City of Lafayette, 1969.

Ditchy, Jay K., ed.; George F. Reinecke, trans. "Early Louisiana French Life and Folklore from the Anonymous Breaux Manuscript," *Louisiana Folklore Miscellany,* Vol. II, No. 3 (May 1968), pp. 1–58. Believed to have been written by the state supreme court judge who claimed to have "found" it.

Doucet, Carol James. "The Acadian French of Lafayette." Master's thesis, USL, 1970.

Duffy, McFadden. "From Rigs to Reefs," *Louisiana Conservationist,* Vol. 27, Nos. 7–8 (July–August 1975), pp. 18–21.

Dupont, Albert Leonce. "The Career of Paul Octave Hébert, Governor of Louisiana, 1853–56," *Louisiana Historical Quarterly,* Vol. 31, No. 2 (April 1948), pp. 491–552.

du Pratz, Le Page. *The History of Louisiana.* Baton Rouge: LSU Press, 1975. Facsimile reissue of the state's earliest history; sponsored by the Louisiana American Bicentennial Commission.

Eaton, Allen H. *Handicrafts of the Southern Highlands.* New York: Dover Publications, 1973.

Egger, Dolores. "Jim Crow Comes to Church: The Establishment of Segregated Catholic Parishes in South Louisiana." Master's thesis, USL, 1965. Tangy exposé of Church politics.

Exner, Beatrice B. "Acadian Brown Cotton," *Handweaver and Craftsman,* Vol. II, No. 4 (Fall, 1960), p. 23.

Faulk, James Donald. *Cajun French I.* Abbeville: The Cajun Press, 1977.

Feibleman, Peter S. *American Cooking, Creole and Acadian.* New York: Time/Life Books, 1971. Excellent recipes, with informative background narrative.

———. *The Bayous.* New York: Time/Life Books, 1973.

Fletcher, Joel L. "The Acadians of Louisiana Today." Cambridge, 1947. Private reprint of an address to the Cambridge, Mass., Historical Society by the late president of USL.

Fontenot, Mary Alice and Rev. Paul B. Freeland. *Acadia Parish, Louisiana: A History to 1900.* Baton Rouge: Claitor's Publishing, 1976.

Fortier, Alcee. *Louisiana.* New Orleans: Century Historical Association, 1914 (three volumes). An encyclopedia of the state, compiled by its foremost Victorian Age scholar, also a founder of the Louisiana Folklore Society in 1892 and the American Folklore Society in 1888.

Gahn, Robert Sr. *A History of Evangeline Parish.* Baton Rouge: Claitor's Publishing, 1972.

Gaidry, Wilson G. III and Bob Dennie. "Riches from the Sea," *Louisiana Conservationist,* Vol. 23, Nos. 7 & 8 (July–August 1971), pp. 5–9.

Gayarre, Charles. *History of Louisiana.* New Orleans: F. F. Hansell, 1903.

Griffin, Harry Lewis. *A Brief History of the Acadians.* Baton Rouge: Department of Commerce and Industry, 1952. Written by Dean Emeritus of USL College of Liberal Arts.

———. *The Attakapas Country: A History of Lafayette Parish, La.* Gretna: Pelican Publishing, 1959.

Griffiths, Naomi. "Acadians in Exile: The Experience of the Acadians in the British Seaports," *Acadiensis,* Vol. IV, No. 1 (Autumn, 1974), pp. 67–84.

———. *The Acadians: Creation of a People.* Toronto: McGraw-Hill Ryerson Ltd., 1973. Sixth volume in the Frontenac Library series on Canadian history.

Guidry, Sherwin. *Land of the Houmas.* Houma, La.: Daily Courier Publishing Co., 1977. Folklore, oral history, and original fiction, compiled by an enterprising Cajun mailman from Chauvin, La., published originally as a series of newspaper articles.

Hardy, Florent Jr. "A Brief History of the University of Southwestern Louisiana, 1900–1960." Master's thesis, USL, 1969.

Hardy, Lady Helen and Raymond J. Martinez. *Louisiana's Fabulous Foods and How to Cook Them.* Jefferson, La.: Hope Publications, 1957.

Hodges, David Julian. "Cajun Culture of Southwest Louisiana: A Study in Cultural Isolation and Role Adaptation in the Fusion of Black African and French Acadian Cultural Traits." Ph.D. dissertation, New York University, 1972.

Holden, Jack and Robert Smith. *Early French Louisiana Furnishings, 1700–1830.* Lafayette: Art Center for Southwest Louisiana, 1974. Catalogue for bicentennial furniture show.

Hollier, Neil. "Crawfish Folklore in Southwest Louisiana," *Attakapas Gazette,* Vol. VI, No. 3 (September 1971), pp. 95–111.

Holmes, Irense Therese Whitfield. *Louisiana French Folk Songs.* Baton Rouge: LSU Press, 1939. The first book ever published on Cajun music.

———. "Acadian Music and Dances," *Attakapas Gazette,* Vol. XI, No. 4 (Winter, 1976), pp. 181–86.

Hudson, Marilyn. *Acadiana Unlimited.* Baton Rouge: Claitor's Publishing, 1969. Typical of the over-romanticism of Cajun history common in some Louisiana circles.

Hynes, Gisa. "Some Aspects of the Demography of Port Royal, 1650–1755," *Acadiensis,* Vol. III, No. 1 (Autumn, 1973), pp. 3–17. Focuses on consanguinity problems before the Expulsion.

Jaenen, Cornelius J. *The Role of the Church in New France.* Toronto: McGraw-Hill Ryerson Ltd., 1976. Seventh volume in the Frontenac Library series in Canadian history, and a good prelude to Baudier's tome.

Jannise, Harry and Randall P. Whatley. *Conversational French I.* Baton Rouge: The Chicot Press, 1978.

Johnson, Jerah. "The Louisiana French," *Contemporary French Civilization,* Vol. 1, No. 1 (Fall, 1976), pp. 19–35. The chairman of the History Department at the University of New Orleans predicts that all native French-speaking in Louisiana will disappear by the turn of the century.

Johnston, William Preston, ed. *In Acadia.* New Orleans: F. F. Hansell, 1893.

Jones, Elaine Douglass. *Gourmet's Guide to New Orleans, Creole Cookbook, and Directory of New Orleans Restaurants.* Baton Rouge: Claitor's Publishing, 1933.

Kilman, Grady W. "Slavery and Forced Labor in Colonial Louisiana, 1699–1803." Master's thesis, USL, 1972.

Kniffen, Fred B. *Louisiana: Its Land and People.* Baton Rouge: LSU Press, 1968. The definitive text by the state's premier geographer, whose work has influenced all subsequent scholarship on the Cajuns.

Knipmeyer, William. "Settlement Succession in Eastern French Louisiana." Master's thesis, LSU, 1947. Timeless after three decades, and written by a Kniffen protégé, this invaluable document has, unfortunately, never been published.

Lagarde, Marie-Louise, William S. Chute and George F. Reinecke. "Six Avoyelles Songs from the Saucier Collection," *Louisiana Folklore Miscellany,* Vol. II, No. 2 (April 1965), pp. 1–26. Regrettably, the remainder of the Corinne Saucier collection still awaits publication.

LeBlanc, Bernard, et al. *La Maison Helen et Roma Bourgeois.* Moncton, N.B.: DHA, Inc. (A la Découverte de l'Habitation Acadienne), 1977. Collaborative research effort to document what could be the earliest surviving Acadian house in the Maritime Provinces. Hand-lettered by LeBlanc, and in French.

LeBlanc, Dudley J. *The Acadian Miracle.* Lafayette: Evangeline Publishing Co., 1966. Colorful history by the late Hadacol king and state senator from Abbeville.

Le Breton, Clarence. "L'Habitat et le Meuble en Acadie d'Autrefois." Unpublished article, 1977. Le Breton directs the staff at the Village Historique Acadien in Caraquet, N.B.

Long, Sister Callista M. "Kate Chopin." Master's thesis, Notre Dame, 1941. Chopin, recently rediscovered in feminist circles, produced a series of short fictional portraits of Louisiana's Cajuns.

"Louisiana's State Tree—Cypress." Baton Rouge: Louisiana Forestry Commission, 1976. Brochure on the sequoia of the South.

Louisiana Tobacco: A Chapter in America's Industrial Growth. New York: The Tobacco Institute, 1975. Description of pungent perique tobacco, which grows only in the former Acadian Coast area of the state.

Loustalot, Kenneth. "Acadian Names and Nicknames," *Attakapas Gazette,* Vol. VII, No. 4 (December 1972), pp. 170–81.

Love, Frances and John Love. *Allons à l'Acadie.* Lafayette: Tribune Co., 1957. See Marilyn Hudson, above.

McCaleb, Thomas. *The Louisiana Book: Selection from the Literature of the State.* New Orleans: R. F. Straughan, 1894.

McIlheny, Louise Westfeldt. "French Culture in Rural Louisiana." Master's thesis, Tulane University, 1935.

Mamalakis, Mario. "Breaux Bridge and the Telephone," *Attakapas Gazette,* Vol. X,

No. 2 (Summer, 1975), pp. 111–12. Discusses the use of *'tit noms* in telephone-directory listings.

Marchand, Sidney A. *The Story of Ascension Parish, La.* Donaldsonville, 1931.

_____. *The Flight of a Century, 1800–1900 in Ascension Parish, La.* Donaldsonville, 1936.

Moore, John Preston. *Revolt in Louisiana: The Spanish Occupation, 1766–1770.* Baton Rouge: LSU Press, 1976.

Morison, Samuel Eliot. *The European Discovery of America.* New York: Oxford University Press, 1971.

Nelson, Robin, ed. *The Doug Kershaw Songbook: Lou'siana Man.* New York: Macmillan, 1971.

Olivier, Louise V. "Archives of the Acadian Handicraft Association, 1939–1962." LSU Library, Baton Rouge. Letters, order forms, scrapbooks, and other memorabilia.

Olmstead, Frederick Law. *Journey in the Seaboard Slave States.* New York: G. P. Putnam's Sons, 1904. Reissue of the 1857 original.

Ott, Thomas O. *The Haitian Revolution, 1789–1804.* Knoxville: University of Tennessee Press, 1973.

"Our Acadian History: Let's Keep It." Baton Rouge: Louisiana State Department of Commerce and Industry, with Louisiana Trade Development Commission, 1955.

Palardy, Jean. *The Early Furniture of French Canada.* Toronto: Macmillan, 1973.

Parenton, Vernon J. "The Rural French-speaking People of Quebec and South Louisiana: A Comparative Study of Social Structure and Organization, with Emphasis on the Role of the Catholic Church." Ph.D. dissertation, Harvard University, 1948.

Pecot, Marguerite A. "The Cajun." Baton Rouge: Federal Writers' Project, 1932.

Pellaprat, Henri Paul. *The Great Book of French Cuisine.* New York: Crowell, 1966.

Periou, Harris J. "The Acadian Flower and Herb Garden," *Attakapas Gazette,* Vol. VII, No. 1 (March 1972), pp. 20–22.

Petitjean, Irene M. "Acadian Songs." Master's thesis, Columbia University, 1930.

"The Petroleum Archives." Southwestern Archives, USL, Lafayette. Letters, photographs, brochures, magazines, catalogues, and newspaper clippings, gathered principally by the Heywood family of Jennings.

Post, Lauren C. *Cajun Sketches from the Prairies of Southwest Louisiana.* Baton Rouge: LSU Press, 1962. The most readable Cajun book published in Louisiana, though limited to the prairie experiences and folklore.

Proctor, Samuel, ed. *18th Century Florida and Its Borderlands.* Gainesville: University Presses of Florida, 1975. Discusses architecture and other subjects relating to the original Florida territory that is now part of Louisiana.

Rafuse, Maxwell Churchill. "French Fortification Systems in North America." Master's thesis, Acadian University, 1975.

Read, William A. *Louisiana French.* Baton Rouge: LSU Press, 1931.

Reed, Revon. "Cajun Music . . . An Acadian Tradition," *Acadiana Profile,* Vol. IV, No. 3 (October-November 1974), pp. 4–5.

_____. *Lâche pas la Patate: Portrait des Acadiens de la Louisiane.* Montreal: Editions Parti

Pris, 1976. Delightful account of Cajun customs and characters. The title translates: "Don't drop the potato," meaning "Don't give up."

Reeves, Miriam G. *The Governors of Louisiana.* Gretna: Pelican Publishing, 1972.

Ricard, Ulysse. *Lagniappe: A Louisiana French Reader.* Privately printed, 1978 (Available from Department of Languages, Louisiana State University).

Richard, Valex. "Louisiana Acadian Handicrafts." Master's thesis, LSU, 1951.

Rickels, Patricia. "The Folklore of Sacraments and Sacramentals in South Louisiana," *Louisiana Folklore Miscellany,* Vol. II, No. 2 (April 1965), pp. 27–42.

River Road Cookbook. Baton Rouge: Junior League of Baton Rouge, 1959.

Rodrigue, George. *The Cajuns of George Rodrigue.* Birmingham, Ala.: Oxmoor House, 1976.

Roy, Edison Peter. "The Indians of Dulac: A Descriptive Study of a Racial Hybrid Community in Terrebonne Parish, La." Master's thesis, LSU, 1959.

Rushton, William F. "Will Texas Annex Southwest Louisiana: The Atchafalaya Basin, Our Last Wilderness, Is Up for Grabs," *Courier,* Vol. XI, No. 45 (April 17–23, 1975).

––––––. "Oil: Coming, the Biggest Offshore Spill of All Time?" *Courier,* Vol. XII, No. 46 (May 20–26, 1976).

––––––. "Indians on the Warpath? Troubles Are Brewing with Louisiana's Bayou Houmas," *Courier,* Vol. XIV, No. 7 (August 11–17, 1977).

––––––. "Voyage du Nord" (five-part series), *Courier,* Vol. XIV, Nos. 8–12 (August 18–September 21, 1977).

Russell, Richard Joel. *Louisiana, Our Treasure Ground.* Baton Rouge: LSU College of Education, 1951.

Saxon, Lyle, and Robert Tallant and Edward Dreyer, eds. *Gumbo Ya-Ya.* New York: Houghton Mifflin, 1945.

Segura, Pearl Mary. "Origins or Meaning of Some South Louisiana Personal Names or Surnames." *Attakapas Gazette,* Vol. VI, No. 2 (June 1971), pp. 53–68.

––––––. *The Acadians in Fact and Fiction: A Classified Bibliography of Writing on the Subject of Acadians in Stephens Memorial Library, SLI.* Baton Rouge: Department of Commerce, 1955. (SLI is now USL.)

Sevier, Mrs. Richard. *Talk About Good: Le Livre de la Cuisine de Lafayette.* Lafayette: Junior League of Lafayette, 1969. Best of the mass-contribution "grass roots" recipe books.

Shugg, Roger W. *Origins of the Class Struggle in Louisiana.* Baton Rouge: LSU Press, 1939. Highly useful Marxist history of the state, produced during the Huey Long era.

Sibley, J. Ashley Jr. *Louisiana's Ancients of Man.* Baton Rouge: Claitor's Publishing, 1967.

Spell, Aden Ives. *Life in Louisiana Cajun Country.* Asheville, N.C.: Biltmore Press, 1956.

Steen, Mrs. Wesley J. *The Story of Steen's Syrup and Its Famous Recipes.* Abbeville, 1975.

Steward, Kenneth Paul. "Naked Heel Cockfights in Acadiana," *Attakapas Gazette,* Vol. XII, No. 1 (Spring, 1977), pp. 21–26.

Thibodeaux, John-Smith (pseud.), *Les Francophones de Louisiane.* Paris: Editions Entente, 1977. Entertaining analysis of French culture and cultural preservation efforts in Louisiana, by the former French consul in New Orleans, Jean-Jacques Peyronnet.

Thurmon, Theodore F., M.D., and Ellen B. Defraites. "Genetic Studies of the French-Acadians of Louisiana," *Birth Defects,* Vol. X, No. 10 (1974), pp. 201–4.

Treadway, Lionel W. "The Louisiana Oyster," *Louisiana Conservationist,* Vol. 23, Nos. 5 & 6 (May–June 1971), pp. 4–9.

Van Sickle, Virginia, et al. *Barataria Basin: Salinity Changes and Oyster Distribution,* LSU Center for Wetland Resources, Technical Bulletin No. 20. Baton Rouge, 1976.

Villiers, Baron Marc de (trans. Warrington Dawson). "A History of the Foundation of New Orleans, 1717–1722," *Louisiana Historical Quarterly,* Vol. III, No. 2 (April 1920), pp. 151–251.

Vlach, John. "Shotgun Houses," *Natural History,* Vol. LXXXVII, No. 2 (February 1977), pp. 50–58.

Voorhies, Felix. *Acadian Reminiscences.* New Orleans: E. P. Rivas, 1907. The earliest-known work of Cajun oral history.

Webster, John Clarence, ed. *Acadia at the End of the 17th Century.* St. John, N.B.: The New Brunswick Museum, 1934.

Western, John Charles. "Social Groups and Activity Patterns: Houma, Louisiana." Master's thesis, University of Western Ontario, 1971.

What's Really Cooking in Crowley. Crowley: St. Margaret's Guild, Trinity Episcopal Church, 1976.

Williams, Lyle Givens. "Spanish Moss Gathering in Pierre Part." *Attakapas Gazette,* Vol. VIII, No. 3 (1973), pp. 97–102.

Wilson, Justin. *The Justin Wilson Cookbook.* Gretna: Pelican Publishing, 1975.

Winzerling, Oscar William. *Acadian Odyssey.* Baton Rouge: LSU Press, 1955. French and Spanish court intrigue surrounding Acadian migration to Louisiana during Spanish times.